Git Version Control Cookbook
Second Edition

Leverage version control to transform your development workflow and boost productivity

Kenneth Geisshirt
Emanuele Zattin
Aske Olsson
Rasmus Voss

BIRMINGHAM - MUMBAI

Git Version Control Cookbook
Second Edition

Copyright © 2018 Packt Publishing

All rights reserved. No part of this book may be reproduced, stored in a retrieval system, or transmitted in any form or by any means, without the prior written permission of the publisher, except in the case of brief quotations embedded in critical articles or reviews.

Every effort has been made in the preparation of this book to ensure the accuracy of the information presented. However, the information contained in this book is sold without warranty, either express or implied. Neither the authors, nor Packt Publishing or its dealers and distributors, will be held liable for any damages caused or alleged to have been caused directly or indirectly by this book.

Packt Publishing has endeavored to provide trademark information about all of the companies and products mentioned in this book by the appropriate use of capitals. However, Packt Publishing cannot guarantee the accuracy of this information.

Commissioning Editor: Aaron Lazar
Acquisition Editor: Shriram Shekhar
Content Development Editor: Pooja Parvatkar
Technical Editor: Subhalaxmi Nadar
Copy Editor: Safis Editing
Project Coordinator: Ulhas Kambali
Proofreader: Safis Editing
Indexer: Rekha Nair
Graphics: Tania Dutta
Production Coordinator: Deepika Naik

First published: July 2014
Second edition: July 2018

Production reference: 1240718

Published by Packt Publishing Ltd.
Livery Place
35 Livery Street
Birmingham
B3 2PB, UK.

ISBN 978-1-78913-754-5

www.packtpub.com

mapt.io

Mapt is an online digital library that gives you full access to over 5,000 books and videos, as well as industry leading tools to help you plan your personal development and advance your career. For more information, please visit our website.

Why subscribe?

- Spend less time learning and more time coding with practical eBooks and Videos from over 4,000 industry professionals

- Improve your learning with Skill Plans built especially for you

- Get a free eBook or video every month

- Mapt is fully searchable

- Copy and paste, print, and bookmark content

PacktPub.com

Did you know that Packt offers eBook versions of every book published, with PDF and ePub files available? You can upgrade to the eBook version at www.PacktPub.com and as a print book customer, you are entitled to a discount on the eBook copy. Get in touch with us at service@packtpub.com for more details.

At www.PacktPub.com, you can also read a collection of free technical articles, sign up for a range of free newsletters, and receive exclusive discounts and offers on Packt books and eBooks.

Contributors

About the authors

Kenneth Geisshirt is a chemist, by education, and a strong free-software advocate. He spent his Christmas holidays in 1992 installing SLS Linux, and GNU/Linux has been his favorite operating system ever since. Currently, he does consultancy work in fields such as scientific computing and Linux clusters. He lives in Copenhagen, Denmark, with his partner and their two children.

> *As a programmer, I have used many versioning systems. I began with CVS, followed by Subversion and Telelogic Synergy. During the last 7 years, Git has become an integral part of my life. Over the years, many people have been kind with their support, especially my wife and children, who always let me be the geek I am.*

Emanuele Zattin is the Continuous Integration Specialist at Realm Inc. with experience in software development and design. He is respected for his work in designing and developing a CM Synergy to Git history conversion tool and rolling out Git-Gerrit-Jenkins in several Nokia divisions.

> *I would like to thank my coauthor, Kenneth, for convincing me to embark on this adventure; my wife, Cecilie; and our children, Sebastian and Mia, for their patience and support. I would also like to thank Aske and Rasmus, the authors of the first edition of this book, whose work has proven to be an incredibly strong base for the current edition.*

Aske Olsson has more than 14 years of experience in the software industry. As an electrical engineer, he has been using every tool available for development, from a soldering iron over Assembly, C, Java Groovy, Python and various DSLs for programming to different SCMs and build-, CI- and issue-tracking systems. He has worked for Nokia for 6 years and, currently, works at Keylane. Aske has experience with Git; he has been teaching Git in regular training sessions, from basic Git to advanced usage.

Rasmus Voss has been working with continuous integration, continuous delivery, automatic testing, and DevOps, in various industries. He has always strived to ensure that where developers, testers, project leaders, and managers can work with the system instead of against the system. Typically, the processes and solutions he develops are clear, precise, and well documented, with relevant feedback to all parts of the software development process.

About the reviewer

Chen Mulong has been working on mobile development for over 10 years. He has coded for all different kinds of mobile devices, from the ancient feature phone platform, which is made of plain C, to the modern smart device platform, Android. Open source is his first choice for solving daily problems.

He has experienced the chaos of being part of a team of 100+ developers and the peace brought about by excellent SCM tools. He loves to tell others how good Git is at making every developer's life easier. He now works as a freelancer in Beijing, China.

> *Thanks to the writers for giving me the chance to review this book and learn so many things I hadn't tried before with Git. The book not only helped me to refresh my knowledge of Git basic, but also inspired me to get more work done by combining various simple Git commands into an automatic script. I enjoyed reading the tricks and examples contained in the book even as entertainment.*

Packt is searching for authors like you

If you're interested in becoming an author for Packt, please visit `authors.packtpub.com` and apply today. We have worked with thousands of developers and tech professionals, just like you, to help them share their insight with the global tech community. You can make a general application, apply for a specific hot topic that we are recruiting an author for, or submit your own idea.

Table of Contents

Preface   1

Chapter 1: Navigating Git   7
  Introduction   7
  Git's objects   9
    Getting ready   10
    How to do it...   10
      The commit object   10
      The tree object   11
      The blob object   12
      The branch object   12
      The tag object   13
    How it works...   13
    There's more...   14
  The three stages   14
    Getting ready   14
    How to do it...   15
    How it works...   17
    See also   18
  Viewing the DAG   18
    Getting ready   19
    How to do it...   20
    How it works...   22
  Extracting fixed issues   22
    Getting ready   22
    How to do it...   23
    How it works...   25
    There's more...   25
  Getting a list of the changed files   25
    Getting ready   25
    How to do it...   26
    How it works...   26
    There's more...   26
    See also   27
  Viewing the history with gitk   27
    Getting ready   27
    How to do it...   28
    How it works...   28
    There's more...   29
  Finding commits in the history   29

Getting ready	29
How to do it...	29
How it works...	30
There's more...	30
Searching through the history code	**31**
Getting ready	31
How to do it...	32
How it works...	32
There's more...	32
Chapter 2: Configuration	**35**
Introduction	**35**
Configuration targets	**35**
Getting ready	36
How to do it...	36
How it works...	38
There's more...	38
Querying the existing configuration	**38**
Getting ready	38
How to do it...	39
How it works...	39
There's more...	40
Templates	**41**
Getting ready	41
How to do it...	41
How it works...	42
A .git directory template	**42**
Getting ready	43
How to do it...	44
How it works...	45
See also	45
A few configuration examples	**45**
Getting ready	46
How to do it...	46
Rebase and merge setup	46
Expiry of objects	47
Autocorrect	48
How it works...	49
There's more...	49
Git aliases	**49**
Getting ready	49
How to do it...	50
How it works...	53
There's more...	53
The refspec exemplified	**53**
Getting ready	53

How to do it...	54
How it works...	56

Chapter 3: Branching, Merging, and Options — 57
Introduction — 57
Managing your local branches — 58
- Getting ready — 58
- How to do it... — 58
- How it works... — 59
- There's more... — 60

Branches with remotes — 61
- Getting ready — 61
- How to do it... — 63
- There's more... — 64

Forcing a merge commit — 65
- Getting ready — 66
- How to do it... — 66
- There's more... — 68

Using git reuse recorded resolution (rerere) to merge Git conflicts — 69
- How to do it... — 70
- There's more... — 73

Compute the difference between branches — 75
- Getting ready — 75
- How to do it... — 75

Orphan branches — 77
- Getting ready — 77
- How to do it... — 78
- There's more... — 80

Chapter 4: Rebasing Regularly and Interactively, and Other Use Cases — 81
Introduction — 81
Rebasing commits to another branch — 82
- Getting ready — 82
- How to do it... — 82
- How it works... — 83

Continuing a rebase with merge conflicts — 83
- How to do it... — 83
- How it works... — 85
- There's more... — 85

Rebasing selected commits interactively — 86
- Getting ready — 86
- How to do it... — 86
- There's more... — 88

Squashing commits using an interactive rebase — 89
- Getting ready — 89

How to do it...	90
There's more...	92
Changing the author of commits using a rebase	**94**
Getting ready	94
How to do it...	94
How it works...	97
Autosquashing commits	**97**
Getting ready	98
How to do it...	98
There's more...	102

Chapter 5: Storing Additional Information in Your Repository — 103
Introduction	103
Adding your first Git note	**104**
Getting ready	104
How to do it...	104
There's more...	107
Separating notes by category	**108**
Getting ready	109
How to do it...	109
How it works...	112
Retrieving notes from the remote repository	**112**
Getting ready	113
How to do it...	114
How it works...	115
Pushing Git notes to a remote repository	**116**
How to do it...	116
There's more...	118
Tagging commits in the repository	**118**
Getting ready	118
How to do it...	119
There's more...	121

Chapter 6: Extracting Data from the Repository — 123
Introduction	123
Extracting the top contributor	**123**
Getting ready	124
How to do it...	124
There's more...	127
Finding bottlenecks in the source tree	**127**
Getting ready	128
How to do it...	128
There's more...	132
Grepping the commit messages	**133**
Getting ready	134

How to do it...	134
The contents of the releases	**136**
How to do it...	136
How it works...	138
Finding what has been achieved in the repository in the last period	**138**
How to do it...	139
How it works...	141
There's more...	141

Chapter 7: Enhancing Your Daily Work with Git Hooks, Aliases, and Scripts — 143

Introduction	**143**
Using a branch description in a commit message	**144**
Getting ready	144
How to do it...	145
Creating a dynamic commit message template	**147**
Getting ready	148
How to do it...	148
There's more...	151
Using external information in a commit message	**153**
Getting ready	154
How to do it...	154
Preventing the push of specific commits	**157**
Getting ready	158
How to do it...	158
There's more...	161
Configuring and using Git aliases	**162**
How to do it...	162
How it works...	167
Configuring and using Git scripts	**167**
How to do it...	167
Setting up and using a commit template	**168**
Getting ready	168
How to do it...	169

Chapter 8: Recovering from Mistakes — 171

Introduction	**171**
Undo – Remove a commit completely	**172**
Getting ready	172
How to do it...	173
How it works...	174
Undo – Remove a commit and retain changes to files	**175**
Getting ready	175
How to do it...	176
How it works...	177

Table of Contents

Undo – Remove a commit and retain changes in the staging area — 177
   Getting ready — 177
   How to do it... — 178
   How it works... — 179

Undo – Working with a dirty area — 180
   Getting ready — 180
   How to do it... — 181
   How it works... — 183

Redo – Recreate the latest commit with new changes — 183
   Getting ready — 183
   How to do it... — 184
   How it works... — 186
   There's more... — 186

Revert – Undo the changes introduced by a commit — 187
   Getting ready — 187
   How to do it... — 188
   How it works... — 189
   There's more... — 189

Reverting a merge — 189
   Getting ready — 190
   How to do it... — 191
   How it works... — 193
   There's more... — 193
   See also — 195

Viewing past Git actions with git reflog — 195
   Getting ready — 195
   How to do it... — 196
   How it works... — 197

Finding lost changes with git fsck — 198
   Getting ready — 198
   How to do it... — 198
   How it works... — 200

Chapter 9: Repository Maintenance — 201
  Introduction — 201
  Pruning remote branches — 202
   Getting ready — 202
   How to do it... — 203
   How it works... — 204
   There's more... — 204

  Running garbage collection manually — 204
   Getting ready — 205
   How to do it... — 205
   How it works... — 207

  Turning off automatic garbage collection — 208

Getting ready	208
How to do it...	208 |ㅤ

Splitting a repository — 209
- Getting ready — 209
- How to do it... — 211
- How it works... — 213
- There's more... — 213

Rewriting history – changing a single file — 214
- Getting ready — 214
- How to do it... — 215
- How it works... — 215

Creating a backup of your repositories as mirror repositories — 216
- Getting ready — 216
- How to do it... — 216
- How it works... — 218
- There's more... — 218

A quick "how-to" submodule — 219
- Getting ready — 219
- How to do it... — 220
- There's more... — 223

Subtree merging — 224
- Getting ready — 225
- How to do it... — 225
- How it works... — 231
- See also — 231

Submodule versus subtree merging — 232

Chapter 10: Patching and Offline Sharing — 233
Introduction — 233
Creating patches — 234
- Getting ready — 234
- How to do it... — 234
- How it works... — 236
- There's more... — 236

Creating patches from branches — 237
- Getting ready — 237
- How to do it... — 237
- How it works... — 238
- There's more... — 238

Applying patches — 238
- Getting ready — 238
- How to do it... — 239
- How it works... — 240
- There's more... — 240

Sending patches — 241

Getting ready	241
How to do it...	241
How it works...	242
There's more...	243
Creating Git bundles	**244**
Getting ready	244
How to do it...	244
How it works...	246
Using a Git bundle	**246**
Getting ready	247
How to do it...	247
There's more...	249
Creating archives from a tree	**249**
Getting ready	250
How to do it...	250
There's more...	251
Chapter 11: Tips and Tricks	**253**
Introduction	**253**
Using git stash	**254**
Getting ready	254
How to do it...	255
How it works...	256
There's more...	258
Saving and applying stashes	**260**
Getting ready	260
How to do it...	261
There's more...	262
Debugging with git bisect	**263**
Getting ready	263
How to do it...	265
There's more...	267
Using the blame command	**268**
Getting ready	268
How to do it...	269
There's more...	269
Coloring the UI in the prompt	**269**
Getting ready	270
How to do it...	270
There's more...	271
Autocompletion	**271**
Getting ready	271
Linux	272
Mac	272
Windows	272

How to do it...	272
How it works...	272
There's more...	273

Bash prompt with status information — 273
Getting ready	273
How to do it...	273
How it works...	274
There's more...	275
See also	276

More aliases — 276
Getting ready	276
How to do it...	277

Interactive add — 281
Getting ready	282
How to do it...	282
There's more...	285

Interactive add with Git gui — 286
Getting ready	286
How to do it...	287

Ignoring files — 289
Getting ready	290
How to do it...	290
There's more...	292
See also	293

Showing and cleaning ignored files — 293
Getting ready	293
How to do it...	293
There's more...	294

Chapter 12: Git Providers, Integrations, and Clients — 295
Introduction — 295
Setting up an organization at GitHub — 296
Getting ready	296
How to do it...	297
How it works...	298
There's more...	299
See also	299

Creating a repository at GitHub — 299
Getting ready	299
How to do it...	300
How it works...	301
There's more...	302

Adding templates for issues and pull requests — 304
Getting ready	304
How to do it...	305

How it works...	307
Creating a GitHub API key	**307**
Getting ready	307
How to do it...	308
How it works...	310
See also	310
Using GitHub to authenticate at Jenkins	**310**
Getting ready	311
How to do it...	317
How it works...	321
There's more...	321
See also	321
Triggering Jenkins builds	**322**
Getting ready	322
How to do it...	322
How it works...	325
There's more...	325
See also	326
Using Jenkinsfiles	**326**
Getting ready	326
How to do it...	326
How it works...	327
There's more...	328
See also	328
Other Books You May Enjoy	**329**
Index	**333**

Preface

Git is increasingly becoming the *de facto* standard for **Source Control Management (SCM)** in modern software development.

Originally developed by Linus Torvalds as an SCM system for the Linux kernel to replace the proprietary SCM BitKeeper, Git has since conquered most of the open source world and is also used by lots of organizations for their private/proprietary projects.

This book is designed to give you practical recipes for everyday Git usage. The recipes can be used directly or as inspiration. The book will cover the Git data model through practical recipes and in-depth explanations so you get a deeper understanding of the internal workings of Git. This book will show you the following topics:

- Working with the history. With Git, all the history is stored locally. You can search through the history, view the history, find the last commit on a certain branch, and more.
- Using branches effectively with options and strategies to push, pull, and merge them.
- Storing and extracting additional metadata in the Git repository.
- Disaster recovery: local and global.

Git Version Control Cookbook gives you precise, step-by-step instructions for various common and uncommon Git operations. The book will make your daily work with Git easier by providing recipes for common issues, useful tips and tricks, and in-depth clarifications of why and how they work.

Who this book is for

This book targets developers, professional build/release managers, and DevOps practitioners who want a practical guide for the next level of Git. Starting with the Git data model and advancing through branching to metadata and hooks, all through an easy-to-read recipe structure, the transition from simple, everyday use cases to advanced repository handling is smooth. The book can be easily read and understood by readers from the target audience. You need basic knowledge of common GNU/Linux tools and Shell/Bash scripting to get the most from this book.

What this book covers

Chapter 1, *Navigating Git*, shows how Git stores files and commits. Examples will visually show you the data model and how to navigate the history and database with simple commands.

Chapter 2, *Configuration*, shows how a lot can be configured in Git, how configuration targets are set, the different configuration levels, and some useful targets.

Chapter 3, *Branching, Merging, and Options*, will give you a deeper understanding of branching and the options for easy push/pull targets. It also shows you the different merge strategies and some tips on how to record merge resolutions.

Chapter 4, *Rebasing Regularly and Interactively, and Other Use Cases*, shows you how rebasing can be used instead of merging, along with a lot of other use cases of rebasing, such as cleaning up the history before publishing, and testing single commits.

Chapter 5, *Storing Additional Information in Your Repository*, takes you on a tour of Git notes. It will show you how to tie additional information to a commit, and how to use and see this information again.

Chapter 6, *Extracting Data from the Repository*, shows you how to extract statistics and other metadata from the repository.

Chapter 7, *Enhancing Your Daily Work with Git Hooks, Aliases, and Scripts*, contains a collection of recipes that will help you automate much of the tedious daily work.

Chapter 8, *Recovering from Mistakes*, walks you through several recovery scenarios, from local undo, to where-is-my-old-commit, to global recovery scenarios.

Chapter 9, *Repository Maintenance*, is a collection of recipes that relate to the maintenance and management of repositories, from forcing garbage collection, over-splitting, and joining repositories, to completely rewriting history.

Chapter 10, *Patching and Offline Sharing*, shows you how to work offline with Git and share the work by means other than pushing and pulling.

Chapter 11, *Tips and Tricks*, is a collection of recipes that cover various topics, from simple tips to displaying the current branch in your prompt to advanced Git tools, such as bisect and stash.

Chapter 12, *Git Providers, Integrations, and Clients*, introduces the largest Git-hosting site, GitHub. Moreover, the chapter will discuss how to integrate Jenkins for automated builds and tests.

To get the most out of this book

To follow and recreate the recipes from this book, you will need a computer preferably running a *nix operating system. You will need Git installed, preferably Git Version 2.x or later.

If you are a Windows user, we recommend the Git Extensions package, which ships both a graphical and textual (Bash) Git interface. The latter is required for the recipes in this book.

Download the color images

We also provide a PDF file that has color images of the screenshots/diagrams used in this book. You can download it here: `https://www.packtpub.com/sites/default/files/downloads/GitVersionControlCookbookSecondEdition_ColorImages.pdf`.

Conventions used

There are a number of text conventions used throughout this book.

`CodeInText`: Indicates code words in text, database table names, folder names, filenames, file extensions, pathnames, dummy URLs, user input, and Twitter handles. Here is an example: "The most recent commit is the `3061dc6 Adds Java version of 'hello world'` commit."

Any command-line input or output is written as follows:

```
$ git checkout master && git reset --hard b14a939
```

Bold: Indicates a new term, an important word, or words that you see onscreen. For example, words in menus or dialog boxes appear in the text like this. Here is an example: "Select **System info** from the **Administration** panel."

Warnings or important notes appear like this.

Tips and tricks appear like this.

Sections

In this book, you will find several headings that appear frequently (*Getting ready*, *How to do it...*, *How it works...*, *There's more...*, and *See also*).

To give clear instructions on how to complete a recipe, use these sections as follows:

Getting ready

This section tells you what to expect in the recipe and describes how to set up any software or anypreliminary settings required for the recipe.

How to do it...

This section contains the steps required to follow the recipe.

How it works...

This section usually consists of a detailed explanation of what happened in the previous section.

There's more...

This section consists of additional information about the recipe in order to make you more knowledgeable about the recipe.

See also

This section provides helpful links to other useful information for the recipe.

Get in touch

Feedback from our readers is always welcome.

General feedback: Email `feedback@packtpub.com` and mention the book title in the subject of your message. If you have questions about any aspect of this book, please email us at `questions@packtpub.com`.

Errata: Although we have taken every care to ensure the accuracy of our content, mistakes do happen. If you have found a mistake in this book, we would be grateful if you would report this to us. Please visit `www.packtpub.com/submit-errata`, selecting your book, clicking on the Errata Submission Form link, and entering the details.

Piracy: If you come across any illegal copies of our works in any form on the internet, we would be grateful if you would provide us with the location address or website name. Please contact us at `copyright@packtpub.com` with a link to the material.

If you are interested in becoming an author: If there is a topic that you have expertise in and you are interested in either writing or contributing to a book, please visit `authors.packtpub.com`.

Reviews

Please leave a review. Once you have read and used this book, why not leave a review on the site that you purchased it from? Potential readers can then see and use your unbiased opinion to make purchase decisions, we at Packt can understand what you think about our products, and our authors can see your feedback on their book. Thank you!

For more information about Packt, please visit `packtpub.com`.

Navigating Git

In this chapter, we will cover the following topics:

- Git's objects
- The three stages
- Viewing the DAG
- Extracting fixed issues
- Getting a list of the changed files
- Viewing the history with gitk
- Finding commits in the history
- Searching through the history code

Introduction

In this chapter, we will take a look at Git's data model. We will learn how Git references its objects and how the history is recorded. We will learn how to navigate the history, from finding certain text snippets in commit messages, to the introducing a particular string in the code.

The data model of Git is different from other common **version control systems** (**VCSs**) in the way Git handles its data. Traditionally, a VCS will store its data as an initial file, followed by a list of patches for each new version of the file:

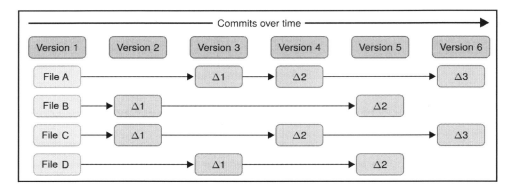

Git is different: Instead of the regular file and patches list, Git records a snapshot of all the files tracked by Git and their paths relative to the repository root—that is, the files tracked by Git in the filesystem tree. Each commit in Git records the full tree state. If a file does not change between commits, Git will not store the file again. Instead, Git stores a link to the file. This is shown in the diagram below where you see how the files will be after every commit/version.

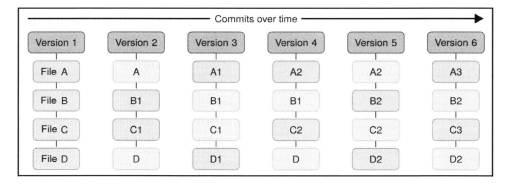

This is what makes Git different from most other VCSs, and, in the following chapters, we will explore some of the benefits of this powerful model.

The way Git references files and directories is directly built into the data model. In short, the Git data model can be summarized as shown in the following diagram:

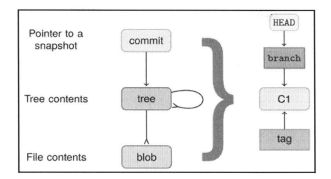

The `commit` object points to the root tree. The root tree points to subtrees and files.

Branches and tags point to a `commit` object and the `HEAD` object points to the **branch** that is currently checked out. So, for every commit, the full tree state and snapshot are identified by the root tree.

Git's objects

Now, since you know that Git stores every commit as a full tree state or snapshot, let's take a closer look at the object's Git store in the repository.

Git's object storage is a key-value storage, the key being the ID of the object and the value being the object itself. The key is an SHA-1 hash of the object, with some additional information, such as size. There are four types of objects in Git, as well as branches (which are not objects, but which are important) and the special `HEAD` pointer that refers to the branch/commit currently being checked out. The four object types are as follows:

- Files, or blobs as they are also called in the Git context
- Directories, or trees in the Git context
- Commits
- Tags

We will start by looking at the most recent `commit` object in the repository we just cloned, keeping in mind that the special `HEAD` pointer points to the branch that is currently being checked out.

Getting ready

To view the objects in the Git database, we first need a repository to be examined. For this recipe, we will clone an example repository in the following location:

```
$ git clone
https://github.com/PacktPublishing/Git-Version-Control-Cookbook-Second-Edit
ion.git
$ cd Git-Version-Control-Cookbook-Second-Edition
```

Now you are ready to look at the objects in the database. We will start by looking first at the commit object, followed by the trees, the files, and finally, the branches and tags.

How to do it...

Let's take a closer look at the object's Git stores in the repository.

The commit object

The Git's special HEAD object always points to the current snapshot/commit, so we can use that as the target for our request of the commit that we want to have a look at:

```
$ git cat-file -p HEAD
tree 34fa038544bcd9aed660c08320214bafff94150b
parent 5c662c018efced42ca5e9cce709787c40a849f34
author John Doe <john.doe@example.com> 1386933960 +0100
committer John Doe <john.doe@example.com> 1386941455 +0100
```

This is the subject line of the commit message. It should be followed by a blank line and then the body, which is this text. Here, you can use multiple paragraphs to explain your commit. It's like an email with a subject and a body to try to attract people's attention to the subject.

The cat-file command with the -p option prints the object given on the command line; in this case, HEAD, points to master, which, in turn, points to the most recent commit on the branch.

We can now see the commit object, consisting of the root tree (tree), the parent commit object's ID (parent), the author and timestamp information (author), the committer and timestamp information (committer), and the commit message.

The tree object

To see the `tree` object, we can run the same command on the tree, but with the tree ID (`34fa038544bcd9aed660c08320214bafff94150b`) as the target:

```
$ git cat-file -p 34fa038544bcd9aed660c08320214bafff94150b
100644 blob f21dc2804e888fee6014d7e5b1ceee533b222c15    README.md
040000 tree abc267d04fb803760b75be7e665d3d69eeed32f8    a_sub_directory
100644 blob b50f80ac4d0a36780f9c0636f43472962154a11a    another-file.txt
100644 blob 92f046f17079aa82c924a9acf28d623fcb6ca727    cat-me.txt
100644 blob bb2fe940924c65b4a1cefcbdbe88c74d39eb23cd    hello_world.c
```

We can also specify that we want the `tree` object from the commit pointed to by `HEAD` by specifying `git cat-file -p HEAD^{tree}`, which would give the same results as the previous command. The special notation `HEAD^{tree}` means that from the reference given, `HEAD` recursively dereferences the object at the reference until a `tree` object is found.

The first `tree` object is the root `tree` object found from the commit pointed to by the `master` branch, which is pointed to by `HEAD`. A generic form of the notation is `<rev>^<type>`, and will return the first object of `<type>`, searching recursively from `<rev>`.

From the `tree` object, we can see what it contains: the file type/permissions, type (`tree`/`blob`), ID, and pathname:

Type/Permissions	Type	ID/SHA-1	Pathname
100644	blob	f21dc2804e888fee6014d7e5b1ceee533b222c15	README.md
040000	tree	abc267d04fb803760b75be7e665d3d69eeed32f8	a_sub_directory
100644	blob	b50f80ac4d0a36780f9c0636f43472962154a11a	another-file.txt
100644	blob	92f046f17079aa82c924a9acf28d623fcb6ca727	cat-me.txt
100644	blob	bb2fe940924c65b4a1cefcbdbe88c74d39eb23cd	hello-world.c

The blob object

Now, we can investigate the `blob` (file) object. We can do this using the same command, giving the `blob` ID as the target for the `cat-me.txt` file:

```
$ git cat-file -p 92f046f17079aa82c924a9acf28d623fcb6ca727
```

The content of the file is `cat-me.txt`.

```
Not really that exciting, huh?
```

This is simply the content of the file, which we can also get by running a normal `cat cat-me.txt` command. So, the objects are tied together, blobs to trees, trees to other trees, and the root tree to the `commit` object, all connected by the SHA-1 identifier of the object.

The branch object

The `branch` object is not really like any other Git objects; you can't print it using the `cat-file` command as we can with the others (if you specify the `-p` pretty print, you'll just get the `commit` object it points to), as shown in the following code:

```
$ git cat-file master
usage: git cat-file (-t|-s|-e|-p|<type>|--textconv) <object>
   or: git cat-file (--batch|--batch-check) < <list_of_objects>
<type> can be one of: blob, tree, commit, tag.
...
$ git cat-file -p master
tree 34fa038544bcd9aed660c08320214bafff94150b
parent a90d1906337a6d75f1dc32da647931f932500d83
...
```

Instead, we can take a look at the branch inside the `.git` folder where the whole Git repository is stored. If we open the text file `.git/refs/heads/master`, we can actually see the commit ID that the `master` branch points to. We can do this using `cat`, as follows:

```
$ cat .git/refs/heads/master
13dcada077e446d3a05ea9cdbc8ecc261a94e42d
```

We can verify that this is the latest commit by running `git log -1`:

```
$ git log -1
commit 34acc370b4d6ae53f051255680feaefaf7f7850d (HEAD -> master, origin/master, origin/HEAD)
Author: John Doe <john.doe@example.com>
Date:   Fri Dec 13 12:26:00 2013 +0100
```

```
This is the subject line of the commit message
...
```

We can also see that HEAD is pointing to the active branch by using `cat` with the `.git/HEAD` file:

```
$ cat .git/HEAD
ref: refs/heads/master
```

The `branch` object is simply a pointer to a commit, identified by its SHA-1 hash.

The tag object

The last object to be analyzed is the `tag` object. There are three different kinds of tag: a lightweight (just a `label`) tag, an annotated tag, and a signed tag. In the example repository, there are two annotated tags:

```
$ git tag
v0.1
v1.0
```

Let's take a closer look at the `v1.0` tag:

```
$ git cat-file -p v1.0
object f55f7383b57ad7c11cf56a7c55a8d738af4741ce
type commit
tag v1.0
tagger John Doe <john.doe@example.com> 1526017989 +0200

We got the hello world C program merged, let's call that a release 1.0
```

As you can see, the tag consists of an object—which, in this case, is the latest commit on the master branch—the object's type (commits, blobs, and trees can be tagged), the tag name, the tagger and timestamp, and finally the tag message.

How it works...

The Git command `git cat-file -p` will print the object given as an input. Normally, it is not used in everyday Git commands, but it is quite useful to investigate how it ties the objects together.

We can also verify the output of `git cat-file` by rehashing it with the Git command `git hash-object`; for example, if we want to verify the `commit` object at `HEAD` (`34acc370b4d6ae53f051255680feaefaf7f7850d`), we can run the following command:

```
$ git cat-file -p HEAD | git hash-object -t commit --stdin
13dcada077e446d3a05ea9cdbc8ecc261a94e42d
```

If you see the same commit hash as `HEAD` pointing towards you, you can verify whether it is correct using `git log -1`.

There's more...

There are many ways to see the objects in the Git database. The `git ls-tree` command can easily show the content of trees and subtrees, and `git show` can show the Git objects, but in a different way.

The three stages

We have seen the different objects in Git, but how do we create them? In this example, we'll see how to create a `blob`, `tree`, and `commit` object in the repository. We'll also learn about the three stages of creating a commit.

Getting ready

We'll use the same `Git-Version-Control-Cookbook-Second-Edition` repository that we saw in the last recipe:

```
$ git clone https://github.com/PacktPublishing/Git-Version-Control-Cookbook-Second-Edition.git
$ cd Git-Version-Control-Cookbook-Second-Edition
```

How to do it...

1. First, we'll make a small change to the file and check `git status`:

   ```
   $ echo "Another line" >> another-file.txt
   $ git status
   On branch master
   Your branch is up-to-date with 'origin/master'.
   Changes not staged for commit:
   (use "git add <file>..." to update what will be committed)
   (use "git checkout -- <file>..." to discard changes in working directory)
   modified:   another-file.txt
   no changes added to commit (use "git add" and/or "git commit -a")
   ```

   This, of course, just tells us that we have modified `another-file.txt` and we need to use `git add` to stage it.

2. Let's add the `another-file.txt` file and run `git status` again:

   ```
   $ git add another-file.txt
   $ git status
   On branch master
   Your branch is up-to-date with 'origin/master'.
   Changes to be committed:
   (use "git reset HEAD <file>..." to unstage)
   modified:   another-file.txt
   ```

   The file is now ready to be committed, just as you have probably seen before. But what happens during the `add` command? The `add` command, generally speaking, moves files from the working directory to the staging area; however, this is not all that actually happens, though you don't see it. When a file is moved to the staging area, the SHA-1 hash of the file is created and the `blob` object is written to Git's database. This happens every time a file is added, but if nothing changes for a file, it means that it is already stored in the database. At first, this might seem that the database will grow quickly, but this is not the case. Garbage collection kicks in at times, compressing, and cleaning up the database and keeping only the objects that are required.

3. We can edit the file again and run `git status`:

   ```
   $ echo 'Whoops almost forgot this' >> another-file.txt
   $ git status
   On branch master
   Your branch is up-to-date with 'origin/master'.
   Changes to be committed:
   (use "git reset HEAD <file>..." to unstage)
   modified:   another-file.txt
   Changes not staged for commit:
   (use "git add <file>..." to update what will be committed)
   (use "git checkout -- <file>..." to discard changes in working directory)
   modified:   another-file.txt
   ```

   Now, the file shows up in both the `Changes to be committed` and `Changes not staged for commit` sections. This looks a bit weird at first, but there is, of course, a reason for this. When we added the file the first time, the content of it was hashed and stored in Git's database. The changes arising from the second change to the file have not yet been hashed and written to the database; it only exists in the working directory. Therefore, the file shows up in both the `Changes to be committed` and `Changes not staged for commit` sections; the first change is ready to be committed, the second is not. Let's also add the second change:

   ```
   $ git add another-file.txt
   $ git status
   On branch master
   Your branch is up-to-date with 'origin/master'.
   Changes to be committed:
   (use "git reset HEAD <file>..." to unstage)
   modified:   another-file.txt
   ```

4. Now, all the changes we have made to the file are ready to be committed, and we can record a commit:

   ```
   $ git commit -m 'Another change to another file'
   [master 99fac83] Another change to another file
   1 file changed, 2 insertions(+)
   ```

How it works...

As we learned previously, the `add` command creates the `blob`, `tree`, and `commit` objects; however, they are also created when we run the `commit` command. We can view these objects using the `cat-file` command, as we saw in the previous recipe:

```
$ git cat-file -p HEAD
tree 162201200b5223d48ea8267940c8090b23cbfb60
parent 13dcada077e446d3a05ea9cdbc8ecc261a94e42d
author John Doe <john.doe@example.com> 1524163792 +0200
committer John Doe <john.doe@example.com> 1524163792 +0200
```

Making changes to another file.

The `root-tree` object from the commit is as follows:

```
$ git cat-file -p HEAD^{tree}
100644 blob f21dc2804e888fee6014d7e5b1ceee533b222c15    README.md
040000 tree  abc267d04fb803760b75be7e665d3d69eeed32f8    a_sub_directory
100644 blob 35d31106c5d6fdb38c6b1a6fb43a90b183011a4b    another-file.txt
100644 blob 92f046f17079aa82c924a9acf28d623fcb6ca727    cat-me.txt
100644 blob bb2fe940924c65b4a1cefcbdbe88c74d39eb23cd    hello_world.c
```

From the previous recipe, we know that the SHA-1 of the root tree was `34fa038544bcd9aed660c08320214bafff94150b` and the SHA-1 of the `another-file.txt` file was `b50f80ac4d0a36780f9c0636f43472962154a11a`, and, as expected, they changed in our latest commit when we updated the `another-file.txt` file. We added the same file, `another-file.txt`, twice before we created the commit, recording the changes to the history of the repository. We also learned that the `add` command creates a blob object when called. So, in the Git database, there must have been an object similar to the content of `another-file.txt` the first time we added the file to the staging area. We can use the `git fsck` command to check for dangling objects—that is, objects that are not referred to by other objects or references:

```
$ git fsck --dangling
Checking object directories: 100% (256/256), done.
dangling blob ad46f2da274ed6c79a16577571a604d3281cd6d9
```

Let's check the content of the blob using the following command:

```
$ git cat-file -p ad46f2da274ed6c79a16577571a604d3281cd6d9
This is just another file
Another line
```

The blob was, as expected, similar to the content of `another-file.txt` when we added it to the staging area the first time.

The following diagram describes the tree stages and the commands used to move between the stages:

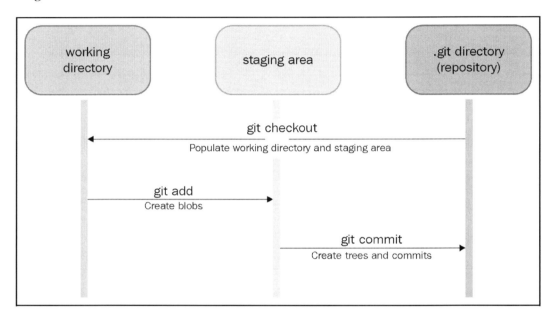

See also

For more examples and information on the `cat-file` and `fsck` commands, please consult the Git documentation at https://git-scm.com/docs/git-cat-file and https://git-scm.com/docs/git-fsck.

Viewing the DAG

The history in Git is formed from the `commit` objects; as development advances, branches are created and merged, and the history will create a directed acyclic graph, the DAG, because of the way that Git ties a commit to its parent commit. The DAG makes it easy to see the development of a project based on the commits.

Please note that the arrows in the following diagram are dependency arrows, meaning that each commit points to its parent commit(s), which is why the arrows point in the opposite direction to the normal flow of time:

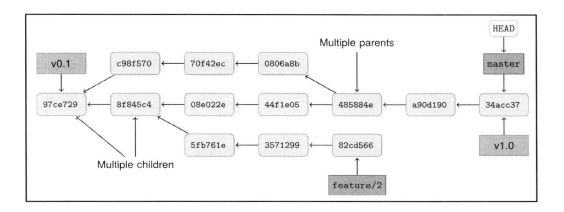

A graph of the example repository with abbreviated commit IDs

You can view the history (the DAG) in Git by using its `git log` command. There are also a number of visual Git tools that can graphically display the history. This section will show some features of `git log`.

Getting ready

We will use the example repository from the last section and ensure that the master branch is pointing to `34acc37`:

```
$ git checkout master && git reset --hard 34acc37
```

In the previous command, we only use the first seven characters (`34acc37`) of the commit ID; this is fine as long as the abbreviated ID that is used is unique in the repository.

How to do it...

1. The simplest way to see the history is to use the `git log` command; this will display the history in reverse chronological order. The output is paged through `less` and can be further limited, for example, by providing only the number of commits in the history to be displayed:

   ```
   $ git log -3
   ```

2. This will display the following result:

   ```
   commit 34acc370b4d6ae53f051255680feaefaf7f7850d
   Author: John Doe <john.doe@example.com>
   Date:   Fri Dec 13 12:26:00 2013 +0100
   This is the subject line of the commit message.
   It should be followed by a blank line then the body, which is this text. Here
   you can have multiple paragraphs etc. and explain your commit. It's like an
   email with subject and body, so try to get people's attention in the subject
   commit a90d1906337a6d75f1dc32da647931f932500d83
   Author: John Doe <john.doe@example.com>
   Date:   Fri Dec 13 12:17:42 2013 +0100
   Instructions for compiling hello_world.c
   commit 485884efd6ac68cc7b58c643036acd3cd208d5c8
   Merge: 44f1e05 0806a8b
   Author: John Doe <john.doe@example.com>
   Date:   Fri Dec 13 12:14:49 2013 +0100
   Merge branch 'feature/1'
   Adds a hello world C program.
   ```

   Turn on colors in the Git output by running `git config --global color.ui auto`.

3. By default, `git log` prints the commit, author's name and email ID, timestamp, and the commit message. However, the information isn't very graphical, especially if you want to see branches and merges. To display this information and limit some of the other data, you can use the following options with `git log`:

   ```
   $ git log --decorate --graph --oneline --all
   ```

Chapter 1

4. The previous command will show one commit per line (`--oneline`), identified by its abbreviated commit ID, and the commit message subject. A graph will be drawn between the commits depicting their dependency (`--graph`). The `--decorate` option shows the branch names after the abbreviated commit ID, and the `--all` option shows all the branches, instead of just the current one(s):

   ```
   $ git log --decorate --graph --oneline --all
   * 34acc37 (HEAD, tag: v1.0, origin/master, origin/HEAD, master)
   This is the sub...
   * a90d190 Instructions for compiling hello_world.c
   *   485884e Merge branch 'feature/1'
   ...
   ```

   This output, however, gives neither the timestamp nor the author information, because of the way the `--oneline` option formats the output.

5. Fortunately, the `log` command gives us the ability to create our own output format. So, we can make a history view similar to the previous one. The colors are made with the `%C<color-name>text-be-colored%Creset` syntax, along with the author and timestamp information and some colors to display it nicely:

   ```
   $ git log --all --graph \
     --pretty=format:'%Cred%h%Creset -%C(yellow)%d%Creset %s
   %Cgreen(%ci) %C(bold blue)<%an>%Creset'
   ```

[21]

6. This is a bit cumbersome to write, but luckily, it can be made as an alias so you only have to write it once:

```
git config --global alias.graph "log --all --graph --pretty=format:'%Cred%h%Creset -%C(yellow)%d%Creset %s %Cgreen(%ci) %C(bold blue)<%an>%Creset'"
```

> Now, all you need to do is call `git graph` to show the history, as you have seen previously.

How it works...

Git traverses the DAG by following the parent IDs (hashes) from the given commit(s). The options passed to `git log` can format the output in different ways; this can serve several purposes—for example, to give a nice graphical view of the history, branches, and tags, as seen previously, or to extract specific information from the history of a repository to use, for example, in a script.

Extracting fixed issues

A common use case of creating a release is to create a release note, containing, among other things, the bugs fixed in the release. A good practice is to write in the commit message whether a bug is fixed by the commit. A better practice is to have a standard way of doing this—for example, a line with the string "`Fixes-bug: `", followed by the bug identifier in the last part of the commit message. This makes it easy to compile a list of bugs fixed for a release note. The JGit project is a good example of this; their bug identifier in the commit messages is a simple "`Bug: `" string followed by the bug ID.

This recipe will show you how to limit the output of `git log` to only list the commits since the last release (tag), which contains a bug fix.

Getting ready

Clone the JGit repository using the following command lines:

```
$ git clone https://git.eclipse.org/r/jgit/jgit
$ cd jgit
```

If you want the exact same output as in this example, reset your `master` branch to `b14a93971837610156e815ae2eee3baaa5b7a44b`:

```
$ git checkout master && git reset --hard b14a939
```

How to do it...

You are now ready to look through the commit log for commit messages that describe the bugs fixed.

1. First, let's limit the log to only look through the history since the last tag (release). To find the last tag, we can use `git describe`:

   ```
   $ git describe
   v3.1.0.201310021548-r-96-gb14a939
   ```

   The preceding output tells us three things:

   - The last tag was `v3.1.0.201310021548-r`
   - The number of commits since the tag was `96`
   - The current commit in abbreviated form is `b14a939`

   Now, the log can be parsed from HEAD to `v3.1.0.201310021548-r`. But just running `git log 3.1.0.201310021548-r..HEAD` will give us all 96 commits, and we just want the commits with the commit messages that contain `"Bug: xxxxxx"` for our release note. The xxxxxx is an identifier for the bug, and will be a number. We can use the `--grep` option with `git log` for this purpose, making the code phrase `git log --grep "Bug: "`. This will give us all the commits containing `"Bug: "` in the commit message; all we need to do now is just to format it to something that we can use for our release note.

2. Now, let's say we want the release note format to look like the following template:

   ```
   Commit-id: Commit subject
   Fixes-bug: xxx
   ```

3. Our command line so far is as follows:

   ```
   $ git log --grep "Bug: " v3.1.0.201310021548-r..HEAD
   ```

Navigating Git

This gives us all the bug fix commits, but we can format this to a format that is easily parsed with the `--pretty` option.

4. First, we will print the abbreviated commit ID (`%h`), followed by a separator of our choice (`|`), and then the commit subject (`%s`, the first line of the commit message), followed by a new line (`%n`), and the body (`%b`):

   ```
   --pretty="%h|%s%n%b"
   ```

   The output, of course, needs to be parsed, but that's easy with regular Linux tools, such as `grep` and `sed`.

5. First, we just want the lines that contain "`|`" or "`Bug: `":

   ```
   grep -E "\||Bug: "
   ```

6. Then, we replace these with `sed`:

   ```
   sed -e 's/|/: /' -e 's/Bug:/Fixes-bug:/'
   ```

7. The entire command put together is as follows:

   ```
   $ git log --grep "Bug: " v3.1.0.201310021548-r..HEAD --pretty="%h|%s%n%b" | grep -E "\||Bug: " | sed -e 's/|/: /' -e 's/Bug:/Fixes-bug:/'
   ```

8. The previous set of commands gives the following output:

   ```
   f86a488: Implement rebase.autostash
   Fixes-bug: 422951
   7026658: CLI status should support --porcelain
   Fixes-bug: 419968
   e0502eb: More helpful InvalidPathException messages (include reason)
   Fixes-bug: 413915
   f4dae20: Fix IgnoreRule#isMatch returning wrong result due to missing reset
   Fixes-bug: 423039
   7dc8a4f: Fix exception on conflicts with recursive merge
   Fixes-bug: 419641
   99608f0: Fix broken symbolic links on Cygwin.
   Fixes-bug: 419494
   ...
   ```

Now, we can extract the bug information from the bug tracker and put the preceding code in the release note as well, if necessary.

How it works...

First, we limit the `git log` command to only show the range of commits we are interested in, and then we further limit the output by filtering the `"Bug: "` string in the commit message. We pretty print the string so we can easily format it to a style we need for the release note, and finally, find `"Bug: "` and replace it by `"Fixes-bug: "` using `grep` and `sed` to completely match the style of the release note.

There's more...

If we just wanted to extract the bug IDs from the commit messages and didn't care about the commit IDs, we could have just used `grep` after the `git log` command, still limiting the log to the last tag:

```
$ git log  v3.1.0.201310021548-r..HEAD | grep "Bug: "
```

If we just want the commit IDs and their subjects, but not the actual bug IDs, we can use the `--oneline` feature of `git log` combined with the `--grep` option:

```
$ git log --grep "Bug: " --oneline  v3.1.0.201310021548-r..HEAD
```

Getting a list of the changed files

As we saw in the previous recipe, where a list of fixed issues was extracted from the history, a list of all the files that have been changed since the last release can also easily be extracted. The files can be further filtered to find those that have been added, deleted, modified, and so on.

Getting ready

The same repository and `HEAD` position (`HEAD` pointing to `b14a939`) that we saw in the previous recipe will be used. The release is also the same, which is `v3.1.0.201310021548-r`.

How to do it...

The following command lists all the files that have changed since the last release (v3.1.0.201310021548-r):

```
$ git diff --name-only v3.1.0.201310021548-r..HEAD
org.eclipse.jgit.packaging/org.eclipse.jgit.target/jgit-4.3.target
org.eclipse.jgit.packaging/org.eclipse.jgit.target/jgit-4.4.target
org.eclipse.jgit.pgm.test/tst/org/eclipse/jgit/pgm/DescribeTest.java
org.eclipse.jgit.pgm.test/tst/org/eclipse/jgit/pgm/FetchTest.java
org.eclipse.jgit.pgm/src/org/eclipse/jgit/pgm/Describe.java
...
```

How it works...

The `git diff` command operates on the same revision range as `git log` did in the previous recipe. By specifying `--name-only`, Git will only give the paths of the files that were changed by the commits in the range specified as output.

There's more...

The output of the command can be further filtered: If we only want to show which files have been deleted in the repository since the last commit, we can use the `--diff-filter` switch with `git diff`:

```
$ git diff --name-only --diff-filter=D  v3.1.0.201310021548-r..HEAD
org.eclipse.jgit.junit/src/org/eclipse/jgit/junit/SampleDataRepositoryTestCase.java
org.eclipse.jgit.packaging/org.eclipse.jgit.target/org.eclipse.jgit.target.target
org.eclipse.jgit.test/tst/org/eclipse/jgit/internal/storage/file/GCTest.java
```

There are also switches for the files that have been added (A), copied (C), deleted (D), modified (M), renamed (R), and so on.

See also

For more information, visit the **Help** page by running the `git help diff` command.

Viewing the history with gitk

We saw earlier how we can view the history (the DAG) and visualize it by using `git log`. However, as the history grows, the terminal representation of the history can be a bit cumbersome to navigate. Fortunately, there are a lot of graphical tools in Git, one of them being gitk, which works on multiple platforms (Linux, Mac, and Windows).

This recipe will show you how to get started with gitk.

Getting ready

Make sure you have `gitk` installed:

```
$ which gitk
/usr/local/bin/gitk
```

If nothing shows up, then gitk is not installed on your system, or at least is not available on your `$PATH`.

Change the directory to the `Git-Version-Control-Cookbook-Second-Edition` repository from the objects and DAG examples. Make sure the master branch is checked out and pointing to `13dcad`:

```
$ git checkout master && git reset --hard 13dcad
```

How to do it...

In the repository, run `gitk --all &` to bring up the `gitk` interface. You can also specify the commit range or branches you want, just as you did with `git log` (or provide `--all` to see everything):

```
$ gitk --all &
```

Gitk shows the commit history of the repository:

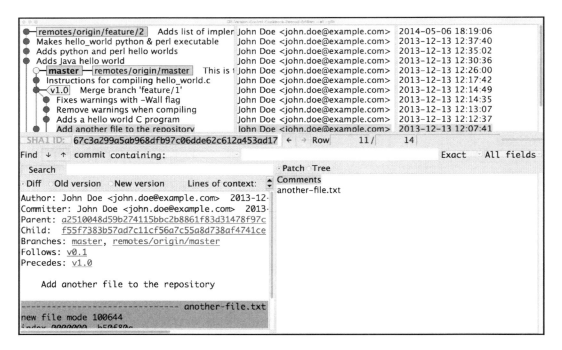

How it works...

Gitk parses the information for every commit and the objects attached to it to provide an easy graphical information screen that shows a graph of the history, author, and timestamp for each commit. In the bottom half is the result of selecting a commit. The commit message and the patches for each file that has changed . Moreover, a list of files that have been changed is displayed to the right.

Though very lightweight and fast, gitk is a very powerful tool. There are many different context menus that appear after the user clicks on a commit, a branch, or a tag in the history view. You can create and delete branches, revert and cherry-pick commits, `diff` selected commits, and much more.

There's more...

From the interface, you can perform a find and search operation. **Find** looks through the history and **Search** looks through the information displayed in the lower half of gitk for the commit that is currently highlighted.

Finding commits in the history

You already saw in the previous recipe how we can filter the output of `git log` to only list commits with the `"Bug: "` string in the commit message. In this example, we will use the same technique to find specific commits in the entire history.

Getting ready

Again, we will use the JGit repository, trying to find commits related to the `"Performance"` keyword. In this recipe, we will look through the entire history, so we don't need the master branch to point to a specific commit.

How to do it...

As we tried earlier, we can use the `--grep` option to find specific strings in commit messages. In this recipe, we look at the entire history and search every commit that has `"Performance"` in its commit message:

```
$ git log --grep "Performance" --oneline --all
e3f19a529 Performance improvement on writing a large index
83ad74b6b SHA-1: collision detection support
48e245fc6 RefTreeDatabase: Ref database using refs/txn/committed
087b5051f Skip redundant 'OR-reuse' step in tip commit bitmap setup
9613b04d8 Merge "Performance fixes in DateRevQueue"
84afea917 Performance fixes in DateRevQueue
7cad0adc7 DHT: Remove per-process ChunkCache
d9b224aeb Delete DiffPerformanceTest
```

```
e7a3e590e Reuse DiffPerformanceTest support code to validate algorithms
fb1c7b136 Wait for JIT optimization before measuring diff performance
```

How it works...

In this example, we specifically ask Git to consider all of the commits in the history by supplying the `--all` switch. Git runs through the DAG and checks whether the `"Performance"` string is included in the commit message. For an easy overview of the results, the `--oneline` switch is also used to limit the output to just the subject of the commit message. Hopefully then, the commit(s) we needed to find can be identified from this, much shorter, list of commits.

Note that the search is case sensitive—had we searched for `"performance"` (all in lower case), the list of commits would have been very different:

```
$ git log --grep "performance" --oneline --all
d7deda98d Skip ignored directories in FileTreeIterator
5a87d5040 Teach UploadPack "include-tag" in "fetch"
7d9246f16 RawParseUtils#lineMap: Simplify by using null sentinel internally
4bfc6c2ae Significantly speed up FileTreeIterator on Windows
4644d15bc GC: Replace Files methods with File alternatives
d3021788d Use bitmaps for non-commit reachability checks
6b1e3c58b Run auto GC in the background
db7761025 Pack refs/tags/ with refs/heads/
30eb6423a Add GC_REST PackSource to better order DFS packs
... more output
```

There's more...

We also could have used the **Find** feature in gitk to find the same commits. Open gitk with the `--all` switch, type `Performance` in the **Find** field, and hit *Enter*. This will highlight the commits in the history view, and you can navigate to the previous/next result by pressing *Shift* + up arrow, *Shift* + down arrow, or the buttons next to the **Find** field. You will still, however, be able to see the entire history in the view with the matching commits highlighted:

Searching through the history code

Sometimes, it is not enough to list the commit messages. You may want to know which commits touched a specific method or variable. This is also possible using `git log`. You can perform a search for a string, for example, or a variable or method, and `git log` will give you the commits, adding or deleting the string from the history. In this way, you can easily get the full commit context for the piece of code.

Getting ready

Again, we will use the JGit repository with the master branch pointing to `b14a939`:

```
$ git checkout master && git reset --hard b14a939
```

How to do it...

We would like to find all the commits that have had changes made to the lines that contain the "isOutdated" method. Again, we will just display the commits on one line each; we can then check them individually later:

```
$ git log -G"isOutdated" --oneline
f32b861 JGit 3.0: move internal classes into an internal subpackage
c9e4a78 Add isOutdated method to DirCache
797ebba Add support for getting the system wide configuration
ad5238d Move FileRepository to storage.file.FileRepository
4c14b76 Make lib.Repository abstract and lib.FileRepository its
implementation
c9c57d3 Rename Repository 'config' as 'repoConfig'
5c780b3 Fix unit tests using MockSystemReader with user configuation
cc905e7 Make Repository.getConfig aware of changed config
```

We can see that eight commits have patches that involve the string "isOutdated".

How it works...

Git looks over the history (the DAG) looking at each commit for the "isOutdated" string in the patch between the parent commit and the current commit. This method is quite convenient to use in finding out when a given string was introduced or deleted, and to get the full context and commit at that point in time.

There's more...

The -G option used with git log will look for differences in the patches that contain added or deleted lines that match the given string. However, these lines could also have been added or removed because of some other refactoring/renaming of a variable or method. There is another option that can be used with git log, namely -S, which will look through the difference in the patch text in a similar way to the -G option, but will only match commits where there is a change in the number of occurrences of the specified string—that is, a line added or removed, but not added and removed.

Let's see the output of the -S option:

```
$ git log -S"isOutdated" --oneline
f32b861 JGit 3.0: move internal classes into an internal subpackage
c9e4a78 Add isOutdated method to DirCache
797ebba Add support for getting the system wide configuration
ad5238d Move FileRepository to storage.file.FileRepository
4c14b76 Make lib.Repository abstract and lib.FileRepository its
implementation
5c780b3 Fix unit tests using MockSystemReader with user configuation
cc905e7 Make Repository.getConfig aware of changed config
```

The search matches seven commits, whereas the search with the -G option matches eight commits. The difference is that the commit with the ID c9c57d3 is only found with the -G option in the first list. A closer look at this commit shows that the isOutdated string is only touched because of the renaming of another object, and this is why it is filtered away from the list of matching commits in the last list when using the -S option. We can see the content of the commit with the git show command, and use grep -C4 to limit the output to just the four lines before and after the search string:

```
$ git show c9c57d3 | grep -C4 "isOutdated"
@@ -417,14 +417,14 @@ public FileBasedConfig getConfig() {
            throw new RuntimeException(e);
        }
    }
-   if (config.isOutdated()) {
+   if (repoConfig.isOutdated()) {
        try {
-           loadConfig();
+           loadRepoConfig();
        } catch (IOException e) {
```

2
Configuration

In this chapter, we will cover the following recipes:

- Configuration targets
- Querying the existing configuration
- Templates
- A .git directory template
- A few configuration examples
- Git aliases
- The refspec exemplified

Introduction

Git, while serving a basic and crucial role in the life of a developer, is also quite complex and highly configurable. This chapter will give an overview of the most important options available and will provide the right tools for learning and navigating the multitude of configuration flags and fields available, in order to tailor your Git experience to your own needs.

Configuration targets

In this section, we will look at the different layers that can be configured. The layers are as follows:

- `SYSTEM`: This layer is system-wide and can be found in `/etc/gitconfig`
- `GLOBAL`: This layer is global for the user and can be found in `~/.gitconfig`
- `LOCAL`: This layer is local to the current repository and can be found in `.git/config`

Configuration

Getting ready

We will use the `jgit` repository for this example; clone it, or use the clone you already have from Chapter 1, *Navigating Git*, as shown in the following command:

```
$ git clone https://git.eclipse.org/r/jgit/jgit
$ cd jgit
```

How to do it...

In the previous chapter, we saw how we could use the command `git config --list` to list configuration entries. This list is actually made from three different levels of configuration that Git offers: system-wide configuration, `SYSTEM`; global configuration for the user, `GLOBAL`; and local repository configuration, `LOCAL`.

1. For each of the configuration layers, we can query the existing configuration. On a Windows box with a default installation of the Git extensions, the different configuration layers will look something like the following:

    ```
    $ git config --list --system
    core.symlinks=false
    core.autocrlf=true
    color.diff=auto
    color.status=auto
    color.branch=auto
    color.interactive=true
    pack.packsizelimit=2g
    help.format=html
    http.sslcainfo=/bin/curl-ca-bundle.crt
    sendemail.smtpserver=/bin/msmtp.exe
    diff.astextplain.textconv=astextplain
    rebase.autosquash=true

    # list the global configuration
    $ git config --list --global
    merge.tool=kdiff3
    mergetool.kdiff3.path=C:/Program Files (x86)/KDiff3/kdiff3.exe
    diff.guitool=kdiff3
    difftool.kdiff3.path=C:/Program Files (x86)/KDiff3/kdiff3.exe
    core.editor="C:/Program Files (x86)/GitExtensions/GitExtensions.exe" fileeditor
    core.autocrlf=true
    credential.helper=!"C:/Program Files (x86)/GitExtensions/GitCredentialWinStore/git-credential-winstore.exe"
    ```

```
user.name=John Doe
user.email=john.doe@example.com

# list the configuration for this repository
$ git config --list --local
core.repositoryformatversion=0
core.filemode=false
core.bare=false
core.logallrefupdates=true
core.symlinks=false
core.ignorecase=true
core.hidedotfiles=dotGitOnly
remote.origin.url=https://git.eclipse.org/r/jgit/jgit
    remote.origin.fetch=+refs/heads/*:refs/remotes/origin/*
    branch.master.remote=origin
    branch.master.merge=refs/heads/master
```

2. We can also query a single key and limit the scope to one of the three layers, by using the following command:

```
$ git config --global user.email
john.doe@example.com
```

3. We can set the email address of the user to a different one for the current repository:

```
$ git config --local user.email john@example.com
```

Now, listing the GLOBAL layer user.email will return john.doe@example.com, listing LOCAL will give john@example.com, and listing user.email without specifying the layer will give the effective value that is used in the operations on this repository; in this case, the LOCAL value john@example.com. The effective value will take precedence when needed. When two or more values are specified for the same key, but on different layers, the lowest layer takes precedence. When a configuration value is needed, Git will first look in the LOCAL configuration. If not found here, the GLOBAL configuration is queried. If it is not found in the GLOBAL configuration, the SYSTEM configuration is used.

If none of this works, the default value in Git is used.

In the previous example, user.email is specified in both the GLOBAL and LOCAL layers. Therefore, the LOCAL layer will be used.

Configuration

How it works...

Querying the three layers of configuration simply returns the content of the configuration files; `/etc/gitconfig` for system-wide configuration, `~/.gitconfig` for user-specific configuration, and `.git/config` for repository-specific configuration. When not specifying the configuration layer, the returned value will be the effective value.

There's more...

Instead of setting all the configuration values on the command line by the key value, it is possible to set them by just editing the configuration file directly. Open the configuration file in your favorite editor and set the configuration you need, or use the built-in `git config -e` repository to edit the configuration directly in the Git-configured editor. You can set the editor to the editor of your choice either by changing the `$EDITOR` environment variable or with the `core.editor` configuration target, for example:

```
$ git config --global core.editor vim
```

Querying the existing configuration

In this example, we will look at how we can query the existing configuration and set the configuration values.

Getting ready

We'll use `jgit` again by using the following command:

```
$ cd jgit
```

How to do it...

You can use `git config` to query your local and global Git configuration. In this section, we will show a couple of examples.

1. To view all the effective configurations for the current Git repository, run the following command:

   ```
   $ git config --list
   user.name=John Doe
   user.email=john.doe@example.com
   core.repositoryformatversion=0
   core.filemode=false
   core.bare=false
   core.logallrefupdates=true
   remote.origin.url=https://git.eclipse.org/r/jgit/jgit
       remote.origin.fetch=+refs/heads/*:refs/remotes/origin/*
       branch.master.remote=origin
       branch.master.merge=refs/heads/master
   ```

   The previous output will, of course, reflect the user running the command. Instead of `John Doe` as the name and the email, the output should reflect your settings.

2. If we are just interested in a single configuration item, we can just query it by its `section.key` or `section.subsection.key`:

   ```
   $ git config user.name
   John Doe
   $ git config remote.origin.url
   https://git.eclipse.org/r/jgit/jgit
   ```

How it works...

Git's configuration is stored in plain text files and works like a key-value storage. You can set/query by key and get the value back. An example of the text-based configuration file is shown as follows (from the `jgit` repository):

```
$ cat .git/config
  [core]
    repositoryformatversion = 0
    filemode = false
    bare = false
    logallrefupdates = true
  [remote "origin"]
```

Configuration

```
    url = https://git.eclipse.org/r/jgit/jgit
    fetch = +refs/heads/*:refs/remotes/origin/*
[branch "master"]
    remote = origin
    merge = refs/heads/master
```

There's more...

It is also easy to set configuration values. You can use the same syntax as you did when querying the configuration, except you need to add an argument to the value. To set a new email address on the LOCAL layer, we can execute the following command line:

```
git config user.email john.doe@example.com
```

The LOCAL layer is the default, if nothing else is specified. If you require whitespaces in the value, you can enclose the string in quotation marks, as you would do when configuring your name:

```
git config user.name "John Doe"
```

You can even set your own configuration, which does not have any effect on the core Git, but which can be useful for scripting/builds, and so on:

```
$ git config my.own.config "Whatever I need"
```

List the value:

```
$ git config my.own.config
Whatever I need
```

It is also very easy to delete/unset configuration entries:

```
$ git config --unset my.own.config
```

List the value:

```
$ git config my.own.config
```

Templates

In this example, we will see how to create a template commit message that will be displayed in the editor when creating a commit. The template is only for the local user and not distributed with the repository in general.

Getting ready

In this example, we will use the example repository from Chapter 1, *Navigating Git*:

```
$ git clone
https://github.com/PacktPublishing/Git-Version-Control-Cookbook-Second-Edition.git
$ cd Git-Version-Control-Cookbook-Second-Edition
```

We'll use the following command as a commit message template for commit messages:

```
Short description of commit

Longer explanation of the motivation for the change

Fixes-Bug: Enter bug-id or delete line
Implements-Requirement: Enter requirement-id or delete line
```

Save the commit message template in $HOME/.gitcommitmsg.txt. The filename isn't fixed and you can choose a filename of your liking.

How to do it...

1. To let Git know about our new commit message template, we can set the configuration variable commit.template to point at the file we just created with that template; we'll do it globally so it is applicable to all our repositories:

    ```
    $ git config --global commit.template $HOME/.gitcommitmsg.txt
    ```

2. Now, we can try to change a file, add it, and create a commit. This will bring up our preferred editor with the commit message template preloaded:

    ```
    $ git commit
    Short description of commit
    Longer explanation of the motivation for the change
    Fixes-Bug: Enter bug-id or delete line
    Implements-Requirement: Enter requirement-id or delete line
    ```

Configuration

```
# Please enter the commit message for your changes. Lines starting
# with '#' will be ignored, and an empty message aborts the commit.
# On branch master
# Changes to be committed:
#   (use "git reset HEAD <file>..." to unstage)
#
# modified:   another-file.txt
#
~
~
".git/COMMIT_EDITMSG" 13 lines, 396 characters
```

3. We can now edit the message according to our commit and save to complete the commit.

How it works...

When `commit.template` is set, Git simply uses the content of the template file as a starting point for all commit messages. This is quite convenient if you have a commit-message policy, as it greatly increases the chances of the policy being followed. You can even have different templates tied to different repositories since you can just set the configuration at the local level.

A .git directory template

Sometimes, having a global configuration isn't enough. You will also need to trigger the execution of scripts (also known as Git hooks), exclude files, and so on. It is possible to achieve this with the template option set to `git init`. It can be given as a command-line option to `git clone` and `git init`, or as the `$GIT_TEMPLATE_DIR` environment variable, or as the configuration option `init.templatedir`. It defaults to `/usr/share/git-core/templates`. The template option works by copying files in the template directory to the `.git` (`$GIT_DIR`) folder after it has been created. The default directory contains sample hooks and some suggested exclude patterns. In the following example, we'll see how we can set up a new template directory, and add a commit message hook and an exclude file.

Getting ready

First, we will create the template directory. We can use any name we want, and we'll use `~/.git_template`, as shown in the following command:

```
$ mkdir ~/.git_template
```

Now, we need to populate the directory with some template files. This could be a hook or an exclude file. We will create one hook file and one exclude file. The hook file is located in `.git/hooks/name-of-hook` and the exclude file in `.git/info/exclude`. Create the two directories needed, `hooks` and `info`, as shown in the following command:

```
$ mkdir ~/.git_template/{hooks,info}
```

To keep the sample hooks provided by the default template directory (the Git installation), we copy the files in the default template directory to the new one. When we use our newly created template directory, we'll override the default one. So, copying the default files to our template directory will make sure that, excepting our specific changes, the template directory is similar to the default one, as shown in the following command:

```
$ cd ~/.git_template/hooks
$ cp /usr/share/git-core/templates/hooks/* .
```

We'll use the `commit-msg` hook as the example hook:

```
#!/bin/sh
MSG_FILE="$1"
echo "\nHi from the template commit-msg hook" >> $MSG_FILE
```

The hook is very simple and will just add `Hi from the template commit-msg hook` to the end of the commit message. Save it as `commit-msg` in the `~/.git_template/hooks` directory and make it executable by using the following command:

```
chmod +x ~/.git_template/hooks/commit-msg
```

Now that the commit message hook is done, let's also add an exclude file to the example. The exclude file works like the `.gitignore` file, but is not tracked in the repository.

We'll create an exclude file that excludes all the `*.txt` files, as follows:

```
$ echo "*.txt" > ~/.git_template/info/exclude
```

Now, our template directory is ready for use.

Configuration

How to do it...

1. Our template directory is ready, and we can use it, as described earlier, as a command-line option, an environment variable or, as in this example, to be set as a configuration:

   ```
   $ git config --global init.templatedir ~/.git_template
   ```

2. Now, all Git repositories we create using `init` or `clone` will have the default files of the template directory. We can test whether it works by creating a new repository as follows:

   ```
   $ git init template-example
   $ cd template-example
   ```

3. Let's try to create a `.txt` file and see what `git status` tells us. It should be ignored by the exclude file from the template directory:

   ```
   $ echo "this is the readme file" > README.txt
   $ git status
   ```

   The exclude file worked! You can put in the file endings yourself, or just leave it blank and keep to the `.gitignore` files.

4. To test whether the `commit-msg` hook works, let's try to create a commit. First, we need a file to commit. So, let's create that and commit it as follows:

   ```
   $ echo "something to commit" > somefile
   $ git add somefile
   $ git commit -m "Committed something"
   ```

5. We can now check the history with `git log`:

   ```
   $ git log -1
   commit 1f7d63d7e08e96dda3da63eadc17f35132d24064
   Author: John Doe <john.doe@example.com>
   Date:   Mon Jan 6 20:14:21 2014 +0100
     Committed something
     Hi from the template commit-msg hook
   ```

How it works...

When Git creates a new repository, either via `init` or `clone`, it will copy the files from the `template` directory (the default location is `/usr/share/git-core/templates`) to the new repository when creating the directory structure. The template directory can be defined either by a command-line argument, an environment variable, or a configuration option. If nothing is specified, the default template directory will be used (distributed with the Git installation). By setting the configuration as a `--global` option, the template directory defined will apply to all of the user's (new) repositories. This is a very nice way to distribute the same hooks across repositories, but it also has some drawbacks. As the files in the template directory are only copied to the Git repositories, updates to the template directory do not affect the existing repositories. This can be solved by running `git init` in each existing repository to reinitialize the repository, but this can be quite cumbersome. Also, the template directory can enforce hooks on some repositories where you don't want them. This is quite easily solved by simply deleting the hook files in `.git/hooks` of that repository.

See also

For more information on hooks in Git, please refer to `Chapter 7`, *Enhancing Your Daily Work with Git Hooks, Aliases, and Scripts*.

A few configuration examples

There are configuration targets in the core Git system. In this section, we'll take a closer look at a few of them that might be useful in your daily work.

We'll look at the following three different configuration areas:

- Rebase and merge setup
- Expiry of objects
- Autocorrect

Configuration

Getting ready

In this exercise, we'll just set a few configurations. We'll use the data model repository from `Chapter 1`, *Navigating Git*:

```
$ cd Git-Version-Control-Cookbook-Second-Edition
```

How to do it...

Let's take a closer look at the previously mentioned configuration areas.

Rebase and merge setup

By default, when performing `git pull`, a merge commit will be created if the history of the local branch has diverged from the remote one. However, to avoid all these merge commits, a repository can be configured so that it will default to rebase instead of merging when doing `git pull`. Several configuration targets related to the option are available as follows:

- `pull.rebase`: This configuration, when set to `true`, will pull to rebase the current branch on top of the fetched one when performing a `git pull`. It can also be set to `preserve` so that the local merge commit will not be flattened in the rebase, by passing `--preserve-merges` to `git rebase`. The default value is `false`, as the configuration is not set. To set this option in your local repository, run the following command:

    ```
    $ git config pull.rebase true
    ```

- `branch.autosetuprebase`: When this configuration is set to `always`, any new branch created with `<git branch` or `git checkout` that tracks another branch will be set up to pull to rebase (instead of merge). The valid options are as follows:
    - `never`: This is set to pull to rebase (default)
    - `local`: This is set to pull to rebase for local tracked branches
    - `remote`: This is set to pull to rebase for remote tracked branches

- `always`: This is set to pull to rebase for all tracked branches
- To set this option for all the new branches regardless of tracking remote or local branches, run the following command:

   ```
   $ git config branch.autosetuprebase always
   ```

- `branch.<name>.rebase`: This configuration, when set to `true`, applies only to the `<name>` branch and tells Git to pull to rebase when performing `git pull` on the given branch. It can also be set to `preserve` so that the local merge commit will not be flattened when running `git pull`. By default, the configuration is not set for any branch. To set the `feature/2` branch in the repository to default to rebase, instead of merge, we can run the following command:

   ```
   $ git config branch.feature/2.rebase true
   ```

Expiry of objects

By default, Git will perform garbage collection on unreferenced objects and clean `reflog` for entries that are more than 90 days old. For an object to be referenced, something must point to it; a tree, a commit, a tag, a branch, or some of the internal Git bookkeeping, such as `stash` or `reflog`. There are three settings that can be used to change this time as follows:

- `gc.reflogexpire`: This is the general setting to know for how long a branch's history is kept in `reflog`. The default time is 90 days. The setting is a length of time, for example, `10 days`, `6 months`, and it can be turned completely with the value `never`. The setting can be set to match a `refs` pattern by supplying the pattern in the configuration setting. `gc.<pattern>.reflogexpire`: This pattern can, for example, be `/refs/remotes/*`, and the expire setting would then only apply for those refs.
- `gc.reflogexpireunreachable`: This setting controls how long the `reflog` entries that are not a part of the current branch history should be available in the repository. The default value is `30 days`, and similar to the previous option, it is expressed as a length of time or set to `never` in order to turn it off. This setting can, as the previous one, be set to match a `refs` pattern.

- `gc.pruneexpire`: This option tells `git gc` to prune objects older than the value. The default is `2.weeks.ago`, and the value can be expressed as a relative date, such as `3.months.ago`. To disable the grace period, the value `now` can be used. To set a non-default expiry date on remote branches only, use the following command:

  ```
  $ git config gc./refs/remote/*.reflogexpire never
  $ git config gc./refs/remote/*.reflogexpireunreachable "2 months"
  ```

- We can also set a date so `git gc` will prune objects sooner:

  ```
  $ git config gc.pruneexpire 3.days.ago
  ```

Autocorrect

This configuration is useful when you get tired of messages such as the following one just because you made a typo on the keyboard:

```
$ git statis
git: 'statis' is not a git command. See 'git --help'.
Did you mean this?
    status
```

By setting the configuration to `help.autocorrect`, you can control how Git will behave when you accidentally send a typo to it. By default, the value is `0` and it means to list the possible options similar to the input (if `statis` is given, `status` will be shown). A negative value means to immediately execute the corresponding command. A positive value means to wait the given number of deciseconds (0.1 sec) before running the command (so there is an amount of time in which to cancel it). If several commands can be deduced from the text entered, nothing will happen. Setting the value to half a second gives you some time to cancel a wrong command, as follows:

```
$ git config help.autocorrect 5
$ git statis
WARNING: You called a Git command named 'statis', which does not exist.
Continuing under the assumption that you meant 'status'
in 0.5 seconds automatically...
# On branch master
# Changes to be committed:
#   (use "git reset HEAD <file>..." to unstage)
#
#       modified:   another-file.txt
#
```

How it works...

Setting the configuration targets will change the way Git behaves. The previous examples describe a few useful methods to get Git to act differently than its default behavior. You should be sure when you are changing a configuration that you completely understand what that configuration does. Therefore, check the Git configuration help page by using `git help config`.

There's more...

There are a lot of configuration targets available in Git. You can run `git help config` and all of them will be displayed and explained over a few pages.

Git aliases

An alias is a nice way to configure long and/or complicated Git commands to represent short useful ones. An alias is simply a configuration entry under the alias section. It is usually configured to `--global` to apply it everywhere.

Getting ready

In this example, we will use the `jgit` repository, which was also used in Chapter 1, *Navigating Git*, with the `master` branch pointing at `b14a93971837610156e815ae2eee3baaa5b7a44b`. Either use the clone from Chapter 1, *Navigating Git*, or clone the repository again, as follows:

```
$ git clone https://git.eclipse.org/r/jgit/jgit
$ cd jgit
$ git checkout master && git reset --hard b14a939
```

Configuration

How to do it...

1. First, we'll create a few simple aliases, then a couple of more special ones, and finally, a couple of aliases using external commands. Instead of writing `git checkout` every time we need to switch branches, we can create an alias of that command and call it `git co`. We can do the same for `git branch`, `git commit`, and `git status` as follows:

   ```
   $ git config --global alias.co checkout
   $ git config --global alias.br branch
   $ git config --global alias.ci commit
   $ git config --global alias.st status
   ```

2. Now, try to run `git st` in the `jgit` repository as follows:

   ```
   $ git st
   # On branch master
   nothing to commit, working directory clean
   ```

3. The `alias` method is also good for creating the Git commands you think are missing in Git. One of the common Git aliases is `unstage`, which is used to move a file out of the staging area, as shown in the following command:

   ```
   $ git config --global alias.unstage 'reset HEAD --'
   ```

   Try to edit the `README.md` file in the root of the `jgit` repository and add it to the root.

4. Now, `git status/git st` should display something like the following:

   ```
   $ git st
   # On branch master
   # Changes to be committed:
   #   (use "git reset HEAD <file>..." to unstage)
   #
   #       modified:   README.md
   #
   ```

5. Let's try to unstage `README.md` and then look at `git st` as follows:

   ```
   $ git unstage README.md
   Unstaged changes after reset:
   M       README.md
   $ git st
   # On branch master
   # Changes not staged for commit:
   ```

[50]

```
#       (use "git add <file>..." to update what will be committed)
#       (use "git checkout -- <file>..." to discard changes in working
directory)
#
#       modified:   README.md
#
no changes added to commit (use "git add" and/or "git commit -a")
```

6. A common use case for aliases is to format the history of Git in specific ways. Let's say you want the number of lines added and deleted for each file in the commit displayed along with some common commit data. For this, we can create the following alias so we don't have to type everything each time:

    ```
    $ git config --global alias.ll "log --
    pretty=format:"%C(yellow)%h%Cred%d %Creset%s %Cgreen(%cr) %C(bold
    blue)<%an>%Creset" --numstat"
    ```

7. Now, we can execute `git ll` in the terminal and get a nice stat output, as shown in the following command:

    ```
    $ git ll
    b14a939 (HEAD, master) Prepare 3.3.0-SNAPSHOT builds (8 days ago)
    <Matthias Sohn>
    6       6       org.eclipse.jgit.ant.test/META-INF/MANIFEST.MF
    1       1       org.eclipse.jgit.ant.test/pom.xml
    3       3       org.eclipse.jgit.ant/META-INF/MANIFEST.MF
    1       1       org.eclipse.jgit.ant/pom.xml
    4       4       org.eclipse.jgit.archive/META-INF/MANIFEST.MF
    2       2       org.eclipse.jgit.archive/META-INF/SOURCE-
    MANIFEST.MF
    1       1       org.eclipse.jgit.archive/pom.xml
    6       6       org.eclipse.jgit.console/META-INF/MANIFEST.MF
    1       1       org.eclipse.jgit.console/pom.xml
    12      12      org.eclipse.jgit.http.server/META-INF/MANIFEST.MF
    ...
    ```

8. It is also possible to use an external command instead of a Git command. So, small shell scripts and so on can be embedded. To create an `alias` method with an external command, the alias must start with an exclamation mark `!`. The examples can be used when resolving conflicts from a rebase or merge. In your `~/.gitconfig` file under `[alias]`, add the following:

    ```
    editconflicted = "!f() {git ls-files --unmerged | cut -f2 | sort -u
    ; }; $EDITOR 'f'"
    ```

Configuration

This will bring up your configured $EDITOR with all the files that are in the conflict state due to the merge/rebase. This quickly allows you to fix the conflicts and get on with the merge/rebase.

9. In the `jgit` repository, we can create two branches at an earlier point in time and merge these two branches:

```
$ git branch A 03f78fc
$ git branch B 9891497
$ git checkout A
Switched to branch 'A'
$ git merge B
```

Now, you'll see that this fails to perform the merge, and you can run `git st` to check the statuses of a lot of files that are in a conflicted state, `both modified`. To open and edit all the conflicted files, we can now run `git editconflicted`. This brings up $EDITOR with the files. If your environment variable isn't set, use the `EDITOR=<your-favorite-editor>` export to set it.

For this example, we don't actually resolve the conflicts. Just check that the alias works and you're ready for the next alias.

10. Now that we have solved all the merge conflicts, it is time to add all of those files before we conclude the merge. Luckily, we can create an `alias` method that can help us with that, as follows:

```
addconflicted = "!f() { git ls-files --unmerged | cut -f2 | sort -u ; }; git add 'f'"
```

11. Now, we can run `git addconflicted`. Later, `git status` will tell us that all the conflicted files are added:

```
$ git st
On branch A
All conflicts fixed but you are still merging.
  (use "git commit" to conclude merge)
Changes to be committed:
  modified:   org.eclipse.jgit.console/META-INF/MANIFEST.MF
  modified:   org.eclipse.jgit.console/pom.xml
  modified:   org.eclipse.jgit.http.server/META-INF/MANIFEST.MF
  modified:   org.eclipse.jgit.http.server/pom.xml
  modified:   org.eclipse.jgit.http.test/META-INF/MANIFEST.MF
  modified:   org.eclipse.jgit.http.test/pom.xml
  ...
Now we can conclude the merge with git commit:
$ git commit
```

```
[A 94344ae] Merge branch 'B' into A
```

How it works...

Git simply runs the command the alias is short for. It is very convenient for long Git commands, or Git commands that are hard to remember exactly how to write. Now, all you have to remember is the alias and you can always look in the configuration file for it.

There's more...

Another way to create a kind of Git alias is to make a shell script and save the file with the name `git-<your-alias-name>`. Make the file executable and place it somewhere in your `$PATH`. You can now run that file simply by running `git<your-alias-name>` from the command line.

The refspec exemplified

Though the `refspec` isn't the first thing that comes to mind when thinking about the Git configuration, it is actually quite close. In a lot of the Git commands, the `refspec` is used, but often implicitly, that is, the `refspec` is taken from the configuration file. If you don't remember setting a `refspec` configuration, you are probably right, but if you cloned the repository or added a remote, you'll have a section in `.git/config` that looks something like the following (this is for the `jgit` repository):

```
[remote "origin"]
  url = https://git.eclipse.org/r/jgit/jgit
  fetch = +refs/heads/*:refs/remotes/origin/*
```

The fetch line contains the configured `refspec` to fetch in relation to this repository.

Getting ready

In this example, we'll be using the `jgit` repository as our server repository, but we have to make a clone of it to a bare repository so we can push it. You can't push to the checked-out branch on a non-bare repository, as this can overwrite the work area and index.

Configuration

Create a bare repository from the jgit repository and create a new Git repository where we can play with the refspec as follows:

```
$ git clone --bare https://git.eclipse.org/r/jgit/jgit jgit-bare.git
$ git init refspec-tests
Initialized empty Git repository in /Users/john.doe/refspec-tests/.git/
$ cd refspec-tests
$ git remote add origin ../jgit-bare.git
```

We also need to change the branch names on some of the branches to match the example for namespacing; the following will rename the stable-xxx branches to stable/xxx:

```
$ for br in $(git branch  -a | grep "stable-"); do new=$(echo $br| sed 's/-///'); git branch $new $br; done
```

In the previous shell scripting, the $new and $br variables aren't placed in double quotes ("), as good practice for shell scripting would otherwise suggest. This is okay, as the variables reflect the names of the branches in the repository and branch names cannot contain spaces.

How to do it...

1. Let's set up our new repository to only fetch the master branch. We do this by changing the fetch line under [remote "origin"] in the configuration file (.git/config), as follows:

   ```
   [remote "origin"]
     url = ../jgit-bare.git
     fetch = +refs/heads/master:refs/remotes/origin/master
   ```

2. Now, we will only fetch the master branch and not all the other branches when executing a git fetch, git pull, or a git remote update origin, as follows:

   ```
   $ git pull
   remote: Counting objects: 44033, done.
   remote: Compressing objects: 100% (6927/6927), done.
   remote: Total 44033 (delta 24063), reused 44033 (delta 24063)
   Receiving objects: 100% (44033/44033), 9.45 MiB | 5.70 MiB/s, done.
   Resolving deltas: 100% (24063/24063), done.
   From ../jgit-bare
        * [new branch]      master     -> origin/master
   From ../jgit-bare
        * [new tag]         v0.10.1    -> v0.10.1
        * [new tag]         v0.11.1    -> v0.11.1
   ```

```
    * [new tag]            v0.11.3    -> v0.11.3
    ...
$ git branch -a
    * master
      remotes/origin/master
```

3. Let's also set up a separate refspec to fetch all the `stable/*` branches to the local repository as follows:

```
[remote "origin"]
  url = ../jgit-bare.git
  fetch = +refs/heads/master:refs/remotes/origin/master
  fetch = +refs/heads/stable/*:refs/remotes/origin/stable/*
```

4. Now, fetch the branches locally, as shown in the following command:

```
$ git fetch
From ../jgit-bare
    * [new branch]      stable/0.10 -> origin/stable/0.10
    * [new branch]      stable/0.11 -> origin/stable/0.11
    * [new branch]      stable/0.12 -> origin/stable/0.12
    * [new branch]      stable/0.7  -> origin/stable/0.7
    * [new branch]      stable/0.8  -> origin/stable/0.8
    * [new branch]      stable/0.9  -> origin/stable/0.9
    * [new branch]      stable/1.0  -> origin/stable/1.0
    * [new branch]      stable/1.1  -> origin/stable/1.1
    * [new branch]      stable/1.2  -> origin/stable/1.2
    * [new branch]      stable/1.3  -> origin/stable/1.3
    * [new branch]      stable/2.0  -> origin/stable/2.0
    * [new branch]      stable/2.1  -> origin/stable/2.1
    * [new branch]      stable/2.2  -> origin/stable/2.2
    * [new branch]      stable/2.3  -> origin/stable/2.3
    * [new branch]      stable/3.0  -> origin/stable/3.0
    * [new branch]      stable/3.1  -> origin/stable/3.1
    * [new branch]      stable/3.2  -> origin/stable/3.2
```

5. We can also set up a push `refspec` that specifies where branches are pushed to by default. Let's create a branch called `develop` and create one commit, as shown in the following commands:

```
$ git checkout -b develop
Switched to a new branch 'develop'
$ echo "This is the developer setup, read carefully" > readme-dev.txt
$ git add readme-dev.txt
```

Configuration

```
$ git commit -m "adds readme file for developers"
[develop ccb2f08] adds readme file for developers
 1 file changed, 1 insertion(+)
 create mode 100644 readme-dev.txt
```

6. Now, let's create a push `refspec` that will send the content of the `develop` branch to `integration/master` on origin:

   ```
   [remote "origin"]
     url = ../jgit-bare.git
     fetch = +refs/heads/master:refs/remotes/origin/master
     fetch = +refs/heads/stable/*:refs/remotes/origin/stable/*
     push = refs/heads/develop:refs/remotes/origin/integration/master
   ```

7. Let's push our commit on `develop` as follows:

   ```
   $ git push
   Counting objects: 4, done.
   Compressing objects: 100% (2/2), done.
   Writing objects: 100% (3/3), 345 bytes | 0 bytes/s, done.
   Total 3 (delta 1), reused 0 (delta 0)
   To ../jgit-bare.git
    * [new branch]      develop -> origin/integration/master
   ```

   As the `integration/master` branch didn't exist on the remote side, it was created for us.

How it works...

The format of the `refspec` is in the form of `<source>:<destination>`. For a fetch `refspec`, this means that `<source>` is the source on the remote side and `<destination>` is `local`. For a push `refspec`, `<source>` is `local` and `<destination>` is `remote`. The `refspec` can be prefixed by a + to indicate that the `ref` pattern can be updated even though it isn't a fast-forward update. It is not possible to use partial globs in the `refspec` pattern, as shown in the following line:

```
fetch = +refs/heads/stable*:refs/remotes/origin/stable*
```

However, it is possible to use namespacing. That's why we had to rewrite the `stable-xxx` branches to `stable/xxx` to fit into a namespace pattern:

```
fetch = +refs/heads/stable/*:refs/remotes/origin/stable/*
```

3
Branching, Merging, and Options

In this chapter, we will cover the following recipes:

- Managing your local branches
- Branches with remotes
- Forcing a merge commit
- Using git reuse recorded resolution (rerere) to merge Git conflicts
- Computing the difference between branches
- Orphan branches

Introduction

If you are developing a small application in a big corporation as a developer, or you are trying to wrap your head around an open source project from GitHub, you have already been using branches with Git.

Most of the time, you may have just been working on a local development or master branch, and so didn't care so much about other branches.

In this chapter, we will show you different branch types and how to work with them.

Managing your local branches

Suppose you just have your local Git repository, and, at the moment, you have no intention of sharing the code with others; you can, however, easily share the knowledge you have while working with a repository with one or more remotes. Local branches with no remotes work exactly in this fashion. As you can see in the examples, we are cloning a repository, and thus we have a remote.

Let's start by creating a few local branches.

Getting ready

Use the following command to clone the jgit repository to match:

```
$ git clone https://git.eclipse.org/r/jgit/jgit
$ cd jgit
```

How to do it...

Perform the following steps to manage your local branches:

1. Whenever you start working on a bug fix or a new feature in your project, you should create a branch. You can do so using the following code:

   ```
   $ git branch newBugFix
   $ git branch
   * master
     newBugFix
   ```

2. The newBugFix branch points to the current HEAD you were on at the time of the creation. You can see the HEAD with git log -1:

   ```
   $ git log -1 newBugFix --format=format:%H
   25fe20b2dbb20cac8aa43c5ad64494ef8ea64ffc
   ```

3. If you want to add a description to the branch, you can do this with the --edit-description option for the git branch command:

   ```
   $ git branch --edit-description newBugFix
   ```

4. The previous command will open an editor where you can type in a description:

   ```
   Refactoring the Hydro controller

   The hydro controller code is currently horrible needs to be
   refactored.
   ```

5. Close the editor and the message will be saved.

How it works...

Git stores the information in the local `git config` file; this also means that you cannot push this information to a remote repository.

To retrieve the description for the branch, you can use the `--get` flag for the `git config` command:

```
$ git config --get branch.newBugFix.description
Refactoring the Hydro controller

The hydro controller code is currently horrible and needs to be refactored.
```

This will be beneficial when we automate some tasks in Chapter 7, *Enhancing Your Daily Work with Git Hooks, Aliases, and Scripts*.

Remember to perform a checkout of `newBugFix` before you start working on it. This must be done with the Git checkout of `newBugFix`. If you are in a hurry, you can create and checkout a new branch in a single command. Just give the option `-b` to `checkout`.

The branch information is stored as a file in `.git/refs/heads/newBugFix`:

```
$ cat .git/refs/heads/newBugFix
25fe20b2dbb20cac8aa43c5ad64494ef8ea64ffc
```

Note that it is the same commit hash we retrieved with the `git log` command.

Branching, Merging, and Options

There's more...

Perhaps you want to create specific branches from specific commit hashes. The first thought might be to check out the commit, and then create a branch; however, it is much easier to use the `git branch` command to create the branches without checking out the commits:

1. If you need a branch from a specific commit hash, you can create it with the `git branch` command as follows:

   ```
   $ git branch anotherBugFix 979e346
   $ git log -1 anotherBugFix --format=format:%h
   979e346

   $ git log -1 anotherBugFix --format=format:%H
   979e3467112618cc787e161097986212eaaa4533
   ```

2. As you can see, the abbreviated commit hash is shown when you use `%h`, and the full commit hash is shown when you use `%H`. You can see that the abbreviated commit hash is the same as the one used to create the branch. Most of the time, you want to create and start working on the branch immediately:

   ```
   $ git checkout -b lastBugFix 979e346
   Switched to a new branch 'lastBugFix'
   ```

3. Git switches to the new branch immediately after it creates the branch. Verify with `gitk` to see whether the `lastBugFix` branch is checked out and another `BugFix` branch is at the same commit hash:

   ```
   $ gitk
   ```

   This can be shown via a screenshot as follows:

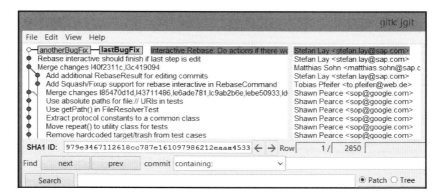

[60]

4. Instead of using Gitk, you can also add -v to the `git branch` command or even another -v:

   ```
   $ git branch -v
   
     anotherBugFix 979e346 Interactive Rebase: Do actions if
   * lastBugFix    979e346 Interactive Rebase: Do actions if
     master        25fe20b Add missing package import for jg
     newBugFix     25fe20b Add missing package import for jg
   ```

5. With -v, you can see the abbreviated commit hash for each branch, and with -vv, you can also see that the master branch tracks the origin/master branch:

   ```
   $ git branch -vv
   
     anotherBugFix 979e346 Interactive Rebase: Do actions if e
   * lastBugFix    979e346 Interactive Rebase: Do actions if e
     master        25fe20b [origin/master] Add missing package
     newBugFix     25fe20b Add missing package import for g
   ```

Branches with remotes

At some point, it is very likely that you have cloned somebody's repository. This means that you have an associated remote. The remote is usually called origin because it is where the source originated from.

While working with Git and remotes, you will get some benefits from Git.

We can start with git status and see what we get while working with the remote.

Getting ready

Follow these steps:

1. We will start by checking out a local branch that tracks a remote branch:

   ```
   $ git checkout -b remoteBugFix --track origin/stable-3.2
   Branch remoteBugFix set up to track remote branch stable-3.2 from origin.
   Switched to a new branch 'remoteBugFix'
   ```

Branching, Merging, and Options

2. The previous command creates and checks out the `remoteBugFix` branch that will track the `origin/stable-3.2` branch. Therefore, for instance, executing `git status` will automatically show how different your branch is from `origin/stable-3.2`, and it will also show whether your branch's `HEAD` can be fast forwarded to the `HEAD` of the remote branch or not.

3. To provide an example of how the previous step works, we need to do some manual work that will simulate this situation. First, we find a commit:

   ```
   $ git log -10 origin/stable-3.2 --oneline
   f839d383e (HEAD -> remoteBugFix, origin/stable-3.2) Prepare post 3.2.0 builds
   699900c30 (tag: v3.2.0.201312181205-r) JGit v3.2.0.201312181205-r
   0ff691cdb Revert "Fix for core.autocrlf=input resulting in modified file..."
   1def0a125 Fix for core.autocrlf=input resulting in modified file and unsmudge
   0ce61caef Canonicalize worktree path in BaseRepositoryBuilder if set via config
   be7942f2b Add missing @since tags for new public methods in Config
   ea04d2329 Don't use API exception in RebaseTodoLine
   3a063a0ed Merge "Fix aborting rebase with detached head" into stable-3.2
   e90438c0e Fix aborting rebase with detached head
   2e0d17885 Add recursive variant of Config.getNames() methods
   ```

4. The command will list the last 10 commits on the `stable-3.2` branch from the remote origin. The `--oneline` option will show the abbreviated commit hash and the commit subject. For this recipe, we will be using the following commit:

   ```
   $ git reset --hard 2e0d178
   HEAD is now at 2e0d178 Add recursive variant of Config.getNames() methods
   ```

5. This will reset the `remoteBugFix` branch to the `2e0d178` commit hash. We are now ready to continue using the free benefits of Git when we have a remote tracking branch.

We are resetting to a commit that is accessible from the `origin/stable-3.2` remote tracking branch; this is done to simulate that we have performed a Git fetch and new commits were downloaded for the `origin/stable-3.2` branch.

How to do it...

Here, we will try a few commands that assist you when you have a remote tracking branch:

1. Start by executing `git status`:

   ```
   $ git status
   
   On branch remoteBugFix
   Your branch is behind 'origin/stable-3.2' by 9 commits, and can be
   fast-forwarded.
     (use "git pull" to update your local branch)
   
   nothing to commit, working directory clean
   ```

   Git is very descriptive when you have a tracking branch and you use `git status`.

   As you can see from the message, you can use `git pull` to update your local branch, which we will try in the next example. The message says it can be fast-forwarded. It simply means that Git can advance the HEAD without merging. Now, we will just perform the merge:

   > The `git pull` command is just a `git fetch` command and then a `git merge` command with the remote tracking branch.

   ```
   $ git merge origin/stable-3.2
   
   Updating 2e0d178..f839d38
   Fast-forward
    .../org/eclipse/jgit/api/RebaseCommandTest.java     | 213 ++++++++++++++
    .../src/org/eclipse/jgit/api/RebaseCommand.java     |  31 +--
    .../jgit/errors/IllegalTodoFileModification.java    |  59 ++++++
    .../eclipse/jgit/lib/BaseRepositoryBuilder.java     |   2 +-
    .../src/org/eclipse/jgit/lib/Config.java            |   2 +
    .../src/org/eclipse/jgit/lib/RebaseTodoLine.java    |  16 +-
   6 files changed, 266 insertions(+), 57 deletions(-)
    create mode 100644
   org.eclipse.jgit/src/org/eclipse/jgit/errors/IllegalTodoFileModific
   ation.java
   ```

[63]

Branching, Merging, and Options

2. From the output, you can see it is a fast-forward merge, as Git predicted in the output of `git status`.

There's more...

You can also add a remote to an existing branch, which is very handy when you realize that you actually wanted a remote tracking branch but forgot to add the tracking information while creating the branch:

1. Start by creating a local branch at the `2e0d17` commit:

   ```
   $ git checkout -b remoteBugFix2 2e0d17
   Switched to a new branch 'remoteBugFix2'
   ```

2. The `remoteBugFix2` branch is just a local branch at the moment with no tracking information; to set the tracking branch, we need to use `--set-upstream-to` or `-u` as a flag to the `git branch` command:

   ```
   $ git branch --set-upstream-to origin/stable-3.2
   Branch remoteBugFix2 set up to track remote branch stable-3.2 from origin.
   ```

3. As you can see from the Git output, we are now tracking the `stable-3.2` branch from the origin:

   ```
   $ git status
   On branch remoteBugFix2
   Your branch is behind 'origin/stable-3.2' by 9 commits, and can be fast-forwarded.
     (use "git pull" to update your local branch)
   nothing to commit, working directory clean
   ```

4. You can see from the Git output that you are nine commits ahead, and you can use `git pull` to update the branch. Remember that a `git pull` command is just a `git fetch` command, followed by a `git merge` command with the upstream branch, which we also call the remote tracking branch:

   ```
   $ git pull

   Updating 2e0d17885..f839d383e
   Fast-forward
   org.eclipse.jgit.test/tst/org/eclipse/jgit/api/RebaseCommandTest.java | 213
   ++++++++++++++++++++++++++++++++++++++++++++++++++++++++++++++++++++++
   +++++++++++++----------------
   ```

```
  org.eclipse.jgit/src/org/eclipse/jgit/api/RebaseCommand.java   | 31
++++++++------
 org.eclipse.jgit/src/org/eclipse/jgit/errors/IllegalTodoFileModific
ation.java | 59 +++++++++++++++++++++++++++
 org.eclipse.jgit/src/org/eclipse/jgit/lib/BaseRepositoryBuilder.jav
a |  2 +-
  org.eclipse.jgit/src/org/eclipse/jgit/lib/Config.java          |  2 +
  org.eclipse.jgit/src/org/eclipse/jgit/lib/RebaseTodoLine.java  | 16
++++----
 6 files changed, 266 insertions(+), 57 deletions(-)
 create mode 100644
org.eclipse.jgit/src/org/eclipse/jgit/errors/IllegalTodoFileModific
ation.java
```

5. From the output, you can see that the branch has been fast forwarded to the `f839d383e` commit hash, which is equivalent to `origin/stable-3.2`. You can verify this with `git log`:

```
$ git log -1 origin/stable-3.2  --format=format:%h
f839d383e
```

Forcing a merge commit

You might have seen a lot of basic examples of software delivery chains and branching models before reading this book. It is very likely that you have been trying to use different strategies and found that none of them completely support your scenario, which is perfectly fine as long as the tool can support your specific workflow.

Git supports almost any workflow. We have often encountered a situation that requires a merge commit while merging a feature, even though it can be done with a fast-forward merge. Those who requested it often use it to indicate that you have actually merged in a feature and want to store the information in the repository.

 Git has fast and easy access to all the commit messages, so the repository should be used as a journal, and not just a backup of the source code.

Branching, Merging, and Options

Getting ready

Start by checking out a local branch `remoteOldbugFix` that tracks `origin/stable-3.1`:

```
$ git checkout -b remoteOldBugFix --track origin/stable-3.1
Branch remoteOldBugFix set up to track remote branch stable-3.1 from
Switched to a new branch 'remoteOldBugFix'
```

How to do it...

The following steps will show you how to force a merge commit:

1. To force a merge commit, you need to use the `--no-ff` flag; *no-ff* means no fast forward. We will also use the `--quiet` flag to minimize the output and `--edit` to allow us to edit the commit message. Unless you have a merge conflict, Git will create the merge commit for you automatically:

   ```
   $ git merge origin/stable-3.2 --no-ff --edit --quiet

   Auto-merging
   org.eclipse.jgit.test/tst/org/eclipse/jgit/test/resources/SampleDat
   Removing
   org.eclipse.jgit.test/tst/org/eclipse/jgit/internal/storage/file/GC
   Te
   Auto-merging
   org.eclipse.jgit.packaging/org.eclipse.jgit.target/jgit-4.3.target
   ```

2. The commit message editor will open, and you can write a commit message. Closing the editor creates the merge commit and we are done.

3. To verify this, you can reset back to `origin/stable-3.1` and perform the merge without the `--no-ff` flag:

   ```
   $ git reset --hard  remotes/origin/stable-3.1
   HEAD is now at da6e87b Prepare post 3.1.0 builds
   ```

4. Now, perform the merge with the following command:

   ```
   $ git merge origin/stable-3.2 --quiet
   ```

5. You can see the difference using Gitk. The following screenshot shows the fast-forward merge; as you can see, our `remoteOldBugFix` branch points to `origin/stable-3.2`:

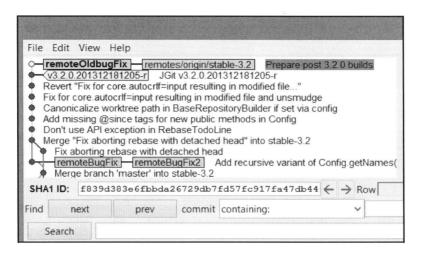

6. The next screenshot shows the merge commit we forced Git to create. Our branch `remoteOldBugFix` is ahead of `remotes/origin/stable-3.2`, and then we performed the commit:

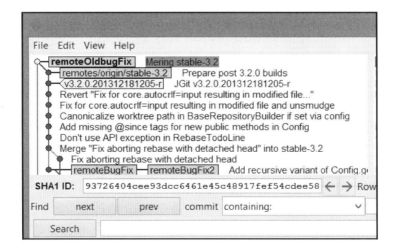

Branching, Merging, and Options

There's more...

Although most branching scenarios expect you to completely merge branches, there are situations when, while working in a real environment, you only need to merge specific pieces of one branch into another branch. Using the `--no-commit` option, Git will make the merge and stop before committing, allowing you to modify and add files to the merge commit before committing.

For example, we have been working with projects where versions of strings have been updated in the feature branch but not in the master branch. So, an automatic merge into master would replace the current version string used on the master branch, which, in this case, was not the intention. In the following example, we will use a simple Git repository with a few commits and files:

1. Start by checking out a local `remotePartlyMerge` branch that tracks `origin/release/1.0`:

    ```
    $ git clone
    https://github.com/PacktPublishing/Git-Version-Control-Cookbook-Sec
    ond-Edition_hello_world_flow_model.git
    $ cd Git-Version-Control-Cookbook-Second-
    Edition_hello_world_flow_model
    $ git checkout -b remotePartlyMerge --track origin/release/1.0
    Branch remotePartlyMerge set up to track remote branch release/1.0
    from origin.
    Switched to a new branch 'remotePartlyMerge'
    ```

2. Then, to create the merge and allow you to decide what will be part of the commit, you can use `--no-commit`:

    ```
    $ git merge origin/master   --no-ff --no-commit
      Automatic merge went well; stopped before committing as requested
    ```

3. Again, Git is very informative; you can see from the output that everything went well and Git stopped before committing as requested. To continue, let's pretend we didn't want the `LICENSE` file to be part of the merge commit.
   To achieve this, we reset the directory using the `git reset <path>` command:

    ```
    $ git reset LICENSE
    ```

4. You can see from the output that you have unstaged changes after the reset; this is exactly what we want. You can check which unstaged changes you have by running `git status`. Now, we will just finish the merge:

   ```
   $ git commit -m "Merging without LICENSE"
   [remotePartlyMerge f138175] Merging without LICENSE
   ```

5. The merge commit is complete. If you run a `git status` command now, you will still have the unstaged changes in you work area. To verify whether the result is as expected, we can compute the difference for this using `git diff` to show that the files are as they are on the `origin/master` branch, excluding the `LICENSE` file:

   ```
   $ git diff origin/master !(LICENSE)
   ```

6. There is no output from diff; this is the expected result. We are telling the `diff` command to `diff` our current `HEAD` commit and branch `origin/master`, and we do not care about the diffs in `LICENSE`

> If you don't specify `HEAD`, you will `diff` with your current `WA`, and the `diff` command will have a lot of output as you have unstaged changes.

Using git reuse recorded resolution (rerere) to merge Git conflicts

While working on a feature branch, you probably like to merge daily or perhaps more often, but when you work on long-living feature branches, you end up in a situation where you have the same conflicts occurring repeatedly.

Here, you can use `git rerere`, which stands for *reuse recorded resolution*. Git rerere is not enabled by default, but can be enabled with the following command:

```
$ git config rerere.enabled true
```

Branching, Merging, and Options

 You can configure it globally by adding `--global` to the `git config` command.

How to do it...

Perform the following steps to merge the known conflicts:

1. In the `jgit` repository folder, start by checking out a branch that tracks `origin/stable-2.2`:

   ```
   $ git checkout -b rerereExample --track origin/stable-2.2
   ```

2. Now, change the maven-compiler-plugin version to something personalized, such as 2.5.2, as this is in line 211 in `pom.xml`. If you run `git diff`, you should get a result very similar to the following:

   ```
   $ git diff

   diff --git a/pom.xml b/pom.xml
   index 085e00f..d5aec17 100644
   --- a/pom.xml
   +++ b/pom.xml
   @@ -208,7 +208,7 @@
             <plugin>
               <artifactId>maven-compiler-plugin</artifactId>
   -           <version>2.5.1</version>
   +           <version>2.5.2</version>
             </plugin>

             <plugin>
   ```

3. Now add the file and create a commit:

   ```
   $ git add pom.xml
   $ git commit -m "Update maven-compiler-plugin to 2.5.2"
   [rerereExample d474848] Update maven-compiler-plugin to 2.5.2
    1 file changed, 1 insertion(+), 1 deletion(-)
   ```

4. Store your current commit in a backup branch named `rerereExample2`:

   ```
   $ git branch rerereExample2
   ```

Here, `git branch rerereExample2` is just storing the current commit as a branch, as we need to use that for the second rerere example.

5. Now, we need to perform the first merge that will fail on auto merge. Then we can solve that. After solving it, we can reuse the merge resolution to solve the same problem in the future:

    ```
    $ git merge --no-ff v3.0.2.201309041250-rc2

    A lot of output ...

    Automatic merge failed; fix conflicts and then commit the result.
    ```

6. As we have `git rerere` enabled, we can use `git rerere status` to see which files or paths will be recorded:

    ```
    $ git rerere status
    pom.xml
    ```

7. Edit the `pom.xml` file (around line 229) and solve the merge conflict so that you can get the `diff` output shown as follows. You have to remove the line with 3.1 and the merge markers:

> Merge markers are lines that begin with <<<<<<, >>>>>>, or ======; these lines indicate the points where Git could not perform an auto merge.

```
$ git diff v3.0.2.201309041250-rc2 pom.xml

diff --git a/pom.xml b/pom.xml
index 60cb0c8..faa7618 100644
--- a/pom.xml
+++ b/pom.xml
@@ -226,7 +226,7 @@

        <plugin>
            <artifactId>maven-compiler-plugin</artifactId>
-           <version>3.1</version>
+           <version>2.5.2</version>
        </plugin>

        <plugin>
```

[71]

Branching, Merging, and Options

8. Mark the merge as complete by adding `pom.xml` to the staging area using `git add` and then run `git commit` to finish the merge:

   ```
   $ git commit
   Recorded resolution for 'pom.xml'.
   [rerereExample 9b8725f] Merge tag 'v3.0.2.201309041250-rc2' into rerereExample
   ```

9. Note the recorded resolution for the `pom.xml` output from Git; this will not be here without enabling `git rerere`. Git has recorded this resolution to this particular merge conflict and will also record how to resolve this. Now, we can try to `rebase` the change to another branch.

10. Start by checking out the `rerereExample2` branch from our repository:

    ```
    $ git checkout rerereExample2

    Switched to branch 'rerereExample2'
    ```

11. Try to rebase your change on top of the `origin/stable-3.2` branch:

    ```
    $ git rebase origin/stable-3.2
    First, rewinding head to replay your work on top of it...
    Applying: Update maven-compiler-plugin to 2.5.2
    Using index info to reconstruct a base tree...
    M pom.xml
    Falling back to patching base and 3-way merge...
    Auto-merging pom.xml
    CONFLICT (content): Merge conflict in pom.xml
    Resolved 'pom.xml' using previous resolution.
    error: Failed to merge in the changes.
    Patch failed at 0001 Update maven-compiler-plugin to 2.5.2
    The copy of the patch that failed is found in: .git/rebase-apply/patch

    Resolve all conflicts manually, mark them as resolved with
    "git add/rm <conflicted_files>", then run "git rebase --continue".
    You can instead skip this commit: run "git rebase --skip".
    To abort and get back to the state before "git rebase", run "git rebase --abort".
    ```

12. You should notice the following output:

    ```
    CONFLICT (content): Merge conflict in pom.xml
    Resolved 'pom.xml' using previous resolution
    ```

[72]

13. As the merge conflict is the same in pom.xml, Git can solve the conflict in the file for you. This is very clear when you open the file and see there are no merge markers, as the resolution Git had recorded has been applied. Finish the merge by adding pom.xml and continue the rebase:

    ```
    $ git add pom.xml
    $ git rebase --continue
    Applying: Update maven-compiler-plugin to 2.5.2
    ```

14. Start Gitk to see that the commit has been rebased on top of the origin/stable-3.2 branch:

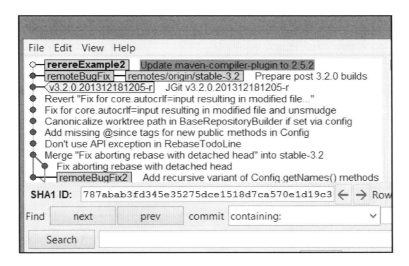

You can try the same scenario with merging and it will merge the file automatically for you.

There's more...

When you merge different branches often and you are not sure which branch a specific error fix is a part of, it is actually quite easy to find out:

1. You need to find a commit for which you are interested in getting this information. Then, use the --contains flag for the git branch command:

    ```
    $ git branch --contains 699900c308
    
    anotherBugFix
    lastBugFix
    ```

```
  master
  newBugFix
  remoteBugFix
  remoteBugFix2
  remoteOldbugFix
* rerereExample2
```

2. The previous command lists all the branches that have the specific commit. If you leave out the commit argument (8e2886897), Git will check HEAD. So, for instance, checking out the rerereExample2 branch and executing the following command, you will see the commit is present only on that branch:

```
$ git checkout rerereExample2
Switched to branch 'rerereExample2'

$ git branch -a --contains
* rerereExample2
```

The -a option indicates that you wish to check all the remote branches as well. If you leave this out, it will check only local branches.

However, as you can see, our commit is not on any remote branch, as the commit has just been created locally and has not been pushed to any remotes yet.

You can use tags, branch names, or commit hashes while using the git branch -a --contains command.

3. Let's try to see the branches where the v2.3.0.201302130906 tag is present:

```
$ git branch -a --contains v2.3.0.201302130906
  anotherBugFix
  lastBugFix
  master
  newBugFix
  remoteBugFix
  remoteBugFix2
  remoteOldbugFix
  remotePartlyMerge
* rerereExample2
  remotes/origin/HEAD -> origin/master
  remotes/origin/master
```

[74]

```
    remotes/origin/stable-2.3
    remotes/origin/stable-3.0
    remotes/origin/stable-3.1
    remotes/origin/stable-3.2

... and many more
```

That tag can be found in quite a lot of branches.

Compute the difference between branches

Checking the difference between branches can show valuable information before merging.

A regular `git diff` between two branches will show you all the information, but it can be rather exhausting to sit and look at; maybe you are only interested in one file. Thus, you don't need the long unified diff.

Getting ready

To start with, we decide on two branches, tags, or commits we want to see the difference between. Then, to list files that have changed between these branches, you can use the `--name-only` flag.

How to do it...

Perform the following steps to see the difference between the branches:

1. Diff `origin/stable-3.1` with the `origin/stable-3.2` branch:

    ```
    $ git diff --name-only origin/stable-3.1 origin/stable-3.2
    org.eclipse.jgit/src/org/eclipse/jgit/transport/org.eclipse.jgit/src/org/eclipse/jgit/transport/BasePackFetch
    
    More output..
    ```

2. We are building the command in this pattern, that is, `git diff [options] <commit> <commit> <path>`. Then, we can diff what we care about while looking into the differences between branches. This is very useful if you are responsible for a subset of the source code, and you wish to diff that area only.

3. Let's try the same diff between branches, but this time we will diff the entire branches, not just a sub-directory; however, we only want to show the deleted or added files between the branches. This is done by using the `--diff-filter=DA` and `--name-status` options. The `--name-status` option will only show the filenames and the type of change. The `--diff-filter=DA` option will only show the deleted and added files:

   ```
   $ git diff --name-status --diff-filter=DA origin/stable-3.1 origin/stable-3.2

   A
   org.eclipse.jgit.packaging/org.eclipse.jgit.target/jgit-4.4.target
   A
   org.eclipse.jgit.pgm.test/tst/org/eclipse/jgit/pgm/DescribeTest.java
   A org.eclipse.jgit.pgm.test/tst/org/eclipse/jgit/pgm/FetchTest.java
   A org.eclipse.jgit.pgm/src/org/eclipse/jgit/pgm/Describe.java
   A
   org.eclipse.jgit.test/tst/org/eclipse/jgit/api/DescribeCommandTest.java
   A org.eclipse.jgit.test/tst/org/eclipse/jgit/api/Sets.java
   D
   org.eclipse.jgit.test/tst/org/eclipse/jgit/internal/storage/file/GCTest.java

     More output..
   ```

4. This shows the files that have been added and deleted while moving from `origin/stable-3.1` to `origin/stable-3.2`.

5. If we switch the branches around, as in the following command, we will get the opposite result:

   ```
   $ git diff --name-status --diff-filter=DA origin/stable-3.2 origin/stable-3.1

   D
   org.eclipse.jgit.packaging/org.eclipse.jgit.target/jgit-4.4.target
   D
   org.eclipse.jgit.pgm.test/tst/org/eclipse/jgit/pgm/DescribeTest.java
   D org.eclipse.jgit.pgm.test/tst/org/eclipse/jgit/pgm/FetchTest.java
   D org.eclipse.jgit.pgm/src/org/eclipse/jgit/pgm/Describe.java
   D
   org.eclipse.jgit.test/tst/org/eclipse/jgit/api/DescribeCommandTest.java
   D org.eclipse.jgit.test/tst/org/eclipse/jgit/api/Sets.java
   ```

```
A
org.eclipse.jgit.test/tst/org/eclipse/jgit/internal/storage/file/GC
Test.java

More output..
```

Note that the indication letters A and D switched places because now we want to know what happens if we move from `origin/stable-3.2` to `origin/stable-3.1`.

Orphan branches

You are now familiar with Git's data model, the DAG. You have seen that objects have a parent. When you create a new branch, the commit is its parent. However, in some situations, it is useful to have a branch with no parent.

One example would be an instance where you have your code base in two separate repositories, but, for some reason, you now want to consolidate it into one. One way is to simply copy the files and add them to one of the repositories, but the disadvantage is that you will lose the histories. The second way is to use an orphan branch that can help you to fetch one repository in another.

Getting ready

It is actually easy to create an orphan branch. The flag `--orphan` to `checkout` will do it. It can be executed as follows:

```
$ git clone
https://github.com/PacktPublishing/Git-Version-Control-Cookbook-Second-Edit
ion.git
$ cd Git-Version-Control-Cookbook-Second-Edition
$ git checkout --orphan fresh-start
Switched to a new branch 'fresh-start'
```

How to do it...

1. We now have a branch with no parent. You can verify it by examining the commit log as follows:

   ```
   $ git log
   fatal: your current branch 'fresh-start' does not have any commits yet
   ```

   `Fresh start` does not mean that you are starting from scratch. The files and directories that have been added to the repository still exist:

   ```
   $ ls
   README.md a_sub_directory another-file.txt cat-me.txt hello_world.c
   $ git status
   On branch fresh-start

   No commits yet

   Changes to be committed:
     (use "git rm --cached <file>..." to unstage)

     new file:   README.md
     new file:   a_sub_directory/readme
     new file:   another-file.txt
     new file:   cat-me.txt
     new file:   hello_world.c
   ```

2. If you need a fresh start, you can delete the files (but remember not to delete `.git`) as follows:

   ```
   $ git rm --cached README.md a_sub_directory/readme another-file.txt cat-me.txt hello_world.c
   $ rm -rf README.md a_sub_directory another-file.txt cat-me.txt hello_world.c
   $ git status
   On branch fresh-start

   No commits yet

   nothing to commit (create/copy files and use "git add" to track)
   ```

3. You have a branch with no files and no commits. Moreover, the branch does not share any commit history with your `master` branch. You could add another repository and fetch all its commits using `git remote add` and `git fetch`. Instead, we will simply add a text file to illustrate it as follows:

    ```
    $ echo "This is from an orphan branch." > orphan.txt
    $ git add orphan.txt
    $ git commit  -m "Orphan"
    ```

    Commit is the only thing in the history that you can verify with the command `git log`. If you fetch another repository into the branch, you will see all the commits and, more importantly you will have a copy of the repository's history.

4. Once you have your commits in place on the orphan branch, it is time to merge them into your master branch. However, your first attempt will fail. For example, check the following:

    ```
    $ git checkout master
    $ git merge fresh-start
    fatal: refusing to merge unrelated histories
    ```

5. As you can see, the orphan branch does not share history with the master branch, and git will not allow you to merge the branch. It shouldn't come as a surprise, since it is basically what an orphan branch is all about. However, you can still merge an orphan branch by allowing unrelated histories to be merged:

    ```
    $ git merge fresh-start --allow-unrelated-histories
    $ git log -3
    commit aa804347c728552f7ce9298a83ab646148078dab (HEAD -> master)
    Merge: 13dcada 45d1798
    Author: John Doe <john.doe@example.com>
    Date: Fri May 11 08:57:45 2018 +0200

    Merge branch 'fresh-start'

    commit 45d179838f8f9f8fd64c6c7bf96147e09ceadbc2 (fresh-start)
    Author: John Doe <john.doe@example.com>
    Date: Fri May 11 08:57:22 2018 +0200

    Orphan

    commit 13dcada077e446d3a05ea9cdbc8ecc261a94e42d (origin/master, origin/HEAD)
    Author: John Doe <john.doe@example.com>
    Date: Fri Dec 13 12:26:00 2013 +0100
    ```

```
      This is the subject line of the commit message

      ... and more output
```

It is unlikely that you will use orphan branches on a daily basis, but it is a strong feature to know when you need to reorganize your code base.

There's more...

There are more options in the help files for Git. Just run `git merge --help` or `git branch --help` to see what other options are available.

4
Rebasing Regularly and Interactively, and Other Use Cases

In this chapter, we will cover the following recipes:

- Rebasing commits to another branch
- Continuing a rebase with merge conflicts
- Rebasing selected commits interactively
- Squashing commits using an interactive rebase
- Changing the author of commits using a rebase
- Autosquashing commits

Introduction

Rebase is an incredibly strong Git feature. Hopefully, you have used it before; if not, you might have heard about it. Rebasing is exactly what the word implies. So, if you have a certain commit, A, which is based on commit B, then rebasing A to C would result in commit A being based on commit C.

As you will see in the different examples in this chapter, it is not always as simple as that.

Rebasing commits to another branch

To start with, we are going to perform a very simple rebase, where we will introduce a new file, commit that file, make a change to it, and then commit it again so that we end up with two new commits.

Getting ready

Before we start, we need a repository to work in. You can use a previous clone of `jgit`, but to get a close-to-identical output from the example, you can clone the `jgit` repository.

The `jgit` repository can be cloned as follows:

```
$ git clone https://git.eclipse.org/r/jgit/jgit chapter4
$ cd chapter4
```

How to do it...

We start by creating a local branch and then make two commits by performing the following steps; these are the commits that we want to rebase onto another branch:

1. Check out a new branch, `rebaseExample`, which tracks `origin/stable-3.1`:

    ```
    $ git checkout -b rebaseExample --track origin/stable-3.1
    Branch rebaseExample set up to track remote branch stable-3.1 from origin.
    Switched to a new branch 'rebaseExample'
    ```

2. Make two commits on the `rebaseExample` branch, as follows:

    ```
    $ echo "My Fishtank
    Gravel, water, plants
    Fish, pump, skeleton" > fishtank.txt
    $ git add fishtank.txt
    $ git commit -m "My brand new fishtank"
    [rebaseExample 4b2c2ec] My brand new fishtank
     1 file changed, 4 insertions(+)
      create mode 100644 fishtank.txt
    $ echo "mosquitos" >> fishtank.txt
    $ git add fishtank.txt
    $ git commit -m "Feeding my fish"
    [rebaseExample 2132d88] Feeding my fish
     1 file changed, 1 insertion(+)
    ```

3. Then, we rebase the change on top of the `origin/stable-3.2` branch instead:

   ```
   $ git rebase origin/stable-3.2
   First, rewinding head to replay your work on top of it...
   Applying: My brand new fishtank
   Applying: Feed the fish
   ```

How it works...

When you execute `git rebase`, Git starts by finding the common ancestor of the current `HEAD` branch and the branch you want to rebase to. When Git finds `merge-base`, it will find the commits that are not available in the branch you are rebasing onto. Git will simply try to apply those commits one by one.

Continuing a rebase with merge conflicts

When you rebase a commit or a branch on top of a different `HEAD`, you may eventually see a conflict.

If there is a conflict, you will be asked to solve the merge conflict and continue with the rebase using `git rebase --continue`.

How to do it...

We will be creating a commit that adds the same `fishtank.txt` file on top of the `origin/stable-3.1` branch; then, we will try to rebase this on top of the `rebaseExample` branch we created in the *Rebasing commits to another branch* section:

1. Check out the branch named `rebaseExample2`, which tracks `origin/stable-3.1`:

   ```
   $ git checkout -b rebaseExample2 --track origin/stable-3.1
   Checking out files: 100% (212/212), done.
   Branch rebaseExample2 set up to track remote branch stable-3.1 from origin.
   Switched to a new branch 'rebaseExample2'
   ```

Rebasing Regularly and Interactively, and Other Use Cases

2. Make a commit on the branch:

    ```
    $ echo "My Fishtank
    Pirateship, Oister shell
    Coconut shell
    ">fishtank.txt
    $ git add fishtank.txt
    $ git commit -m "My brand new fishtank"
    [rebaseExample2 39811d6] My brand new fishtank
     1 file changed, 4 insertions(+)
    create mode 100644 fishtank.txt
    ```

3. Try to rebase the branch on top of the `rebaseExample` branch:

    ```
    $ git rebase rebaseExample
    First, rewinding head to replay your work on top of it...
    Applying: My brand new fishtank
    Using index info to reconstruct a base tree...
    <stdin>:12: new blank line at EOF.
     +
    warning: 1 line adds whitespace errors.
    Falling back to patching base and 3-way merge...
    Auto-merging fishtank.txt
    CONFLICT (add/add): Merge conflict in fishtank.txt
    Failed to merge in the changes.
    Patch failed at 0001 My brand new fishtank
    The copy of the patch that failed is found in:
       /Users/JohnDoe/repos/chapter4/.git/rebase-apply/patch
    When you have resolved this problem, run "git rebase --continue".
    If you prefer to skip this patch, run "git rebase --skip" instead.
    To check out the original branch and stop rebasing, run "git rebase --abort".
    ```

4. You can solve the conflict in your preferred editor. Then, add the file to the index using `git add` and continue with the rebase.

    ```
    $ git add fishtank.txt
    $ git rebase --continue
    Applying: My brand new fishtank
    ```

5. We can now check with `gitk` to see whether our change is rebased on top of the `rebaseExample` branch, as shown in the following screenshot:

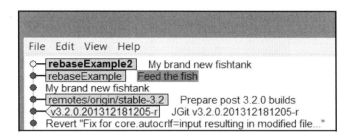

How it works...

As we learned from the first example, Git will apply the commits that are not available in the branch you are rebasing onto. In our example, it is only our commit, as we made it, that is available on the `rebaseExample2` branch.

There's more...

You might have noticed in the output of the failing rebase that you have two extra options for the commit.

When you have resolved this problem, run `git rebase --continue`. If you prefer to skip this patch, run `git rebase --skip` instead. To check out the original branch and stop rebasing, run `git rebase --abort`.

The first extra option we have is to totally ignore this patch by skipping it; you can do this using `git rebase --skip`. In our example, this will cause our branch to be fast-forwarded to the `rebaseExample` branch. So, both our branches will point to the same commit hash.

The second option is to abort the rebasing. If we choose to do this, then we will go back to the branch as it was prior to starting the rebase. This can be done using `git rebase --abort`.

Rebasing selected commits interactively

When you are working on a new feature and have branched from an old release into a feature branch, you might want to rebase this branch onto the latest release. When looking into the list of commits on the feature branch, you may realize that some of the commits are not suitable for the new release. In that case, when you want to rebase the branch onto a new release, you will need to remove some commits. This can be achieved with interactive rebasing, where Git gives you the option to pick the commits you wish to rebase.

Getting ready

To get started with this example, you need to check the previously created branch, `rebaseExample`; if you don't have this branch, follow the steps from the *Rebasing commits to another branch* section and use the following command:

```
$ git checkout rebaseExample
Switched to branch 'rebaseExample'
Your branch is ahead of 'origin/stable-3.1' by 109 commits.
  (use "git push" to publish your local commits)
```

Notice that, because we are tracking `origin/stable-3.1`, the Git checkout will tell us how far ahead we are in comparison with that branch.

How to do it...

We will try to rebase our current branch, `rebaseExample`, on top of the `origin/stable-3.1` branch by performing the following steps. Remember that Git will apply the commits that are not available on the branch we are rebasing to; so, in this case, there will be a lot of commits:

1. Rebase the branch onto `origin/stable-3.1` by using the following command:

    ```
    $ git rebase --interactive origin/stable-3.1
    ```

2. What you will see now is a list of all the commits you will be rebasing onto the origin/stable-3.1 branch. These commits are all the commits between the origin/stable-3.1 and rebaseExample branches. The commits will be applied from top to bottom, hence, the commits will be listed in reverse order—at least compared to what you would normally see in Git. This actually makes good sense. The commits have the keyword pick to the left and then the abbreviated commit hash, and finally the title of the commit subject.

   If you scroll down to the bottom, you will see a list along the lines of the following:

   ```
   pick 43405e6 My brand new fishtank
   pick 08d0906 Feed the fish
   # Rebase da6e87b..08d0906 onto da6e87b
   #
   # Commands:
   #  p, pick = use commit
   #  r, reword = use commit, but edit the commit message
   #  e, edit = use commit, but stop for amending
   #  s, squash = use commit, but meld into previous commit
   #  f, fixup = like "squash", but discard this commit's log message
   #  x, exec = run command (the rest of the line) using shell
   #
   # These lines can be re-ordered; they are executed from top to bottom.
   #
   # If you remove a line here THAT COMMIT WILL BE LOST.
   #
   # However, if you remove everything, the rebase will be aborted.
   #
   # Note that empty commits are commented out
   ```

   So, if we only want our fishtank commits to be based on top of the origin/stable-3.1 branch, we should remove all the commits except for our two.

3. Remove all the lines except for the two commits at the bottom; for now, leave pick as the keyword. Save the file and close the editor, and you will get the following message from Git:

   ```
   Successfully rebased and updated refs/heads/rebaseExample.
   ```

4. Now, with `gitk`, check whether we accomplished what we predicted. The next screenshot shows our two `fishtank` commits on top of the `origin/stable-3.1` branch. The following screenshot is what we expected:

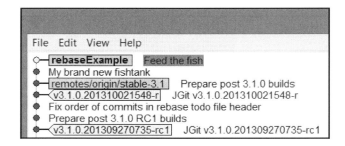

There's more...

The same thing could actually be achieved with a single short Git command. We have been rebasing commits from the `origin/stable-3.2` branch to the `rebaseExample` branch onto the `origin/stable-3.2` branch. This can also be achieved in the following manner:

```
$ git rebase --onto origin/stable-3.1 origin/stable-3.2 rebaseExample
First, rewinding head to replay your work on top of it...
Applying: My brand new fishtank
Applying: Feed the fish
```

The `--onto origin/stable-3.2` flag tells Git to rebase onto `origin/stable-3.2`, and it has to be from `origin/stable-3.1` to the `rebaseExample` branch. So, we end up having the `rebaseExample` branch to the branch of the `origin/stable-3.1` and so on. The next diagram illustrates both before the rebase example, where we have our two commits on top of `origin/stable-3.2`, and after the rebase, where our commits are on top of `origin/stable-3.1`, as we wanted:

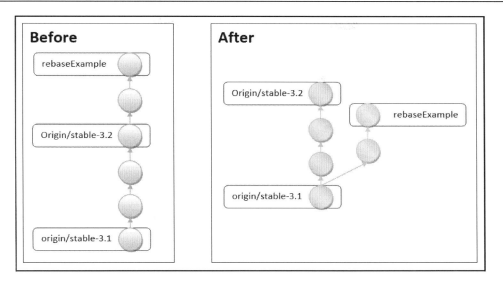

Squashing commits using an interactive rebase

When I work on a local branch, I prefer to commit in small increments with a few comments on what I did in the commits; however, as these commits do not build or pass any test requirements, I cannot submit them for review and verification one by one. I have to merge them in my branch, but still, cherry-picking my fix would require me to cherry-pick twice the number of commits, which is not very handy.

What we can do is rebase and squash the commits into a single commit, or at least fewer commits.

Getting ready

To get started with this example, we need a new branch, namely rebaseExample3, which tracks origin/stable-3.1. Create the branch with the following command:

```
$ git checkout -b rebaseExample3 --track origin/stable-3.1
Branch rebaseExample3 set up to track remote branch stable-3.1 from origin.
Switched to a new branch 'rebaseExample3'
```

How to do it...

To really showcase this Git feature, we will start off six commits ahead of the `origin/stable-3.1` branch. This is to simulate the fact that we have just created six commits on top of the `rebaseExample3` branch; to do this, perform the following steps:

1. Find a commit that is between `origin/stable-3.1` and `origin/stable-3.2`, and list the commits in reverse order. Alternatively, you can scroll down to the bottom of the output and find the commit we will use, as shown in the following snippet:

   ```
   $ git log origin/stable-3.1..origin/stable-3.2 --oneline --reverse
   8a51c44 Do not close ArchiveOutputStream on error
   3467e86 Revert "Close unfinished archive entries on error"
   f045a68 Added the git-describe implementation
   0be59ab Merge "Added the git-describe implementation"
   fdc80f7 Merge branch 'stable-3.1'
   7995d87 Prepare 3.2.0-SNAPSHOT builds
   5218f7b Propagate IOException where possible when getting refs.
   ```

2. Reset the `rebaseExample3` branch to the `5218f7b` commit; this will simulate having six commits on top of the `origin/stable-3.1` branch. This can be tested by running the status of Git as follows:

   ```
   $ git reset --hard 5218f7b
   HEAD is now at 5218f7b Propagate IOException where possible when getting refs.
   $ git status
   On branch rebaseExample3
   Your branch is ahead of 'origin/stable-3.1' by 6 commits.
   (use "git push" to publish your local commits)
   nothing to commit, working directory clean
   ```

3. Now, we have these six commits on top of the `origin/stable-3.1` branch, and we want to squash these commits into two different commits. This can be done by simply running `git rebase --interactive`. Note that we are not specifying which branch we want to rebase to, since we have already set up a tracking branch when we created the branch using `--track`.

To continue, let's execute the rebase command as follows:

```
$ git rebase --interactive
pick 8a51c44 Do not close ArchiveOutputStream on error
pick f045a68 Added the git-describe implementation
pick 7995d87 Prepare 3.2.0-SNAPSHOT builds
pick 5218f7b Propagate IOException where possible when getting refs.
```

4. The editor will open, and you will see four commits, not six as you would expect. This is because the rebase, in general, refuses to take merged commits as part of the rebase scenario. Although you can use the `--preserve-merges` flag, as per the Git **Help** section, this is not recommended.

> According to the Git Help section, instead of ignoring merges, `--preserve-merges` tries to recreate them. The `--preserve-merges` flag uses the `--interactive` machinery internally, but combining it with the `--interactive` option explicitly is generally not a good idea, unless you know what you are doing (see the bugs in the following snippet).

5. Edit the file so that it looks as follows:

```
pick 8a51c44 Do not close ArchiveOutputStream on error
squash f045a68 Added the git-describe implementation
pick 7995d87 Prepare 3.2.0-SNAPSHOT builds
squash 5218f7b Propagate IOException where possible when getting refs.
```

6. Remember that commits are listed in reverse order compared to the Git log. So, when squashing commits, we squash up into the commits we have marked with the `pick`. When you close the editor, Git will start the rebase from top to bottom. First, apply `8a51c44` and then squash `f045a68` into the commit `8a51c44`. This will open the commit message editor, which contains both of the commit messages. You can edit the commit messages, but for now, let's just close the editor to finish with the rebase and the squashing of these two commits. The editor will open one more time to complete the squashing of `5218f7b` into `7995d87`. Use `gitk` to verify the result.

The following screenshot is as expected; now, we only have two commits on top of the `origin/stable-3.1` branch:

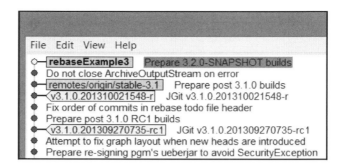

7. If you check the commit message of the HEAD commit, you will see that it has the information of two commits, as shown in the following command. This is because we decided not to change the commit message when we made the change:

```
$ git log -1
commit 9c96a651ff881c7d7c5a3974fa7a19a9c264d0a0
Author: Matthias Sohn <matthias.sohn@sap.com>
Date:   Thu Oct 3 17:40:22 2013 +0200
 Prepare 3.2.0-SNAPSHOT builds
 Change-Id: Iac6cf7a5bb6146ee3fe38abe8020fc3fc4217584
 Signed-off-by: Matthias Sohn <matthias.sohn@sap.com>
 Propagate IOException where possible when getting refs.
 Currently, Repository.getAllRefs() and Repository.getTags()
 silently
 ignores an IOException and instead returns an empty map.
Repository
  is a public API and as such cannot be changed until the next
major
  revision change. Where possible, update the internal jgit APIs to
  use the RefDatabase directly, since it propagates the error.
 Change-Id: I4e4537d8bd0fa772f388262684c5c4ca1929dc4c
```

There's more...

Now we have squashed two commits, but we could have used other keywords when editing the rebase's to-do list.

We will try the fixup functionality, which works like the squash functionality, by performing the following steps; the exception is that Git will select the commit message of the commits using the `pick` keyword:

1. Start by resetting back to our starting point:

   ```
   $ git reset --hard 5218f7b
   HEAD is now at 5218f7b Propagate IOException where possible when getting refs.
   $ git status
   On branch rebaseExample3
   Your branch is ahead of 'origin/stable-3.1' by 6 commits.
   (use "git push" to publish your local commits)
   nothing to commit, working directory clean
   ```

2. As you can see, we are back at the starting point, that is, we're six commits ahead of the `origin/stable-3.1` branch. Now we can try the fixup functionality. Start the interactive rebase and change the file according to the following output. Notice that you can use `f` instead of `fixup`:

   ```
   $ git rebase --interactive
   pick 8a51c44 Do not close ArchiveOutputStream on error
   f    f045a68 Added the git-describe implementation
   pick 7995d87 Prepare 3.2.0-SNAPSHOT builds
   f    5218f7b Propagate IOException where possible when getting refs.
   ```

3. Once you close the editor, you will see rebase's progress through Git. As predicted, the commit message editor will not open. Git will just rebase the changes into two commits on top of the `origin/stable-3.1` branch. Using `git status`, you can confirm that you have just two commits:

   ```
   $ git status
   On branch rebaseExample3
   Your branch is ahead of 'origin/stable-3.1' by 2 commits.
     (use "git push" to publish your local commits)

   nothing to commit, working tree clean
   ```

4. Another difference is that the commit message from the two commits we marked with fixup has disappeared. So, if you compare this with the previous example, it's very clear what the difference is; it's shown in the following command:

   ```
   $ git log -1
   commit c5bc5cc9e0956575cc3c30c3be4aecab19980e4d
   Author: Matthias Sohn <matthias.sohn@sap.com>
   Date:   Thu Oct 3 17:40:22 2013 +0200
   ```

```
Prepare 3.2.0-SNAPSHOT builds
Change-Id: Iac6cf7a5bb6146ee3fe38abe8020fc3fc4217584
Signed-off-by: Matthias Sohn matthias.sohn@sap.com
```

5. Finally, we can also confirm that we still have the same source code, but with different commits. This can be done by comparing this commit with the commit we created via `5218f7b`, using the following command:

```
$ git diff 5218f7b
```

As predicted, there is no output from `git diff`, so we still have the same source code.

This check can also be performed on the previous example.

Changing the author of commits using a rebase

When starting to work on a new project, it is common to forget to set the author name and author email address for the specified project. Therefore, you will often have commits in your local branch that have been committed with the wrong username and/or email ID.

Getting ready

Before we begin this exercise, we need a branch, as always with Git. Name the branch `resetAuthorRebase` and make it track `origin/master`. Use the following command to achieve this:

```
$ git checkout -b resetAuthorRebase -t origin/master
Branch resetAuthorRebase set up to track remote branch 'master' from 'origin'.
Switched to a new branch 'resetAuthorRebase'
```

How to do it...

Now, we want to change the author of all the commits from `origin/stable-3.2` to our `HEAD`, which is `master`. This is just an example; you will rarely have to change the author of commits that have already been published to a remote repository.

You can change the author of the `HEAD` commit by using `git commit --amend --reset-author`; however, this will only change the author of `HEAD` and leave the rest of the commits as they were. We will start by changing the author of the `HEAD` commit and then verify why that is wrong by performing the following steps:

1. Change the author of the `HEAD` commit as follows:

   ```
   $ git commit --amend --reset-author
   [resetAuthorRebase b0b2836] Update Kepler target platform to use Kepler SR2 orbit R-build
     1 file changed, 1 insertion(+), 1 deletion(-)
   ```

2. Verify that you have changed it using the Git log command:

   ```
   $ git log --format='format:%h %an <%ae>' origin/stable-3.2..HEAD
   b0b2836 John Doe <john.doe@example.com>
   b9a0621 Matthias Sohn <matthias.sohn@sap.com>
   ba15d82 Matthias Sohn matthias.sohn@sap.com
   ```

3. We will list all the commits from `origin/stable-3.2` to `HEAD` and we will define a format with `%h` as the abbreviated commit hash, `%an` for the author's name, and `%ae` for the author's email address. From the output, you can see that I am now the author of the `HEAD` commit, but what we really wanted was to change the author of all the commits. To do this, we will rebase onto the `origin/stable-3.2` branch; then, for each commit, we will stop to amend and reset the author. Git can do most of that work with `--exec` option for the `git rebase`, as follows:

   ```
   $ git rebase --interactive --exec "git commit --amend --reset-author" origin/stable-3.2
   pick b14a939 Prepare 3.3.0-SNAPSHOT builds
   exec git commit --amend --reset-author
   pick f2abbd0 archive: Prepend a specified prefix to all entry filenames
   exec git commit --amend --reset-author
   ```

4. As you can see, Git has opened the rebase's to-do list for you, and between every commit, you have the `exec` keyword and the command we specified on the command line. You can have more `exec` lines between commits if you have a use case for them. Closing the editor will start the rebase.

5. As you will see, this process is not very good, as the commit message editor opens every time and you have to close the editor to allow Git to continue with the rebase. To stop the rebase, clear the commit message editor and Git will return to the command line; then, you can use `git rebase --abort` as follows:

```
Executing: git commit --amend --reset-author
Aborting commit due to empty commit message.
Execution failed: git commit --amend --reset-author
You can fix the problem, and then run
        git rebase --continue
$ git rebase --abort
```

To achieve what we really want, you can add the `--reuse-message` option for `git commit`; this will reuse the commit message for the commit you will specify. We want to use the message of HEAD, as we are going to amend it to the HEAD commit. So, try again, as shown in the following command:

```
$ git rebase --interactive --exec "git commit --amend --reset-author --reuse-message=HEAD" origin/stable-3.2
Executing: git commit --amend --reset-author --reuse-message=HEAD
[detached HEAD 0cd3e87] Prepare 3.3.0-SNAPSHOT builds
 51 files changed, 291 insertions(+), 291 deletions(-)
 rewrite org.eclipse.jgit.java7.test/META-INF/MANIFEST.MF (62%)
 rewrite org.eclipse.jgit.junit/META-INF/MANIFEST.MF (73%)
 rewrite org.eclipse.jgit.pgm.test/META-INF/MANIFEST.MF (61%)
 rewrite org.eclipse.jgit.test/META-INF/MANIFEST.MF (76%)
 rewrite org.eclipse.jgit.ui/META-INF/MANIFEST.MF (67%)
    Executing: git commit --amend --reset-author --reuse-message=HEAD
    [detached HEAD faaf25e] archive: Prepend a specified prefix to all entry filenames
     5 files changed, 115 insertions(+), 1 deletion(-)
    Executing: git commit --amend --reset-author --reuse-message=HEAD
    [detached HEAD cfd743e] [CLI] Add option --millis / -m to debug-show-dir-cache c
    Command
    Successfully rebased and updated refs/heads/resetAuthorRebase.
```

6. Git provides an output indicating that the action was a success; however, to verify this, you can execute the previous Git log command and you should see that the email address has changed on all the commits, as shown in the following command:

```
$ git log --format='format:%h %an <%ae>' origin/stable-3.2..HEAD
9b10ff9 John Doe <john.doe@example.com>
d8f0ada John Doe <john.doe@example.com>
53df2b7 John Doe <john.doe@example.com>
```

How it works...

It works as you would expect! There is one thing to remember: when using the `exec` option, Git will check the work area for unstaged and staged changes. Consider the following command line:

```
exec echo rainy_day > weather_main.txt
exec echo sunny_day > weather_california.txt
```

If you were to have a line as illustrated in the preceding command, the first `exec` would be executed and you would then have an unstaged change in your work area. Git would complain and you would have to solve that before continuing with the next `exec`.

So, if you want to do something like this, you must create a single exec line that executes all the things you want. Besides this, the rebase functionality is fairly simple; it just tries to apply the changes in the order specified in the rebase's to-do list. Git will only apply the changes specified in the list, so if you remove some of them, they will not be applied. This is a way to clean up a feature branch for unwanted commits, for instance, commits that enable you to debug.

Autosquashing commits

When I work with Git, I often create a lot of commits for a single bug fix, but when making the delivery to the remote repository, I prefer—and recommend—delivering the bug fix as one commit. This can be achieved with an interactive rebase, but since this should be a common workflow, Git has a built-in feature called autosquash, which will help you squash the commits together.

Getting ready

Before we begin with this exercise, we will create a branch from origin/master so we are ready to add commits to our fix.

Let's start with something like this:

```
$ git checkout -b readme_update_developer --track origin/master
Branch readme_update_developer set up to track remote branch master from origin.
Switched to a new branch 'readme_update_developer'
```

How to do it...

After checking the branch, we will create the first commit that we want to squash other commits to. We need to use the abbreviated commit hash from this commit to automatically create other commits that will squash to this commit by performing the following steps:

1. Start by echoing some text into README.md:

   ```
   $ echo "More information for developers" >> README.md
   ```

2. This will append more information to README.md for developers; verify that the file has changed using the Git status as follows:

   ```
   $ git status
   On branch readme_update_developer
   Your branch is up-to-date with 'origin/master'.
   Changes not staged for commit:
     (use "git add <file>..." to update what will be committed)
     (use "git checkout -- <file>..." to discard changes in working directory)
            modified:   README.md
   no changes added to commit (use "git add" and/or "git commit -a")
   ```

3. Now, we want to add and commit this. We can do this with the commit command using the -a flag, which will add any unstaged changes to the commit, as shown in the following command:

   ```
   $ git commit -a -m "Updating information for developers"
   [readme_update_developer d539645] Updating information for developers
    1 file changed, 1 insertion(+)
   ```

4. After you create the commit, remember the abbreviated commit hash; we have highlighted it in bold in the command output. The abbreviation will be different in your environment, and you should have your own abbreviation once you finish the exercise.

5. To continue, we will add three commits to the branch, and we would like to squash two of these with the first commit, as shown in the following command:

```
$ echo "even More information for developers" >> README.md
$ git commit -a --squash=d539645 --no-edit
[readme_update_developer d62922d] squash! Updating information for developers
 1 file changed, 1 insertion(+)
```

6. This is the first commit. Pay attention to why we needed to store the abbreviated hash of the first commit—we used it with the `--squash` option for `git commit`. This option will create the commit with the subject of the commit specified. It will also add `squash!` to the start of the subject. This is to indicate that Git should squash this commit when performing a rebase. Now, create the second commit, as shown in the following command:

```
$ echo "even More information for developers" >> README.md
$ git commit -a --squash=d539645 --no-edit
[readme_update_developer 7d6194d] squash! Updating information for developers
 1 file changed, 1 insertion(+)
```

7. We have added two commits that we would like to squash with the first commit. When committing, I also used the `--no-edit` option; this skips the opening of the commit's message editor. If you leave the flag out, the editor will open as it usually does when committing. The difference is that the commit subject has already been set, and you only need to write the commit message. Now, we will create the last commit; we don't want to squash this commit:

```
$ echo "Adding configuration information" >> README.md
$ git commit -a -m "Updating information on configuration"
[readme_update_developer fd07857] Updating information on configuration
 1 file changed, 1 insertion(+)
```

8. We add the final commit, which does not have anything to do with the first three commits we added. This is why we did not use the `--squash` option. We can now squash the commits together using `git rebase -i`:

```
$ git rebase -i
```

9. You will get the rebase's to-do list up in the configured commit editor. What we would have expected was to have Git configure a squash for the commits we wanted to squash, as shown in the following command:

   ```
   pick d539645 Updating information for developers
   pick d62922d squash! Updating information for developers
   pick 7d6194d squash! Updating information for developers
   pick fd07857 Updating information on configuration
   ```

10. What you can see is that Git inserted `squash` to the subject of two of the commits, but besides this, we did not get what we had expected. Git requires you to specify `--autosquash` to the `git rebase -i` command. Close the editor and Git will perform the rebase and give the following output:

    ```
    Successfully rebased and updated
    refs/heads/readme_update_developer.
    ```

11. Let's try again with `--autosquash` and see what happens with the rebase's to-do list:

    ```
    $ git rebase -i --autosquash
    pick d539645 Updating information for developers
    squash d62922d squash! Updating information for developers
    squash 7d6194d squash! Updating information for developers
    pick fd07857 Updating information on configuration
    ```

12. Now, the rebase's to-do list looks much more as we expected. Git has preconfigured the to-do list to show which commits it will squash and which commits it will keep.

13. Closing the to-do list now will start the rebase, and we don't want that (the next step will show what we really want). If you clear the to-do list (deleting all lines), save and close the editor, the rebase will be aborted. This is what we want. The output will be as follows:

    ```
    Nothing to do
    ```

14. What we really want to do is just run `git rebase -i` and Git will use `--autosquash` as the default. This can be achieved with `git config rebase.autosquash true`; try it and then run `git rebase -i`:

    ```
    $ git config rebase.autosquash true
    $ git rebase -i
    ```

15. The rebase's to-do list pops up, and we have the expected result as follows:

    ```
    pick d539645 Updating information for developers
    squash d62922d squash! Updating information for developers
    squash 7d6194d squash! Updating information for developers
    pick fd07857 Updating information on configuration
    ```

16. Now close the editor and allow the rebase to start. The editor opens and you can change the commit message for the combined message, as shown in the following command:

    ```
    # This is a combination of 3 commits.
    # The first commit's message is:
    Updating information for developers
    # This is the 2nd commit message:
    squash! Updating information for developers
    # This is the 3rd commit message:
    squash! Updating information for developers
    ```

17. Modify the message and close the editor; Git continues with the rebase and ends with the following message:

    ```
    [detached HEAD baadd53] Updating information for developers
      1 file changed, 3 insertions(+)
    Successfully rebased and updated
    refs/heads/readme_update_developer.
    Verify the commit log with git log -3
    $ git log -3
    commit 6d83d44645e330d0081d3679aca49cd9bc20c891
    Author: John Doe <john.doe@example.com>
    Date:   Wed May 21 10:52:03 2014 +0200
        Updating information on configuration
    commit baadd53018df2f6f3cdf88d024c3b9db16e526cf
    Author: John Doe <john.doe@example.com>
    Date:   Wed May 21 10:25:43 2014 +0200
        Updating information for developers
    commit 6d724dcd3355f09e3450e417cf173fcafaee9e08
    Author: Shawn Pearce <spearce@spearce.org>
    Date:   Sat Apr 26 10:40:30 2014 -0700
    ```

18. As expected, we now have two commits on top of the `origin/master` commit.

Hopefully, this will assist you when you are just making changes and committing them, but want to deliver the code as one commit.

There's more...

If you want to avoid opening the commit message editor, as in step 17 of the *Autosquashing commits* recipe, you can use `--fixup=d539645`. This will use the commit message from the first commit and totally disregard any message written in the commits.

5
Storing Additional Information in Your Repository

In this chapter, we will cover the following recipes:

- Adding your first Git note
- Separating notes by category
- Retrieving notes from the remote repository
- Pushing Git notes to a remote repository
- Tagging commits in the repository

Introduction

Git is powerful in many ways. One of the most powerful features of Git is that it has immutable history. This is powerful because nobody can squeeze something into the history of Git without it being noticed by the people who have cloned the repository. This also causes some challenges for developers, as some would like to change the commit messages after a commit has been released. This is possible in many other version control systems, but because of the immutable history with Git, it has Git notes. A Git note is essentially an extra `refs/notes/commits` reference in Git. Here, you add additional information to the commits that can be displayed when running a `git log` command. You can also release the notes into a remote repository so that people can fetch the notes.

Adding your first Git note

We will add some extra information to the already released code. If we were doing it in the actual commits, we would see the commit hashes change.

Getting ready

Before we start, we need a repository to work in; you can use the previous clone of jgit, but to get an output from the example that's almost identical, you can clone the jgit repository as follows:

```
$ git clone https://git.eclipse.org/r/jgit/jgit chapter5
$ cd chapter5
```

How to do it...

We start by creating a local branch, notesMessage, tracking origin/stable-3.2. Then, we will try and change the commit message and see that the commit hash changes:

1. Checkout the branch notesMessage tracking origin/stable-3.2:

    ```
    $ git checkout -b notesMessage --track origin/stable-3.2
    Branch notesMessage set up to track remote branch stable-3.2 from origin.
    Switched to a new branch 'notesMessage'
    ```

2. List the commit hash of the HEAD of your branch:

    ```
    $ git log -1
    commit f839d383e6fbbda26729db7fd57fc917fa47db44
    Author: Matthias Sohn <matthias.sohn@sap.com>
    Date:   Wed Dec 18 21:16:13 2013 +0100
        Prepare post 3.2.0 builds
        Change-Id: Ie2bfdee0c492e3d61d92acb04c5bef641f5f132f
        Signed-off-by: Matthias Sohn <matthias.sohn@sap.com>
    ```

3. Change the commit message by amending the commit using git commit --amend, and, following that, add a line above the Change-Id: line with Update MANIFEST files:

    ```
    $ git commit --amend
    ```

4. Now, we list the commit again and see that the commit hash has changed:

   ```
   $ git log -1
   commit 5ccc9c90d29badb1bd860d29860715e0becd3d7b
   Author: Matthias Sohn <matthias.sohn@sap.com>
   Date:   Wed Dec 18 21:16:13 2013 +0100
       Prepare post 3.2.0 builds
       Update MANIFEST files

       Change-Id: Ie2bfdee0c492e3d61d92acb04c5bef641f5f132f
       Signed-off-by: Matthias Sohn matthias.sohn@sap.com
   ```

5. Notice that the commit parts have changed from `f839d383e6fbbda26729db7fd57fc917fa47db44` to `9fcaa153c4afc6ee95572a58ddfa297f60b7e1cf`, as the commit is derived from the content in the commit, the parents of the commit, and the commit message. So, the commit hash will change when updating the commit message. Since we have changed the content of the HEAD commit, we are no longer based on the HEAD commit of the `origin/stable-3.2` branch. This becomes visible in `gitk` and `git status`:

   ```
   $ git status
   On branch notesMessage
   Your branch and 'origin/stable-3.2' have diverged,
   and have 1 and 1 different commit each, respectively.
     (use "git pull" to merge the remote branch into yours)
   nothing to commit, working directory clean
   ```

6. As you can see from the output, our branch has diverged from `origin/stable-3.2`; this is also visible from `gitk`. Note that we can specify which branches and commits we want to see with `gitk`. In this case, we want to see `origin/stable-3.2` and `HEAD`:

   ```
   $ gitk origin/stable-3.2 HEAD
   ```

Storing Additional Information in Your Repository

The following is the screenshot for this:

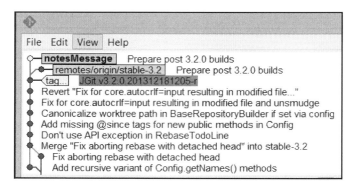

7. To prevent this result, we can add a note to the commit message. Let's start by resetting the branch to `origin/stable-3.2` and then adding a note to the commit:

   ```
   $ git reset --hard origin/stable-3.2
   HEAD is now at f839d38 Prepare post 3.2.0 builds
   ```

8. Now, add the same message as the previous one, but just as a note:

   ```
   $ git notes add -m "Update MANIFEST files"
   ```

9. We have added the note directly from the command line without invoking the editor by using the `-m` flag and then a message. The log will now be visible when running `git log`:

   ```
   $ git log -1
   commit f839d383e6fbbda26729db7fd57fc917fa47db44
   Author: Matthias Sohn <matthias.sohn@sap.com>
   Date:   Wed Dec 18 21:16:13 2013 +0100
       Prepare post 3.2.0 builds
       Change-Id: Ie2bfdee0c492e3d61d92acb04c5bef641f5f132f
       Signed-off-by: Matthias Sohn <matthias.sohn@sap.com>
   Notes:
       Update MANIFEST files
   ```

10. As you can see from the log output, we have a `Notes:` section with our note. Although it does not add the note directly in the commit message as the `--amend` option does, we still have our important addition to the commit message. We can verify with `git status` that we have no longer diverged:

    ```
    $ git status
    On branch notesMessage
    Your branch is up-to-date with 'origin/stable-3.2'.
    nothing to commit, working directory clean
    ```

There's more...

So, you have your notes for your commit and now you want to add to them. You will perhaps expect that you just add the note again with more information. This is not the case. You have the option to append, edit, or force the note to be created:

1. Start by trying to add the note again with additional information:

    ```
    $ git notes add -m "Update MANIFESTS files for next version"
    error: Cannot add notes. Found existing notes for object f839d383e6fbbda26729db7
    fd57fc917fa47db44. Use '-f' to overwrite existing notes
    ```

2. As predicted, we cannot add the note but we can do it with the `-f` flag:

    ```
    $ git notes add -f -m "Update MANIFESTS files for next version"
    Overwriting existing notes for object
    f839d383e6fbbda26729db7fd57fc917fa47db44
    ```

3. Git overwrites the existing notes due to the `-f` flag. You can also use `--force`, which is the same. Verify it with `git log`:

    ```
    $ git log -1
    commit f839d383e6fbbda26729db7fd57fc917fa47db44
    Author: Matthias Sohn <matthias.sohn@sap.com>
    Date:   Wed Dec 18 21:16:13 2013 +0100

        Prepare post 3.2.0 builds

        Change-Id: Ie2bfdee0c492e3d61d92acb04c5bef641f5f132f
        Signed-off-by: Matthias Sohn <matthias.sohn@sap.com>

    Notes:
        Update MANIFESTS files for next version
    ```

4. You can also append a current note with `git notes append`:

   ```
   $ git notes append -m "Verified by John Doe"
   ```

5. There is no output from this unless something goes wrong, but you can verify this by using `git log` again. To keep the output to a minimum, we are using `--oneline`. This will show a minimum output of the commit. But to show the note, we have to add `--notes`, which will show the notes for the commits in the output:

   ```
   $ git log -1 --notes --oneline
   f839d38 Prepare post 3.2.0 builds
   Notes:
       Update MANIFESTS files for next version
       Verified by John Doe
   ```

6. As we can see from the output, we have the line appended to the note. If you try to use the `edit` option, you will see that you can only use this with the `-m` flag. This makes good sense, as you should edit the note and not overwrite or append an already created note:

   ```
   $ git notes edit -m "John Doe"
   The -m/-F/-c/-C options have been deprecated for the 'edit' subcommand.
   Please use 'git notes add -f -m/-F/-c/-C' instead.
   ```

7. In other words, Git rejects editing the note and mentions other ways of doing it.

> The `git notes add` and `git notes edit` commands without any arguments will do exactly the same, that is, open the configured editor and allow you to write a note to the commit.

Separating notes by category

As we saw in the previous example, we can add notes to the commits; however, in some cases, it makes sense to store the information sorted by categories, such as `featureImplemented`, `defect`, and `alsoCherryPick`. As briefly explained at the beginning of the chapter, notes are stored in `refs/notes/commits`, but we can add multiple references so that we can easily sort and list the various scopes of the notes.

Getting ready

To start this example, we need a new branch that tracks the `origin/stable-3.1` branch; we name the branch `notesReferences`, and create and checkout the branch with the following command:

```
$ git checkout -b notesReferences --track origin/stable-3.1
Branch notesReferences set up to track remote branch stable-3.1 from origin.
Switched to a new branch 'notesReferences'
```

How to do it...

Imagine a situation where we have corrected a defect and did everything we could to ensure the quality of the commit before releasing it. Nonetheless, we had to make another fix for the same defect.

So, we want to add a note to the reference `refs/notes/alsoCherryPick`, which should indicate that if you cherry-pick this commit, you should also cherry-pick the other commits as they fix the same defect.

In this example, we will find the commit and add some extra information to the commit in multiple notes' reference specifications:

1. Start by listing the top 10 commits on the branch so we have something to copy and paste from:

    ```
    $ git log -10 --oneline
    da6e87b Prepare post 3.1.0 builds
    16ca725 JGit v3.1.0.201310021548-r
    c6aba99 Fix order of commits in rebase todo file header
    5a2a222 Prepare post 3.1.0 RC1 builds
    6f0681e JGit v3.1.0.201309270735-rc1
    a065a06 Attempt to fix graph layout when new heads are introduced
    b4f07df Prepare re-signing pgm's ueberjar to avoid SecurityException
    aa4bbc6 Use full branch name when getting ref in BranchTrackingStatus
    570bba5 Ignore bitmap indexes that do not match the pack checksum
    801aac5 Merge branch 'stable-3.0'
    ```

Storing Additional Information in Your Repository

2. Add a note for the `da6e87bc3` commit:

   ```
   $ git notes add -m "test note"
   ```

3. Now, to add a note for the `b4f07df` commit in the ref `alsoCherryPick`, we must use the `--ref` option for `git notes`. This has to be specified before the `add` option:

   ```
   $ git notes --ref alsoCherryPick add -m "570bba5" b4f07df
   ```

4. No output indicates success while adding notes. Now that we have a note, we should be able to list it with a single `git log -1` command. However, this is not the case. You actually need to specify that you want to list the notes from the specific ref. This can be done with the `--notes=alsoCherryPick` option for `git log`:

   ```
   $ git log -1 b4f07df357fccdff891df2a4fa5c5bd9e83b4a4a --notes=alsoCherryPick
   commit b4f07df357fccdff891df2a4fa5c5bd9e83b4a4a
   Author: Matthias Sohn <matthias.sohn@sap.com>
   Date:   Tue Sep 24 09:11:47 2013 +0200
       Prepare re-signing pgm's ueberjar to avoid SecurityException
   More output...
       Change-Id: Ia302e68a4b2a9399cb18025274574e31d3d3e407
       Signed-off-by: Matthias Sohn <matthias.sohn@sap.com>
   Notes (alsoCherryPick):
       570bba5
   ```

5. As you see from the output, Git shows the `alsoCherryPick` notes. Git defaults to adding notes to `refs/notes/commits`, but we have explicitly specified to show `alsoCherryPick`. It would be nice if you could show the `alsoCherryPick` notes' reference by default so you don't have to use `--notes=alsoCherryPick`. This can be done by configuring Git as follows:

   ```
   $ git config notes.displayRef "refs/notes/alsoCherryPick"
   ```

6. By configuring this option, you are telling Git to always list these notes. But what about the default notes? Have we overwritten the configuration to list the default `refs/notes/commits` notes? We can check this with `git log -1` to see if we still have the test note displayed:

   ```
   $ git log -1
   commit da6e87bc373c54c1cda8ed563f41f65df52bacbf
   Author: Matthias Sohn <matthias.sohn@sap.com>
   Date:   Thu Oct 3 17:22:08 2013 +0200
       Prepare post 3.1.0 builds
       Change-Id: I306a3d40c6ddb88a16d17f09a60e3d19b0716962
       Signed-off-by: Matthias Sohn <matthias.sohn@sap.com>
   Notes:
       test note
   ```

7. No, we did not overwrite the setting to list notes in the default refs. Knowing that we can have as many `notes.displayRef` configurations as we want, we should add all the refs we want to use in our repository. In some situations, it is even better to just add `refs/notes/*`. This will configure Git to show all the notes:

   ```
   $ git config notes.displayRef 'refs/notes/*'
   ```

8. If we now add another note in `refs/notes/defect`, we should be able to list it without specifying which notes' reference we want to list when using `git log`. We are adding to the commit that already has a note in the `alsoCherryPick` reference:

   ```
   $ git notes --ref defect add -m "Bug:24435"
   b4f07df357fccdff891df2a4fa5c5bd9e83b4a4a
   ```

9. Now, list the commit with `git log`:

   ```
   $ git log -1 b4f07df357fccdff891df2a4fa5c5bd9e83b4a4a
   commit b4f07df357fccdff891df2a4fa5c5bd9e83b4a4a
   Author: Matthias Sohn <matthias.sohn@sap.com>
   Date:   Tue Sep 24 09:11:47 2013 +0200
       Prepare re-signing pgm's ueberjar to avoid SecurityException
       See http://dev.eclipse.org/mhonarc/lists/jgit-dev/msg02277.html
       Change-Id: Ia302e68a4b2a9399cb18025274574e31d3d3e407
       Signed-off-by: Matthias Sohn <matthias.sohn@sap.com>
   Notes (alsoCherryPick):
       570bba5
   Notes (defect):
       Bug:24435
   ```

10. Git shows both notes, which is what we would expect.

How it works...

We have been discussing the `refs/notes/alsoCherryPick` reference and so on. As you know, we refer to the remote branches as references, such as `refs/remotes/origin/stable-3.2`, but the local branches also have references such as `refs/heads/develop`, for instance.

Since you can create a branch that starts at a specific reference, you should be able to create a branch that starts at the `refs/notes/alsoCherrypick` reference:

1. Create a branch that starts from `refs/notes/alsoCherryPick`. Also, checkout the branch:

   ```
   $ git checkout -b myNotes notes/alsoCherryPick
   Switched to a new branch 'myNotes'
   ```

2. The `myNotes` branch now points to `HEAD` on `refs/notes/alsoCherryPick`. Listing the files on the branch will show a file with the commit hash of the commit we have added the notes to:

   ```
   $ ls
   b4f07df357fccdff891df2a4fa5c5bd9e83b4a4a
   ```

3. Showing the file content will show the text we used as note text:

   ```
   $ cat b4f07df357fccdff891df2a4fa5c5bd9e83b4a4a
   570bba5
   ```

4. As you can see, the abbreviated commit hash `570bba5` we added as a note for `b4f07df357fccdff891df2a4fa5c5bd9e83b4a4a` is in the file. If we had a longer message, that message would also be shown here.

Retrieving notes from the remote repository

So far, we have been creating notes in our own local repository, which is fine. But if we want to share those notes, we have to be sure to be able to push them. We would also like to be able to retrieve other people's notes from the remote repository. Unfortunately, this is not so simple.

Getting ready

Before we can start, we need another clone from the local clone we already have. This is to show the push and fetch mechanism of Git with `git notes`:

1. Start by checking out the master branch:

    ```
    $ git checkout master
    Checking out files: 100% (1529/1529), done.
    Switched to branch 'master'
    Your branch is up-to-date with 'origin/master'.
    ```

2. Now, create a local branch of all the `stable-3.1` branches:

    ```
    $ git branch stable-3.1 origin/stable-3.1
    Branch stable-3.1 set up to track remote branch stable-3.1 from origin.
    ```

3. We are checking out all these branches because we want to clone this repository and, by default, all the `refs/heads/*` branches will be cloned. So, when we clone the `chapter5` directory, you will see that we only get the branches we see if you execute `git branch`:

    ```
    $ git branch
    * master
    myNotes
    notesMessage
    notesReference
    stable-3.1
    ```

4. Now, go one directory up so that you can create your new clone from the `chapter5` directory:

    ```
    $ cd ..
    $ git clone ./chapter5 shareNotes
    Cloning into 'shareNotes'...
    done.
    ```

5. Now, enter the `shareNotes` directory and run `git branch -a` to see that the only remote branches we have are the branches we checked out as local branches in the `chapter5` directory. After this, we are ready to fetch some notes:

    ```
    $ cd shareNotes
    $ git branch -a
    * master
    remotes/origin/HEAD -> origin/master
    ```

```
remotes/origin/master
remotes/origin/myNotes
remotes/origin/notesMessage
remotes/origin/notesReference
remotes/origin/stable-3.1
```

6. As predicted, the list matches the Git branch output from the `chapter5` directory.

How to do it...

We have now prepared the setup for pushing and fetching notes. The challenge is that Git is not a default setup for retrieving and pushing notes, and hence you won't usually see other people's notes:

1. We start by showing that we did not receive the notes during the clone:

   ```
   $ git log -1 b4f07df357fccdff891df2a4fa5c5bd9e83b4a4a --notes=alsoCherryPick
   warning: notes ref refs/notes/alsoCherryPick is invalid
   commit b4f07df357fccdff891df2a4fa5c5bd9e83b4a4a
   Author: Matthias Sohn <matthias.sohn@sap.com>
   Date:   Tue Sep 24 09:11:47 2013 +0200
        Prepare re-signing pgm's ueberjar to avoid SecurityException
   ```

2. As expected, the output does not show the note, and the first line makes it clear why. In the `chapter5` directory, we will see the note. To enable the notes to be fetched, we need to create a new fetch rule configuration; it needs to be similar to the fetch rule for `refs/heads`. Take a look at the configuration from `git config`:

   ```
   $ git config --get remote.origin.fetch
   +refs/heads/*:refs/remotes/origin/*
   ```

3. This shows that we are fetching `refs/heads` into the `refs/remotes/origin` reference, but what we also want to do is fetch `refs/notes/*` into `refs/notes/*`:

   ```
   $ git config --add remote.origin.fetch '+refs/notes/*:refs/notes/*'
   ```

4. You should now have it configured. If you leave out the `--add` option from your command, you will overwrite your current settings. Verify that the rule now exists:

   ```
   $ git config --get-all  remote.origin.fetch
   +refs/heads/*:refs/remotes/origin/*
   +refs/notes/*:refs/notes/*
   ```

5. Now, try and fetch the notes:

   ```
   $ git fetch
   From /tmp/chapter5
   * [new ref]    refs/notes/alsoCherryPick -> refs/notes/alsoCherryPick
   * [new ref]    refs/notes/commits -> refs/notes/commits
   * [new ref]    refs/notes/defect -> refs/notes/defect
   ```

6. As the Git output indicates, we have received some new refs. So, let's check whether we have the note on the commit now:

   ```
   $ git log -1 b4f07df357fccdff891df2a4fa5c5bd9e83b4a4a --notes=alsoCherryPick
   commit b4f07df357fccdff891df2a4fa5c5bd9e83b4a4a
   Author: Matthias Sohn <matthias.sohn@sap.com>
   Date:   Tue Sep 24 09:11:47 2013 +0200

       Prepare re-signing pgm's ueberjar to avoid SecurityException
   More output...
       Signed-off-by: Matthias Sohn <matthias.sohn@sap.com>
   Notes (alsoCherryPick):
       570bba5
   ```

7. We now have the notes in our repository, which is what we expected.

How it works...

We fetched the notes. The reason why it works is because of the way we fetched them. By default, Git is configured to fetch `refs/heads/*` into `refs/remotes/origin/*`. This way, we can easily keep track of what is remote and what is local. The branches in our local repository are in `refs/heads/*`. These branches are also listed when you execute `git branch`.

For notes, we need to fetch `refs/notes/*` into `refs/notes/*` since we want to get the notes from the server and use them with the `git show`, `git log`, and `git notes` Git commands.

Pushing Git notes to a remote repository

We have, successfully, tried to retrieve the notes from the remote repository, but what about your notes? How can you push them to the server? This has to be done with the push command just as with any other references, such as branches and commits.

How to do it...

Before we can push the notes from the `shareNotes` repository, we have to create a note to be pushed, as the notes we have now are all available on the remote repository. The remote repository in this case is the `chapter5` directory:

1. You have found a commit you would like to add a note to, and you want to add the note to the `verified` reference:

    ```
    $ git notes --ref verified add -m "Verified by john.doe@example.com" 871ee53b52a
    ```

2. Now that we have added the note, we can list it with the `git log` command:

    ```
    $ git log --notes=verified -1 871ee53b52a
    commit 871ee53b52a7e7f6a0fe600a054ec78f8e4bff5a
    Author: Robin Rosenberg <robin.rosenberg@dewire.com>
    Date:   Sun Feb 2 23:26:34 2014 +0100

        Reset internal state canonical length in WorkingTreeIterator when moving
        Bug: 426514
        Change-Id: Ifb75a4fa12291aeeece3dda129a65f0c1fd5e0eb
        Signed-off-by: Matthias Sohn <matthias.sohn@sap.com>
    Notes (verified):
        Verified by john.doe@example.com
    ```

3. As expected, we can see the note. If you cannot see the note, you probably missed `--notes=verified` for the `git log` command, since we have not configured `verified` as `notes.displayRef`. To push the note, we must use the `git push` command, because the default push rule in Git is to push branches to `refs/heads/<branchname>`.

So, if we just try to push the note to the remote, nothing happens:

```
$ git push
Everything up-to-date
```

4. You will probably see a warning about `git push.default` not being configured; you can safely ignore this for these examples. The important part is that Git shows that everything is up-to-date. But we know we have created a Git note for a commit. So, to push these notes, we need to push our note references to the remote notes, references. This can be done as follows:

```
$ git push origin refs/notes/*
Counting objects: 3, done.
Delta compression using up to 4 threads.
Compressing objects: 100% (2/2), done.
Writing objects: 100% (3/3), 294 bytes | 294.00 KiB/s, done.
Total 3 (delta 0), reused 0 (delta 0)
To /Users/kneth/tmp/./chapter5
 * [new branch]      refs/notes/verified -> refs/notes/verified
```

5. Now, something happened; we have a new branch on the remote named `refs/notes/verified`. This is because we have pushed the notes to the remote. What we can do in order to verify it is go to the `chapter5` directory and check whether the `871ee53b52a` commit has a Git note:

```
$ cd ../chapter5/
$ git log --notes=verified -1 871ee53b52a
commit 871ee53b52a7e7f6a0fe600a054ec78f8e4bff5a
Author: Robin Rosenberg <robin.rosenberg@dewire.com>
Date:   Sun Feb 2 23:26:34 2014 +0100

    Reset internal state canonical length in WorkingTreeIterator
when moving
    Bug: 426514
    Change-Id: Ifb75a4fa12291aeeece3dda129a65f0c1fd5e0eb
    Signed-off-by: Matthias Sohn <matthias.sohn@sap.com>
Notes (verified):
    Verified by john.doe@example.com
```

6. As predicted, we can see the note in this directory.

There's more...

Since Git notes do not work as normal branches, it can be a little cumbersome to push them back and forth to a repository when you are trying to collaborate on them. Since you cannot just fetch and merge the Git notes branches as easily as with other branches, a clear recommendation is to build some tools to add these notes so that you only have one server adding the notes.

A simple, but value adding, note could be information about Jenkins builds and testing. This can be valuable when you have to reopen a defect. You can then actually see in the repository which tests were executed on the commit hash.

Tagging commits in the repository

If you are releasing software with Git, you are bound to deal with tags. Tags describe the different software releases in the repository. There are two types of tags, a lightweight tag and an annotated tag. The lightweight tag is very similar to a branch, since it is just a named reference, such as `refs/tags/version123`. This points to the commit hash of the commit you are tagging; whereas if it were a branch, it would be `refs/heads/version123`. The difference is that the branch moves forward when you work and commit to it. A tag will always point to the same commit hash. We will discuss the annotated tag shortly.

Getting ready

Before we start, you must go to the `chapter5` directory, where we made the original clone for this chapter.

We should start by tagging the commit that is ten commits behind `origin/stable-2.3` and is not a merge. In order to find that commit, we will use the `git log` command.

For the `git log` command, we are using the `--no-merges` option, which will show commits that only have one parent. The `--oneline` option we have used before tells Git to limit the output to one line per commit. Moreover, `-11` shows us the last 11 commits (10 commits before the latest).

Find the commit as follows:

```
$ git checkout stable-2.3
$ git log -11 --no-merges --oneline
49ec6c1 Prepare 2.3.2-SNAPSHOT builds
63dcece JGit v2.3.1.201302201838-r
3b41fcb Accept Change-Id even if footer contains not well-formed entries
5d7b722 Fix false positives in hashing used by PathFilterGroup
9a5f4b4 Prepare post 2.3.0.201302130906 builds
19d6cad JGit v2.3.0.201302130906
3f8ac55 Replace explicit version by property where possible
1c4ee41 Add better documentation to DirCacheCheckout
e9cf705 Prepare post 2.3rc1 builds
ea060dd JGit v2.3.0.201302060400-rc1
60d538f Add getConflictingNames to RefDatabase
```

How to do it...

Now that we have found the `60d538f` commit, we should make it a lightweight tag:

1. Use the `git tag` command to give a meaningful release name:

   ```
   $ git tag 'v2.3.0.201302061315rc1' ea060dd
   ```

2. Since there is no output, it is a success. To see whether the tag is available, use the `git tag` command:

   ```
   $ git tag -l "v2.3.0.2*"
   v2.3.0.201302061315rc1
   v2.3.0.201302130906
   ```

3. We are using the `git tag` command with `-l` as a flag, since we want to list the tags and not tag the current HEAD. Some repositories have a lot of tags; so to prevent the list from becoming too long, you can specify which tags you want to list and use a * wildcard as we did previously. Our tag is available, but all it really says is that we have a tag in the repository with the name `v2.3.0.201302061315rc1`, and if you are using `git show v2.3.0.201302061315rc1`, you will see that the output is the same as `git show ea060dd`:

   ```
   $ git show v2.3.0.201302061315rc1
   commit ea060dd8e74ab588ca55a4fb3ff15dd17343aa88
   Author: Matthias Sohn <matthias.sohn@sap.com>
   Date:   Wed Feb 6 13:15:01 2013 +0100
           JGit v2.3.0.201302060400-rc1
   ```

Storing Additional Information in Your Repository

```
        Change-Id: Id1f1d174375f7399cee4c2eb23368d4dbb4c384a
        Signed-off-by: Matthias Sohn <matthias.sohn@sap.com>
diff --git a/org.eclipse.jgit.ant.test/META-INF/MANIFEST.MF
b/org.eclipse.jgit.a
... More output
$ git show ea060dd
commit ea060dd8e74ab588ca55a4fb3ff15dd17343aa88
Author: Matthias Sohn <matthias.sohn@sap.com>
Date:   Wed Feb 6 13:15:01 2013 +0100
        JGit v2.3.0.201302060400-rc1
        Change-Id: Id1f1d174375f7399cee4c2eb23368d4dbb4c384a
        Signed-off-by: Matthias Sohn <matthias.sohn@sap.com>
diff --git a/org.eclipse.jgit.ant.test/META-INF/MANIFEST.MF
b/org.eclipse.jgit.a
... More output
```

4. There will also be a lot of file diff information in the output, but it is exactly the same output. So, in order to add more information, we should use an annotated tag. An annotated tag is a tag where you have to add some information to the tag. To create an annotated tag, we use the `--annotate` tag for the `git tag` command:

```
$ git tag --annotate -m "Release Maturity rate 97%"
'v2.3.0.201409022257rc2' 1c4ee41
```

5. The -m flag is the same as `--message`, as we want to give the tag a message. If you leave out the -m flag, Git will open the configured editor and you can write a full release note into the annotation of the tag. We can check the tag information with `git show`:

```
$ git show 'v2.3.0.201409022257rc2'
tag v2.3.0.201409022257rc2
Tagger: John Doe <john.doe@example.com>
Date:   Sun Feb 9 22:58:28 2014 +0100
Release Maturity rate 97%
commit 1c4ee41dc093266c19d4452879afe5c0f7f387f4
Author: Christian Halstrick christian.halstrick@sap.com
... More output
```

6. We can actually see the tag name and information we added with the -m flag. With the lightweight tag, we don't see anything about the tag from the output. We actually don't even see the tag name when using `git show` on a lightweight tag.

There's more...

Tags are very powerful as they can add valuable information to the repository, and since tags should be considered official releases in the repository, we should be very careful when working with them.

Naturally, you can push the tags to a remote area, and contributors to the repository would fetch those tags. This is where you have to be careful. With a legacy version control system, you can go back in time and just change the release, and since these legacy systems are all based on a centralized server where you have to be connected in order to work, changing a release is not that bad, since not so many people use the release or have even downloaded the release. But it is different in Git. If you change a tag that you have already pushed to point to another commit hash, then those developers who have already fetched the tag will not get the new tag unless they delete the tag locally:

1. To prove the dangers of not getting a new tag, we will try to delete a tag and recreate it to point to another commit hash:

   ```
   $ git tag -d v1.3.0.201202121842-rc4
   Deleted tag 'v1.3.0.201202121842-rc4' (was d1e8804)
   ```

2. Now that we have deleted the tag, we are ready to recreate the tag again to point to HEAD:

   ```
   $ git tag -a -m "Local created tag" v1.3.0.201202121842-rc4
   ```

3. We have recreated the tag, and it points to HEAD because we did not specify a commit hash at the end of the command. Now, execute `git fetch` to see whether you can get the tag overwritten from the remote repository:

   ```
   $ git fetch
   ```

4. Since there is no output, the tag was probably not overwritten. Let's verify with `git show`:

   ```
   $ git show v1.3.0.201202121842-rc4
   tag v1.3.0.201202121842-rc4
   Tagger: John Doe <john.doe@example.com>
   Date:   Wed May 2 16:27:25 2018 +0200
   Local created tag
   commit 1c4ee41dc093266c19d4452879afe5c0f7f387f4
   ```

Storing Additional Information in Your Repository

5. As you can see from the output, it is still our locally created tag. To get the tag from the remote again, we need to delete the local tag and do a `git fetch`. To delete a tag, you need to apply the `-d` flag:

```
$ git tag -d v1.3.0.201202121842-rc4
Deleted tag 'v1.3.0.201202121842-rc4' (was 28be24b)
$ git fetch
From https://git.eclipse.org/r/jgit/jgit
 * [new tag]         v1.3.0.201202121842-rc4 -> v1.3.0.201202121842-
rc4
```

6. As you can see, Git has fetched the tag from the server again. We can verify with `git show`:

```
$ git show v1.3.0.201202121842-rc4
tag v1.3.0.201202121842-rc4
Tagger: Matthias Sohn <matthias.sohn@sap.com>
Date:   Mon Feb 13 00:57:56 2012 +0100
JGit 1.3.0.201202121842-rc4
-----BEGIN PGP SIGNATURE-----
Version: GnuPG/MacGPG2 v2.0.14 (Darwin)
iF4EABEIAAYFAk84UhMACgkQWwXM3hQMKHbwewD/VD62MWCVfLCYUIEz20C4Iywx
40O15TedaLFwIOS55HcA/ipDh6NWFvJdWK3Enm2krjegUNmd9zXT+0pNjt1J+Pyi
    =LRoe
-----END PGP SIGNATURE-----
commit 53917539f822afa12caaa55db8f57c29570532f3
```

7. So, as you can see, we have the correct tag again, but it should also be a warning. Once you have pushed a tag to a remote repository, you should never change it, since the developers who are fetching from the repository may never know about the changes unless they clone again or delete the tags locally and fetch them again.

In this chapter, we learned how you can tag your commits and add notes to them. These are powerful methods for storing additional information after a commit has been committed and published to a shared repository. But before you actually publish your commit, you have the chance to add the most valuable information for a commit. The commit message is where you must specify what you are doing and sometimes why you are doing it.

If you are solving a bug, you should list the bug ID; if you are using a special method to solve the problem, it is recommended that you describe why you have used this awesome technique to solve the problem. So, when people look back on your commits, they can also learn a few things about why different decisions were made.

6
Extracting Data from the Repository

In this chapter, we will cover the following recipes:

- Extracting the top contributor
- Finding bottlenecks in the source tree
- Grepping the commit messages
- The contents of the releases
- Finding what has been achieved in the repository in the last period

Introduction

Whether you work in big or small organizations, safeguarding and maintaining data is always important and it keeps track of a fair amount of information for you; it is just a matter of extracting the data. Some of the data is included in the system by you or any other developer when the commit message is filled in with the proper information – for instance, details of the bug you are fixing from the bug tracking system.

The data is not only valid for management but can also be used to add more time to refactor the C files, where almost all bugs are fixed.

Extracting the top contributor

Git has a few built-in stats you can get instantaneously. The `git log` command has different options, such as `--numstat`, that will show the number of files added and lines deleted for each file since each commit. However, for finding the top committer in the repository, we can just use the `git shortlog` command.

Extracting Data from the Repository

Getting ready

For all the examples throughout the book, we are using the `jgit` repository; you can either clone it or go to one of the clones you might already have.

Clone the `jgit` repository as follows:

```
$ git clone https://git.eclipse.org/r/jgit/jgit chapter6
$ cd chapter6
```

How to do it...

The `shortlog` Git command is very simple and does not have a lot of options or flags to use with it. It can show the log but in a boiled-down version, and then it can summarize it for us as follows:

1. Start by showing the last five commits with `shortlog`. We can use `-5` to limit the amount of output:

   ```
   $ git shortlog -5
   Jonathan Nieder (1):
     Update commons-compress to 1.6

   Matthias Sohn (2):
     Update com.jcraft.jsch to 0.1.50 in Kepler target platform
     Update target platforms to use latest orbit build

   SATO taichi (1):
     Add git checkout --orphan implementation

   Stefan Lay (1):
     Fix fast forward rebase with rebase.autostash=true
   ```

2. As you can see, the output is very different from the `git log` output. You can try it for yourself with `git log -5`. The numbers in parentheses are the number of commits by that committer. Beneath the name and number are the commit titles of the commits. Note that no commit hashes are shown. To find the top committer with just those five commits is easy, but when you try running `git shortlog` without `-5`, it is hard to find that person. To sort and find the top committer, we can use the `-n` or `--numbered` option to sort the output; the top committer is on top:

   ```
   $ git shortlog -5 --numbered
   Matthias Sohn (2):
   ```

```
            Update com.jcraft.jsch to 0.1.50 in Kepler target platform
            Update target platforms to use latest orbit build

    Jonathan Nieder (1):
            Update commons-compress to 1.6

    SATO taichi (1):
            Add git checkout --orphan implementation

    Stefan Lay (1):
            Fix fast forward rebase with rebase.autostash=true
```

3. As you can see, the output is nicely sorted. If we don't care about the commit subjects, we can use `-s` or `--summary` to only show the commit count for each developer as follows:

```
$ git shortlog -5 --numbered --summary
     2  Matthias Sohn
     1  Jonathan Nieder
     1  SATO taichi
     1  Stefan Lay
```

4. Finally, we have what we want, except that we don't have the email addresses of the committers; this option is also available with `-e` or `--email`. This will also show the email addresses of the committers in the list. This time, we will try it on the entire repository. Currently, we have only listed it for the HEAD commit. To list it for the repository, we need to add `--all` at the end of the command so as to execute the command for all branches as follows:

```
$ git shortlog  --numbered --summary --email --all
    765  Shawn O. Pearce <spearce@spearce.org>
    399  Matthias Sohn <matthias.sohn@sap.com>
    360  Robin Rosenberg <robin.rosenberg@dewire.com>
    181  Chris Aniszczyk <caniszczyk@gmail.com>
    172  Shawn Pearce <spearce@spearce.org>
    160  Christian Halstrick <christian.halstrick@sap.com>
    114  Robin Stocker <robin@nibor.org>
```

5. So, this is the list now; we know who contributed with the most commits, but this picture can be a little skewed, as the top committer may just happen to be the creator of the project and may not actively contribute to the repository. So, to list the top committers for the last six months, we can add `--since="6 months ago"` to the `git shortlog` command as follows:

```
$ git shortlog  --numbered --summary --email --all --since="6 months ago"
```

Extracting Data from the Repository

```
    73  Matthias Sohn <matthias.sohn@sap.com>
    15  Robin Stocker <robin@nibor.org>
    14  Robin Rosenberg <robin.rosenberg@dewire.com>
    13  Shawn Pearce <sop@google.com>
    12  Stefan Lay <stefan.lay@sap.com>
     8  Christian Halstrick <christian.halstrick@sap.com>
     7  Colby Ranger <cranger@google.com>
```

6. As you can see, the picture has changed since the start of the repository.

You can use *"n weeks ago"*, *"n days ago"*, *"n months ago"*, *" n hours ago"*, and so on for specifying time periods. You can also use specific dates, such as `"1 october 2013"`.

You can also list the top committer for a specific month using the `--until` option, where you can specify the date you wish to list the commit until. This can be done as follows:

```
$ git shortlog  --numbered --summary --email --all --since="30 september 2013" --until="1 november 2013"
    15  Matthias Sohn <matthias.sohn@sap.com>
     4  Kaloyan Raev <kaloyan.r@zend.com>
     4  Robin Rosenberg <robin.rosenberg@dewire.com>
     3  Colby Ranger <cranger@google.com>
     2  Robin Stocker <robin@nibor.org>
     1  Christian Halstrick <christian.halstrick@sap.com>
     1  Michael Nelson <michael.nelson@tasktop.com>
     1  Rüdiger Herrmann <ruediger.herrmann@gmx.de>
     1  Tobias Pfeifer <to.pfeifer@web.de>
     1  Tomasz Zarna <tomasz.zarna@tasktop.com>
```

7. As you can see, we get another list, and it seems like Matthias is the main contributor, at least compared to the initial result. These types of data can also be used to visualize the shift of responsibility in a repository by collecting the data for each month since the repository's initialization.

There's more...

While working with code, it is often useful to know who to go to when you need to perform a fix in the software, especially in an area where you are inexperienced. So, it would be nice to figure out who is the code owner of the file or the files you are changing. The obvious reason is to get some input on the code, but also to know who to go to for a code review. You can again use `git shortlog` to figure this out. You can use the command on the files as well:

1. To do this, we simply add the file to the end of the `git shortlog` command:

   ```
   $ git shortlog  --numbered --summary --email ./pom.xml
       86  Matthias Sohn <matthias.sohn@sap.com>
       21  Shawn O. Pearce <spearce@spearce.org>
        4  Chris Aniszczyk <caniszczyk@gmail.com>
        4  Jonathan Nieder <jrn@google.com>
        3  Igor Fedorenko <igor@ifedorenko.com>
        3  Kevin Sawicki <kevin@github.com>
        2  Colby Ranger <cranger@google.com>
   ```

2. As for `pom.xml`, we also have a top committer. As all the options you have for `git log` are available for `shortlog`, we can also do this on a directory as follows:

   ```
   $ git shortlog  --numbered --summary --email org.eclipse.jgit.lfs.server.test
       35 Matthias Sohn <matthias.sohn@sap.com>
       20 David Pursehouse <david.pursehouse@gmail.com>
        4 Markus Duft <markus.duft@ssi-schaefer.com>
        2 Saša Živkov <sasa.zivkov@sap.com>
        1 David Ostrovsky <david@ostrovsky.org>
        1 Mat Booth <mat.booth@redhat.com>
        1 Karsten Thoms <karsten.thoms@itemis.de>
   ```

3. As you can see, it is fairly simple to get some indication of who to go to for the different files or directories in Git.

Finding bottlenecks in the source tree

Often, the development teams know where the bottleneck in the source tree is, but it can be challenging to convince the management that you need resources to rewrite some code. However, with Git, it is fairly simple to extract that type of data from the repository.

Getting ready

Start by checking out the stable-3.1 release as follows:

```
$ git checkout stable-3.1
Branch stable-3.1 set up to track remote branch stable-3.1 from origin.
Switched to a new branch 'stable-3.1'
```

How to do it...

We want to start by listing some stats for one commit, and then we can extend the examples to larger chunks of commits:

1. The first option we will be using is `--dirstat` for `git log` as follows:

   ```
   $ git log -1 --dirstat
   commit da6e87bc373c54c1cda8ed563f41f65df52bacbf
   Author: Matthias Sohn <matthias.sohn@sap.com>
   Date:   Thu Oct 3 17:22:08 2013 +0200

       Prepare post 3.1.0 builds

       Change-Id: I306a3d40c6ddb88a16d17f09a60e3d19b0716962
       Signed-off-by: Matthias Sohn <matthias.sohn@sap.com>

      5.0% org.eclipse.jgit.http.server/META-INF/
      6.9% org.eclipse.jgit.http.test/META-INF/
      3.3% org.eclipse.jgit.java7.test/META-INF/
      4.3% org.eclipse.jgit.junit.http/META-INF/
      6.6% org.eclipse.jgit.junit/META-INF/
      5.5% org.eclipse.jgit.packaging/
      5.9% org.eclipse.jgit.pgm.test/META-INF/
     13.7% org.eclipse.jgit.pgm/META-INF/
     15.4% org.eclipse.jgit.test/META-INF/
      3.7% org.eclipse.jgit.ui/META-INF/
     13.1% org.eclipse.jgit/META-INF/
   ```

2. The `--dirstat` option shows which directories have changed in the commit and how much they have changed compared to each other. The default setting is to count the number of lines added to or removed from the commit. So, rearranging the code potentially does not count for any change, as the line count might be the same. You can compensate for this slightly by using `--dirstat=lines`. This option will look at each file line by line and see whether they have changed compared to the previous version as follows:

```
$ git log -1 --dirstat=lines
commit da6e87bc373c54c1cda8ed563f41f65df52bacbf
Author: Matthias Sohn <matthias.sohn@sap.com>
Date:   Thu Oct 3 17:22:08 2013 +0200

    Prepare post 3.1.0 builds

    Change-Id: I306a3d40c6ddb88a16d17f09a60e3d19b0716962
    Signed-off-by: Matthias Sohn <matthias.sohn@sap.com>

   4.8% org.eclipse.jgit.http.server/META-INF/
   6.5% org.eclipse.jgit.http.test/META-INF/
   3.2% org.eclipse.jgit.java7.test/META-INF/
   4.0% org.eclipse.jgit.junit.http/META-INF/
   6.1% org.eclipse.jgit.junit/META-INF/
   6.9% org.eclipse.jgit.packaging/
   5.7% org.eclipse.jgit.pgm.test/META-INF/
  13.0% org.eclipse.jgit.pgm/META-INF/
  14.6% org.eclipse.jgit.test/META-INF/
   3.6% org.eclipse.jgit.ui/META-INF/
  13.8% org.eclipse.jgit/META-INF/
```

3. This also gives a slightly different result. If you would like to limit the output to only show directories with a certain percentage or higher, we can limit the output as follows:

```
$ git log -1 --dirstat=lines,10
commit da6e87bc373c54c1cda8ed563f41f65df52bacbf
Author: Matthias Sohn <matthias.sohn@sap.com>
Date:   Thu Oct 3 17:22:08 2013 +0200

    Prepare post 3.1.0 builds
    Change-Id: I306a3d40c6ddb88a16d17f09a60e3d19b0716962
    Signed-off-by: Matthias Sohn <matthias.sohn@sap.com>

  13.0% org.eclipse.jgit.pgm/META-INF/
  14.6% org.eclipse.jgit.test/META-INF/
  13.8% org.eclipse.jgit/META-INF/
```

Extracting Data from the Repository

4. By adding 10 to the `--dirstat=lines` command, we are asking Git to only show the directories that have 10 percent or higher changes; you can use any number you like here. By default, Git does not count the changes in the subdirectories, but only the files in the directory. So, in the following diagram, only changes in **File A1** are counted as changes; for the **Dir A1** directory and the **File B1** file, it is counted as a change in **Dir A2**:

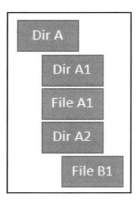

5. To cumulate this, we can add `cumulative` to the `--dirstat=lines,10` command, and this will cumulate the changes and calculate a percentage. Be aware that the percentage can go beyond 100 due to the way it is calculated:

   ```
   $ git log -1 --dirstat=files,10,cumulative
   commit da6e87bc373c54c1cda8ed563f41f65df52bacbf
   Author: Matthias Sohn <matthias.sohn@sap.com>
   Date:   Thu Oct 3 17:22:08 2013 +0200

       Prepare post 3.1.0 builds

       Change-Id: I306a3d40c6ddb88a16d17f09a60e3d19b0716962
       Signed-off-by: Matthias Sohn <matthias.sohn@sap.com>

     31.3% org.eclipse.jgit.packaging/
   ```

6. As you can see, the output is slightly different from what we have seen earlier. By using `git log --dirstat`, you can get some information about what goes on in the repository. Obviously, you can also do this for all the commits between two releases or two commit hashes. Let's try this, but instead of using `git log`, we will be using `git diff`, as Git will show the accumulated `diff` between the two releases, and `git log` will show `dirstat` for each commit between the releases:

```
$ git diff  origin/stable-3.1..origin/stable-3.2 --dirstat
   4.0% org.eclipse.jgit.packaging/org.eclipse.jgit.target/
   3.9% org.eclipse.jgit.pgm.test/tst/org/eclipse/jgit/pgm/
   4.1% org.eclipse.jgit.pgm/
  20.7% org.eclipse.jgit.test/tst/org/eclipse/jgit/api/
  21.3% org.eclipse.jgit.test/tst/org/eclipse/jgit/internal/storage/file/
   5.2% org.eclipse.jgit.test/tst/org/eclipse/jgit/
  14.5% org.eclipse.jgit/src/org/eclipse/jgit/api/
   6.5% org.eclipse.jgit/src/org/eclipse/jgit/lib/
   3.9% org.eclipse.jgit/src/org/eclipse/jgit/transport/
   4.6% org.eclipse.jgit/src/org/eclipse/jgit/
```

7. So, between the `origin/stable-3.1` and `origin/stable-3.2` branches, we can see which directories have the highest percentage of changes. We can then dig a little deeper using `--stat` or `--numstat` for the directory, and again use `git diff`. We will also use `--relative="org.eclipse.jgit.test/tst/org/eclipse/"`, which will show the relative path of the files from `org.eclipse.jgit.test/tst/org/eclipse/`. This will look better on the console. Feel free to try this without using the following option:

```
$ git diff --pretty  origin/stable-3.1..origin/stable-3.2 --numstat --relative="org.eclipse.jgit.test/tst/org/eclipse/jgit/internal/" org.eclipse.jgit.test/

tst/org/eclipse/jgit/internal/
4       2       storage/file/FileRepositoryBuilderTest.java
8       1       storage/file/FileSnapshotTest.java
0       741     storage/file/GCTest.java
162     0       storage/file/GcBasicPackingTest.java
119     0       storage/file/GcBranchPrunedTest.java
119     0       storage/file/GcConcurrentTest.java
85      0       storage/file/GcDirCacheSavesObjectsTest.jav
104     0       storage/file/GcKeepFilesTest.java
180     0       storage/file/GcPackRefsTest.java
120     0       storage/file/GcPruneNonReferencedTest.java
```

Extracting Data from the Repository

```
146        0          storage/file/GcReflogTest.java
 78        0          storage/file/GcTagTest.java
113        0          storage/file/GcTestCase.java
```

8. The first number is the number of lines added, and the second number is the lines removed from the files between the two branches.

There's more...

We have used `git log`, `git diff`, and `git shortlog` to find information about the repository, but there are so many options for those commands on how to find bottlenecks in the source code.

If we want to find the files with the most commits, and these are not necessarily the files with the most line additions or deletions, we can use `git log`:

1. We can use `git log` between the `origin/stable-3.1` and `origin/stable-3.2` branches and list all the files changed in each commit. Then, we just need to sort and accumulate the result with some Bash tools as follows:

   ```
   $ git log origin/stable-3.1..origin/stable-3.2 --format=format: --name-only

   org.eclipse.jgit.ant.test/META-INF/MANIFEST.MF
   org.eclipse.jgit.ant.test/pom.xml
   ```

2. First, we are just executing the command without the use of the Bash tools. You can see from the extensive output that you only see file names and nothing else. This is due to the options used. The `--format=format:` option tells Git to not display any commit-message-related information, and `--name-only` tells Git to list the files for each commit. Now, all we have to do is count them:

   ```
   $ git log origin/stable-3.1..origin/stable-3.2 --format=format: --name-only | sed '/^$/d'  | sort | uniq -c | sort -r | head -10
        12 se.jgit/src/org/eclipse/jgit/api/RebaseCommand.java
        12 est/tst/org/eclipse/jgit/api/RebaseCommandTest.java
         9 org.eclipse.jgit/META-INF/MANIFEST.MF
         7 org.eclipse.jgit.pgm.test/META-INF/MANIFEST.MF
         7 org.eclipse.jgit.packaging/pom.xml
         6 pom.xml
         6 pse.jgit/src/org/eclipse/jgit/api/RebaseResult.java
         6 org.eclipse.jgit.test/META-INF/MANIFEST.MF
         6 org/eclipse/jgit/pgm/internal/CLIText.properties
   ```

```
      6 org.eclipse.jgit.pgm/META-INF/MANIFEST.MF
```

3. Now, we have a list of the top ten files between the two releases, but before we proceed further, let's just go through what we did. We got the list of files, and we used `sed '/^$/d'` to remove empty lines from the output. After this, we used `sort` to sort the list of files. Then, we used `uniq -c`, which counts the occurrences of each item in the files and adds the number from the output. Finally, we sorted in reverse order using `sort -r` and displayed only the top ten results using `head 10`. To proceed from here, we should list all the commits between the branches that are changing the top file as follows:

```
$ git log origin/stable-3.1..origin/stable-3.2 \\
    org.eclipse.jgit/src/org/eclipse/jgit/api/RebaseCommand.java

commit e90438c0e867bd105334b75df3a6d640ef8dab01
Author: Stefan Lay <stefan.lay@sap.com>
Date:   Tue Dec 10 15:54:48 2013 +0100

    Fix aborting rebase with detached head

    Bug: 423670
    Change-Id: Ia6052867f85d4974c4f60ee5a6c820501e8d2427

commit f86a488e32906593903acb31a93a82bed8d87915
```

4. By adding the file to the end of the `git log` command, we will see the commits between the two branches. Now, all we have to do is to grep commits that have the bug, so we can tell our manager the number of bugs we fixed in this file.

Grepping the commit messages

Now we know how to list and sort files that we make frequent changes to and vice versa, but we are also interested in finding out the bugs that we are fixing, the features that we are implementing, and perhaps who is signing the code. All this information is usually available in the commit message. Some companies have a policy that you need to have a referral to a bug, a feature, or some other reference in the commit message. By having this information in the commit message, it is a lot easier to produce a nice release note as well.

Extracting Data from the Repository

Getting ready

As we will mostly be grepping the Git database in these examples, we really don't need to check something out or be at a specific commit for this example. So, if you are still lurking around in the `chapter6` folder, we can continue.

How to do it...

Let's see how many commits in the repository are referring to a bug:

1. First of all, we need to know the pattern for bugs referred to in the commit messages. I did this by looking in the commits, and the pattern for `jgit` is to use `Bug: 6 digits`; so, to find all of these commits, we use the `--grep` option for `git log`, and we can grep for "`[Bb][Uu][gG]: [0-9]+`":

   ```
   $ git log --all --grep="^[bB][uU][gG]: [0-9]"
   commit 3db6e05e52b24e16fbe93376d3fd8935e5f4fc9b
   Author: Stefan Lay <stefan.lay@sap.com>
   Date:   Wed Jan 15 13:23:49 2014 +0100

       Fix fast forward rebase with rebase.autostash=true

       The folder .git/rebase-merge was not removed in this case. The
       repository was then still in rebase state, but neither abort
   nor
       continue worked.

       Bug: 425742
       Change-Id: I43cea6c9e5f3cef9d6b15643722fddecb40632d9
   ```

2. You should get a lot of commits as output, but you should notice that all the commits have a referral to a bug ID. So what was the grep doing? The `^[Bb][Uu][gG]:` part matches any combination of lowercase and uppercase bugs. The `^` character means from the beginning of the line. The `:` character is matching `:`. Then, we have `[0-9]+`, which will match any number between zero and nine, and the `+` part means one or more occurrences. But enough with regular expressions for grep. We have a lot of output (which is valuable), but for now, we just want to count the commits. We can do this by piping it to `wc -l` (word count `-l` is to count the lines):

   ```
   $ git log --all --oneline --grep="^[bB][uU][gG]: [0-9]+" | wc -l
   366
   ```

3. Before piping it to `wc`, remember to use `--oneline` to limit the output to one line for each commit. As you can see, when I was writing this, `jgit` has reference to `366` bugs that have all been fixed and released into the repository. If you are used to using regular expressions in another scripting or programming language, you will see that using `--grep` does not support everything. You can enable a more extensive regular expression support using the `--extended-regexp` option for `git log`; however, the pattern still has to be used with `--grep` as follows:

   ```
   $ git log --all --oneline  --extended-regexp --grep="^[bB][uU][gG]:
   [0-9]{6}"

   3db6e05 Fix fast forward rebase with rebase.autostash=true
   c6194c7 Update com.jcraft.jsch to 0.1.50 in Kepler target platform
   1def0a1 Fix for core.autocrlf=input resulting in modified file and
   unsmudge
   0ce61ca Canonicalize worktree path in BaseRepositoryBuilder if set
   via config
   e90438c Fix aborting rebase with detached head
   2e0d178 Add recursive variant of Config.getNames() methods
   ```

4. We have used it in the preceding example, and you can see that we are getting the same commits. I have used a slightly different expression, and have now added `{6}` instead of `+`; the `{6}` searches for six occurrences of the associated pattern. In our case, it is six digits as it is next to the `[0-9]` pattern. We can verify by counting the lines or commits again with `wc -l` as follows:

   ```
   $ git log --all --oneline  --extended-regexp --grep="^[bB][uU][gG]:
   [0-9]{6}" | wc -l

       366
   ```

5. We get the same number. To shrink the regular expression even more, we can use `--regexp-ignore-case`, which will ignore the case for the pattern:

   ```
   $ git log --all --oneline  --regexp-ignore-case --extended-regexp -
   -grep="^bug: [0-9]{6}"

   3db6e05 Fix fast forward rebase with rebase.autostash=true
   c6194c7 Update com.jcraft.jsch to 0.1.50 in Kepler target platform
   1def0a1 Fix for core.autocrlf=input resulting in modified file and
   unsmudge
   0ce61ca Canonicalize worktree path in BaseRepositoryBuilder if set
   via config
   e90438c Fix aborting rebase with detached head
   2e0d178 Add recursive variant of Config.getNames() methods
   ```

Extracting Data from the Repository

6. Now we have the exact same output, and we no longer have `[bB][uU][Gg]` but just `bug`.

Now you know how to grep the commit messages for information, and you can grep for anything in the commit message and list all the commits where the regular expression matches.

The contents of the releases

While extracting information from Git, one of the natural things to do is to generate release notes. To generate a release note, you need all the valid information from the repository between this release and the previous release.

We can utilize some of the methods we have used earlier to generate the data we want.

How to do it...

We start by listing the commits between two tags, `v2.3.1.201302201838-r` and `v3.0.0.201305080800-m7`, and then we build on that information:

1. By using `git log` with `v3.0.0.201305080800-m7..v3.0.0.201305080800-m7`, we will get the commits between the tags:

   ```
   $ git log --oneline v2.3.1.201302201838-r..v3.0.0.201305080800-m7

   00108d0 JGit v3.0.0.201305080800-m7
   e27993f Add missing @since tags
   d7cc6eb Move org.eclipse.jgit.pgm's resource bundle to internal package
   75e1bdb Merge "URIish: Allow multiple slashes in paths"
   b032623 Remove unused repository field from RevWalk
   a626f9f Merge "Require a DiffConfig when creating a FollowFilter"
   ```

2. As we have a lot of commits between these two tags, let's count them using `wc -l`:

   ```
   $ git log --oneline v2.3.1.201302201838-r..v3.0.0.201305080800-m7 | wc -l

        211
   ```

3. There are 211 commits between the tags. Now, we will show the most modified files between the releases:

   ```
   $ git log  v2.3.1.201302201838-r..v3.0.0.201305080800-m7  --
   format=format:  --name-only | sed '/^$/d'  | sort | uniq -c | sort -
   r | head -10
         11 org.eclipse.jgit/src/org/eclipse/jgit/internal/st
         10 org.eclipse.jgit/src/org/eclipse/jgit/internal/sto
         10 org.eclipse.jgit.pgm/resources/org/eclipse/jgit/p
          9 org.eclipse.jgit.test/META-INF/MANIFEST.MF
          8 pom.xml
          8 org.eclipse.jgit/src/org/eclipse/jgit/storage/pac
          8 org.eclipse.jgit/src/org/eclipse/jgit/internal/sto
          8 org.eclipse.jgit.pgm/src/org/eclipse/jgit/pgm/CLI
          7 org.eclipse.jgit/src/org/eclipse/jgit/storage/dfs/D
          7 org.eclipse.jgit/src/org/eclipse/jgit/storage/dfs/D
   ```

4. This information is useful as we now have an overview of where the majority of the changes are. Then, we can find the commit that refers to bugs so we can list the bug IDs:

   ```
   $ git log --format=format:%h --regexp-ignore-case  --extended-
   regexp --grep="bug: [0-9]{6}"  v2.3.1.201302201838-
   r..v3.0.0.201305080800-m7 | xargs -n1 git log -1 | grep --ignore-
   case -E "commit [0-9a-f]{40}|bug:"

   commit e8f720335f86198d4dc99af10ffb6f52e40ba06f
       Bug: 406722
   commit f448d62d29acc996a97ffbbdec955d14fde5c254
       Bug: 388095
   commit 68b378a4b5e08b80c35e6ad91df25b1034c379a3
       Bug: 388095
   commit 8bd1e86bb74da17f18272a7f2e8b6857c800a2cc
       Bug: 405558
   commit 37f0e324b5e82f55371ef8adc195d35f7a196c58
       Bug: 406722
   commit 1080cc5a0d67012c0ef08d9468fbbc9d90b0c238
       Bug: 403697
   commit 7a42b7fb95ecd2c132b2588e5ede0f1251772b30
       Bug: 403282
   commit 78fca8a099bd2efc88eb44a0b491dd8aecc222b0
       Bug: 405672
   commit 4c638be79fde7c34ca0fcaad13d7c4f1d9c5ddd2
       Bug: 405672
   ```

Extracting Data from the Repository

5. So, what we have here is a nice list of the bugs being fixed and their corresponding commit hashes.

How it works...

We are using some Bash tools to get this list of fixed bugs. I will briefly explain what they are doing in this section:

- The `xargs -n1 git log -1` part will execute `git log -1` on each commit coming from the first `git log` command, `git log --format=format:%h --regexp-ignore-case --extended-regexp --grep="bug: [0-9]{6}" v2.3.1.201302201838-r..v3.0.0.201305080800-m7`.
- The `grep --ignore-case -E "commit [0-9a-f]{40}|bug:"` part will ignore the case in the regular expression and `-E` will enable an extended regular expression. You might see that a lot of these options for the tool grep are the same options we have for git log. The regular expression is matching commit and 40 characters with the `[0-9a-f]` range or bug. The `|` character means or. Remember we are in the output from `git log -1`.

All of this information we have extracted is the basis for a good, solid release note, with information on what has changed from one release to another.

The next natural step would be to look into the bug tracking system and also list the titles for each error being fixed in the commits. However, that is not something we will go through here as it all depends on the system you are using.

Finding what has been achieved in the repository in the last period

Sometimes it's useful to be able to extract what has been achieved in a specific range of time. Let's see how `git log` numerous arguments can help with this task.

How to do it...

1. Let's say we want to know everything that has been done in the last 30 days in the `jgit` repository that we have been analyzing so far:

   ```
   $ git log --all --since="30 days ago"
   commit 6efedb41c6fe3fc6eb88f49afc3e7f481514e806 (HEAD -> master, origin/master, origin/HEAD)
   Author: Jonathan Nieder <jrn@google.com>
   Date: Wed May 2 15:23:31 2018 -0700

       Mark CrissCrossMergeTest as flaky

       It often fails on my machine, both in maven and bazel.

       This patch marks the test flaky[1] in bazel so that "bazel test" can
       run it a few times before declaring failure.

       [1] https://docs.bazel.build/versions/master/be/common-definitions.html#test.flaky

       Bug: 534285
       Change-Id: Ibe5414fefbffe4e8f86af7047608d51cf5df5c47

   commit 5f2ddc8ac0528f2fc9776be822568dff3f065670
   Merge: b1f8ddfb7 3d89622d4
   Author: Matthias Sohn <matthias.sohn@sap.com>
   Date: Sat May 5 19:44:26 2018 -0400

       Merge "Add API filter for "non-API type FileRepository" in tests"

   commit 3d89622d4e32eb24c203b71f4cce49e35dff8e09
   Author: David Pursehouse <david.pursehouse@gmail.com>
   Date: Thu Apr 12 10:53:29 2018 +0900

       Add API filter for "non-API type FileRepository" in tests

       Change-Id: If805ad4a962e48dd16fbc7eff915fd6539839933
       Signed-off-by: David Pursehouse <david.pursehouse@gmail.com>

   [...]
   ```

Extracting Data from the Repository

Here, we use `--all` in order to see the commits in all the branches and not only the current one. We also use `--since` as illustrated previously during this chapter.

2. Now, let's only show the commits by `David Pursehouse`:

```
$ git log --all --since="30 days ago" --oneline --author="David Pursehouse"
3d89622d4 Add API filter for "non-API type FileRepository" in tests
9fb724f1b RefDatabase: add hasRefs convenience method
4dcf2f93d RefDatabase: Introduce getAllRefs method
57f158632 RefDatabase: Update Javadoc for ALL constant
20d431f79 LargePackedWholeObject#openStream: Suppress resource warning
7575cab53 Upgrade error_prone_core to 2.3.1
cbb2e65db PushProcess: Remove unused import of HashMap
5b0129641 Merge "Push: Ensure ref updates are processed in input order"
e5ba2c9bd DirCache: Use constant from StandardCharsets
ec84767c3 Use Constants.CHARACTER_ENCODING in tests
b0ac5f9c8 LargePackedWholeObject: Refactor to open DfsReader in try-with-resource
045799f2e Merge branch 'stable-4.11'
```

We used `--author` to specify the desired commit author and `--oneline` to condense the output to a more manageable format.

If you're looking for your own commits you can pass your name to `--author`, but if you are writing a script or an alias and you want it to be portable, you can, at least on Linux and macOS, use a subshell to retrieve the information automatically: `--author=$(git config user.name)`.

3. It looks like some merge commits are present. These are not really useful to describe the activity of the last month, so let's get rid of those with `--no-merges`:

```
$ git log --all --since="30 days ago" --oneline --author="David Pursehouse" --no-merges
3d89622d4 Add API filter for "non-API type FileRepository" in tests
9fb724f1b RefDatabase: add hasRefs convenience method
4dcf2f93d RefDatabase: Introduce getAllRefs method
57f158632 RefDatabase: Update Javadoc for ALL constant
20d431f79 LargePackedWholeObject#openStream: Suppress resource warning
7575cab53 Upgrade error_prone_core to 2.3.1
cbb2e65db PushProcess: Remove unused import of HashMap
e5ba2c9bd DirCache: Use constant from StandardCharsets
```

```
ec84767c3 Use Constants.CHARACTER_ENCODING in tests
b0ac5f9c8 LargePackedWholeObject: Refactor to open DfsReader in
try-with-resource
```

We finally have the information we need. This simple example also shows the importance of good commit messages as they will make the history managed by Git so much more useful and valuable!

How it works...

In this example, we didn't have to jump through hoops to get the result we needed; we simply used the power of the log command and its options. As a matter of fact, `git log` has almost 200 different arguments, and its help document, reachable with `git log --help`, is composed of more than 11,000 words! Now you know what to do during your next long flight without internet access!

There's more...

What about across repositories? The previous approach can, of course, be scaled with some scripting in order to repeat the operation on a list of repositories, but a better and simpler option is available as a third-party application that leverages the same `git log` capabilities we have been exploring thus far: `git-standup`.

It can easily be installed with a `curl` command:

```
curl -L
https://raw.githubusercontent.com/kamranahmedse/git-standup/master/installe
r.sh | sudo sh
```

Its source code is available on https://github.com/kamranahmedse/git-standup and it features several options that will make daily or weekly team meetings much easier to prepare.

Extracting Data from the Repository

`git-standup` is also able to operate on a single repository, and when applied to the previous example, its output looks like this:

```
$ git-standup -a "David Pursehouse" -d 30
3d89622d4 - Add API filter for "non-API type FileRepository" in tests (6 days ago) <David Pursehouse>
9fb724f1b - RefDatabase: add hasRefs convenience method (12 days ago) <David Pursehouse>
4dcf2f93d - RefDatabase: Introduce getAllRefs method (2 weeks ago) <David Pursehouse>
57f158632 - RefDatabase: Update Javadoc for ALL constant (2 weeks ago) <David Pursehouse>
20d431f79 - LargePackedWholeObject#openStream: Suppress resource warning (2 weeks ago) <David Pursehouse>
7575cab53 - Upgrade error_prone_core to 2.3.1 (3 weeks ago) <David Pursehouse>
cbb2e65db - PushProcess: Remove unused import of HashMap (4 weeks ago) <David Pursehouse>
e5ba2c9bd - DirCache: Use constant from StandardCharsets (4 weeks ago) <David Pursehouse>
```

7
Enhancing Your Daily Work with Git Hooks, Aliases, and Scripts

In this chapter, we will cover the following recipes:

- Using a branch description in a commit message
- Creating a dynamic commit message template
- Using external information in a commit message
- Preventing the push of specific commits
- Configuring and using Git aliases
- Configuring and using Git scripts
- Setting up and using a commit template

Introduction

In order to work efficiently in a corporate environment, there are certain prerequisites, or rules, regarding any code that is produced. It should be able to compile and pass specific sets of unit tests. There should also be certain documentation in the commit messages, such as references to a bug fix ID or an instance. Most of these rules can be automated using scripts. But why not put these rules into the process? In this chapter, you will see some examples of how to transfer data from one location to a commit message before you see the message. You will also learn how you can verify whether you are pushing your code to the right location. Finally, you will see how you can add scripts to Git.

A hook in Git is a script that will be triggered on events, such as pushing, committing, or rebasing. If these scripts exit with a non-zero value, it is probably best to cancel the current Git operation. You can find these hook scripts in the `.git/hooks` folder in any Git clone. If they have the `.sample` file extension, they are not active.

Using a branch description in a commit message

In Chapter 3, *Branching, Merging, and Options*, we mentioned that you can set a description on your branch, and this information can be retrieved from a script using the `git config --get branch.<branchname> description` command. In this example, we will take this information and use it for the commit message.

We will be using the `prepare-commit-msg` hook. The `prepare-commit-msg` hook is executed every time you want to commit, and the hook can be set to anything you wish to check, before you actually see the commit message editor.

Getting ready

We need a clone and a branch to get started on this exercise, hence we will clone `jgit` again to the `chapter7.5` folder, as follows:

```
$ git clone https://git.eclipse.org/r/jgit/jgit chapter7.5
Cloning into 'chapter7.5'...
remote: Counting objects: 2170, done
remote: Finding sources: 100% (364/364)
remote: Total 45977 (delta 87), reused 45906 (delta 87)
Receiving objects: 100% (45977/45977), 10.60 MiB | 1.74 MiB/s, done.
Resolving deltas: 100% (24651/24651), done.
Checking connectivity... done.
Checking out files: 100% (1577/1577), done.
```

Check out a local `descriptioInCommit` branch that tracks the `origin/stable-3.2` branch:

```
$ cd chapter7.5
$ git checkout -b descriptioInCommit  --track origin/stable-3.2
Branch descriptioInCommit set up to track remote branch stable-3.2 from origin.
Switched to a new branch 'descriptioInCommit'
```

How to do it...

We will start by setting the description of our local branch. Then, we will create the hook that can extract this information and put it in the commit message.

We have our local `descriptioInCommit` branch, for which we need to set a description. We will use the `--edit-description` Git branch to add a description to our local branch. This opens the description editor, and you can type in a message by performing the following steps:

1. When you execute the command, the description editor will open and you can type in a message:

    ```
    $ git branch --edit-description descriptioInCommit
    ```

2. Now, type in the following message:

    ```
    Remote agent not connection to server
    When the remote agent is trying to connect
    it will fail as network services are not up
    and running when remote agent tries the first time
    ```

3. You should write your branch description just as you write your commit messages. It make sense then to reuse the description in the commit. Now, we will verify whether we have a message with the following description:

    ```
    $ git config --get branch.descriptioInCommit.description
    Remote agent not connection to server
    When the remote agent is trying to connect
    it will fail as network services are not up
    and running when remote agent tries the first time
    ```

4. As expected, we have the desired output. Now, we can continue creating the hook that will take the description and use it.

    Next, we will check whether we have a description for the hook and, if we do, we will use that description as the commit message.

5. First, we will ensure that we can get the information into the commit message at our desired position. There are many ways to do this and we have settled on the following method: open the `.git/hook/prepare-commit-msg` hook file, type in the following script, and make it executable (`chmod +x`):

    ```
    #!/bin/bash
    BRANCH=$(git branch | grep '*'| sed 's/*//g'| sed 's/ //g')
    DESCRIPTION=$(git config --get branch.${BRANCH}.description)
    ```

```
    if [ -z "$DESCRIPTION" ]; then
      echo "No desc for branch using default template"
    else
      # replacing # with n
      DESCRIPTION=$(echo "$DESCRIPTION" | sed 's/#/\n/g')
      # replacing the first \n with \n\n
      DESCRIPTION=$(echo "$DESCRIPTION" | sed 's/\n/\n\n/')
      # append default commit message
      DESCRIPTION=$(echo "$DESCRIPTION" && cat $1)
      # and write it all to the commit message
      echo "$DESCRIPTION" > $1
    fi
```

6. Now, we can try to create a commit and see whether the message is being displayed as predicted. Use `git commit --allow-empty` to generate an empty commit, but also to trigger the prepare-commit-msg hook:

   ```
   $ git commit --allow-empty
   ```

7. You should get the message editor with our branch description as the commit message, as follows:

   ```
   Remote agent not connection to server
   When the remote agent is trying to connect
   it will fail as network services are not up
   and running when remote agent tries the first time
   # Please enter the commit message for your changes. Lines starting
   # with '#' will be ignored, and an empty message aborts the commit.
   # On branch descriptioInCommit
   # Your branch is up-to-date with 'origin/stable-3.2'.
   #
   # Untracked files:
   #       hen the remote agent is trying to connect
   #
   ```

8. This is as we expected. Save the commit message and close the editor. Try using the `git log -1` command to verify whether we have the following message in our commit:

   ```
   $ git log -1
   commit 92447c6aac2f6d675f8aa4cb88e5abdfa46c90b0
   Author: John Doe <john.doe@example.com>
   Date:   Sat Mar 15 00:19:35 2014 +0100
       Remote agent not connection to server
   ```

```
When the remote agent is trying to connect
it will fail as network services are not up
and running when remote agent tries the first time
```

9. You should get something similar to a commit message that is the same as our branch description. However, what about an empty branch description? How will our hook handle that? We can try again with a new branch named `noDescriptionBranch`. Use `git checkout` to create it, and check it as shown in the following command:

```
$ git checkout -b noDescriptionBranch
Switched to a new branch 'noDescriptionBranch'
```

10. Now, we will make yet another empty commit to see whether the commit message is as follows:

```
$ git commit --allow-empty
```

11. You should get the commit message editor with the default commit message text, as follows:

```
# Please enter the commit message for your changes. Lines starting
# with '#' will be ignored, and an empty message aborts the commit.
#
# On branch noDescriptionBranch
```

This is all as we expected. This script can be combined with the next exercise, which will take content from a defective system as well.

Creating a dynamic commit message template

Developers can be encouraged to do the right thing, or developers can be forced to do the right thing. However, in the end, developers need to spend time coding. So, if a good commit message is required, we can use the `prepare-commit-msg` hook to assist the developer.

In this example, we will create a commit message for developers that contains information about the state of the work area. It will also insert some information from a web page. This could just as well be defect information from Bugzilla.

Getting ready

To start this exercise, we will not be cloning a repository, but creating one. To do this, we will be using `git init`, as shown in the following code. You can use `git init <directory>` to create a new repository somewhere, or you can go to a directory and execute `git init` and Git will create a repository for you.

```
$ git init chapter7
Initialized empty Git repository in /Users/JohnDoe/repos/chapter7/.git/
$ cd chapter7
```

How to do it...

We have our `chapter7` directory, where we just initialized our repository. In this directory, the hooks are already available. Just look in the `.git/hooks` directory. We will be using the `prepare-commit-msg` hook. Perform the following steps:

1. Start by looking in the folder with the following hooks:

   ```
   $ ls .git/hooks/
   applypatch-msg.sample     pre-applypatch.sample
   pre-rebase.sample         commit-msg.sample
   pre-commit.sample         prepare-commit-msg.sample
   post-update.sample        pre-push.sample
   update.sample
   ```

2. As you can see, there are plenty of hooks in each of the hook files. There is an example script, and a short explanation of what the hook does and when it is executed. To enable `prepare-commit-msg`, rename the file as shown in the following code:

   ```
   $ cd .git/hooks/
   $ mv prepare-commit-msg.sample prepare-commit-msg
   $ cd -
   ```

3. Open the `prepare-commit-msg` file in your preferred editor.
4. You can read the information in the file, but for our examples, we will clear the file so that we can include the script.
5. Now, include the following command in the file:

   ```
   #!/bin/bash
   echo "I refuse to commit"
   exit 1
   ```

6. Save the file.
7. Finally, try to commit either something or nothing. Usually, you cannot make a commit that is empty, but with the `--allow-empty` option, you can create an empty commit as follows:

   ```
   $ git commit --allow-empty
   I refuse to commit
   ```

8. As you can see, we get the message we put in the `prepare-commit-msg` script file. You can check whether or not we have a commit by using `git log -1` as follows:

   ```
   $ git log -1
   fatal: your current branch 'master' does not have any commits yet
   ```

   There is no commit, and we get an error message that we have not seen before. The message has to be there because there is no commit so far in this repository. Before we make further changes to the script, we should know that the `prepare-commit-msg` hook takes some arguments, depending on the situation. The first argument is always `.git/COMMIT_EDITMSG`, and the second argument can be merge, commit, squash, or template, depending on the situation. We can use these in the script.

9. Change the script so that we can reject amending commits as follows:

   ```
   #!/bin/bash
   if [ "$2" == "commit" ]; then
     echo "Not allowed to amend"
     exit 1
   fi
   ```

10. Now that we have changed the script, let's create a commit and try to amend it as follows:

    ```
    $ echo "alot of fish" > fishtank.txt
    $ git add fishtank.txt
    $ git commit -m "All my fishes are belong to us"
    [master (root-commit) f605886] All my fishes are belong to us
    1 file changed, 1 insertion(+)
    create mode 100644 fishtank.txt
    ```

11. Now that we have a commit, let's try to amend it using `git commit --amend`:

    ```
    $ git commit --amend
    Not allowed to amend
    ```

12. As we expected, we were not allowed to amend the commit. If we wish to extract some information, for instance, from a bug handling system, we will have to put this information into the file before opening the editor. So, again, we will change the script as follows:

    ```
    #!/bin/bash
    if [ "$2" == "commit" ]; then
      echo "Not allowed to amend"
      exit 1
    fi
    MESSAGE=$(curl -s http://whatthecommit.com/index.txt)
    echo "$MESSAGE" > $1
    ```

13. This script downloads a commit message from http://www.whatthecommit.com/ and inserts it into the commit message. Every time you commit, you will get a new message from the web page. Let's give it a try by using the following command:

    ```
    $ echo "gravel, plants, and food" >>fishtank.txt
    $ git add fishtank.txt
    $ git commit
    ```

14. When the commit message editor opens, you should see a message from whatthecommit.com. Close the editor and, using git log -1, verify whether we have the commit, as follows:

    ```
    $ git log -1
    commit c087f75665bf516af2fe30ef7d8ed1b775bcb97d
    Author: John Doe <john.doe@example.com>
    Date:   Wed Mar 5 21:12:13 2014 +0100
        640K ought to be enough for anybody
    ```

15. As expected, we have succeeded with the commit. Obviously, this is not the best message to have for the committer. A more typical usage is to list the bugs assigned to the developer, as follows, in the commit message:

    ```
    # You have the following artifacts assigned
    # Remove the # to add the artifact ID to the commit message
    #[artf23456] Error 02 when using update handler on wlan
    #[artf43567] Enable Unicode characters for usernames
    #[artf23451] Use stars instead of & when keying pword
    ```

16. This way, the developer can easily select the correct bug ID, or the artefact ID, from TeamForge in this case, using the correct format for the other systems that will look into the commit messages.

There's more...

You can extend the functionality of the `prepare-commit-msg` hook easily, but you should bear in mind that the waiting time for fetching some information should be worth the benefits. One thing that is usually easy to check is a dirty work area.

Here, we need to use the `git status` command in the prepare commit message hook, and we need to predict whether we will have modified files after the commit:

1. To check this, we need to have something staged for committing and some unstaged changes, as follows:

   ```
   $ git status
   On branch master
   nothing to commit, working directory clean
   ```

2. Now, modify the `fishtank.txt` file:

   ```
   $ echo "saltwater" >> fishtank.txt
   ```

3. Use `git status --porcelain` to check the work area:

   ```
   $ git status --porcelain
   M fishtank.txt
   ```

4. Add the file to the staging area using `git add`:

   ```
   $ git add fishtank.txt
   ```

5. Now try `git status --porcelain`:

   ```
   $ git status --porcelain
   M  fishtank.txt
   ```

6. What you should note is the space before `M` the first time we use the `--porcelain` option for Git status. The `porcelain` option provides a machine-friendly output that shows the state of the files for Git status. The first character is the status in the staging area, whereas the second character is the status in the work area. So, `MM fishtank.txt` would mean the file is modified in the work area and in the staging area. So, if you modify `fishtank.txt` again, the following is the result you can expect:

   ```
   $ echo "sharks and oysters" >> fishtank.txt
   $ git status --porcelain
   MM fishtank.txt
   ```

7. As expected, the output from Git status is `MM fishtank.txt`. We can use this in the hook to tell whether or not the work area will have uncommitted changes after we commit. Add the following command to the `prepare-commit-msg` file:

    ```
    for file in $(git status --porcelain)
    do
      if [ ${file:1:1} ]; then
        DIRTY=1
      fi
    done
    if [ "${DIRTY}" ]; then
      # -i '' is not needed on Linux
      sed -i '' "s/# Please/You have a dirty workarea are you sure you wish to commit ?&/" $1
    fi
    ```

8. First, we list all the files that have changed with `git status --porcelain`. Then, for each of these files, we check whether there is a second character. If this is true, we will have a dirty work area after the commit. In the end, we just insert the message into the commit message so that it is available for the developer to see. Let's try and commit the change by using the following command:

    ```
    $ git commit
    ```

9. Check that you have a message similar to the following. The first line might be different, as we still have the message from http://www.whatthecommit.com/:

    ```
    somebody keeps erasing my changes.
    You have a dirty workarea are you sure you wish to commit ?
    # Please enter the commit message for your changes. Lines starting
    # with '#' will be ignored, and an empty message aborts the commit.
    # On branch master
    # Changes to be committed:
    #       modified:   fishtank.txt
    #
    # Changes not staged for commit:
    #       modified:   fishtank.txt
    #
    ```

10. Saving the file and closing the editor will create the commit. Verify this with `git log -1`, as follows:

    ```
    $ git log -1
    commit 70cad5f7a2c3f6a8a4781da9c7bb21b87886b462
    Author: John Doe <john.doe@example.com>
    Date:   Thu Mar 6 08:25:21 2014 +0100
        somebody keeps erasing my changes.
        You have a dirty workarea are you sure you wish to commit ?
    ```

11. We have the information we expected. The text about the dirty work area is in the commit message . To clean up nicely before the next exercise, we should reset our work area to `HEAD`, as follows:

    ```
    $ git reset --hard HEAD
    HEAD is now at 70cad5f somebody keeps erasing my changes.
    ```

Now, it is just a matter of finding out what suits you. Is there any information you would like to check before you commit and potentially push the code to a remote branch? This may include:

- Style checks in code
- Using Pylint to check your Python scripts
- Checking for files that you are not allowed to add to Git

This list is not exhaustive; there is probably something to add for every organization or development team in the world. However, this clearly is one way of taking tedious manual work away from the developer so that he or she can focus on coding.

Using external information in a commit message

The commit hook is executed when you close the commit message editor. It can, among other things, be used to manipulate the commit message or do an automatic review of the commit message to check whether it has a specific format.

In this recipe, we will be manipulating and checking the content of a commit message.

Getting ready

To start this exercise, we just need to create a branch and check it out. We need to disable the current `prepare-commit-msg` hook; we can do this by simply renaming it. Now, we can start working on the `commit-msg` hook by using the following command:

```
$ git checkout -b commit-msg-example
Switched to a new branch 'commit-msg-example'
$ mv .git/hooks/prepare-commit-msg .git/hooks/prepare-commit-msg.example
```

How to do it...

What we want to do in the first example is to check whether or not the defect information is correct. There is no need to release a commit that refers to a defect that does not exist:

1. We will start by testing the `commit-msg` hook. First, make a copy of the current hook, then we will force the hook to exit with a non-zero value that will abort the creation of the commit:

   ```
   $ cp .git/hooks/commit-msg.sample .git/hooks/commit-msg
   ```

2. Now, open the file in your preferred editor and add the following lines to the file:

   ```
   #!/bin/bash
   echo "you are not allowed to commit"
   exit 1
   ```

3. Now, we will try to make a commit and see what happens, as follows:

   ```
   $ echo "Frogs, scallops, and coco shell" >> fishtank.txt
   $ git add fishtank.txt
   $ git commit
   ```

4. The editor will open, you can write a small commit message, and then close the editor. You should see the `you are not allowed to commit` message, and if you check with `git log -1`, you will see that you don't have a commit with the message you just wrote, as follows:

   ```
   you are not allowed to commit
   $ git log -1
   commit 70cad5f7a2c3f6a8a4781da9c7bb21b87886b462
   ```

```
Author: John Doe <john.doe@example.com>
Date:   Thu Mar 6 08:25:21 2014 +0100
    somebody keeps erasing my changes.
You have a dirty workarea are you sure you wish to commit ?
```

5. As you can see, the commit message hook is executed after you close the message editor, whereas the `prepare-commit-msg` hook is executed before the message editor. To validate, if we have a proper reference to the hook in our commit message, we will be checking whether a specific error is available for the Jenkins-CI project. Replace the lines in the `commit-msg` hook so that it looks like the following command:

```
#!/bin/bash
JIRA_ID=$(cat $1 | grep jenkins | sed 's/jenkins //g')
ISSUE_INFO=$(curl -g
"https://issues.jenkins-ci.org/browse/JENKINS-${JIRA_ID}")
if [ -z "${ISSUE_INFO}" ]; then
  echo "Jenkins issue ${JIRA_ID} does not exist"
  echo "Please try again"
  exit 1
else
  TITLE=$(curl -g
"https://issues.jenkins-ci.org/browse/JENKINS-$JIRA_ID}" | grep -E
"<title>.*</title>")
  echo "Jenkins issue ${JIRA_ID}"
  echo "${TITLE}"
  exit 0
fi
```

6. We are using curl to retrieve the web page and, if it is empty, we know that the ID does not exist. Now, we should create a commit and see what happens if we put in the wrong ID, `jenkins 384895`, or an ID that exists as `jenkins 3157`. To check this, we will create a commit as follows:

```
$ echo "more water" >> fishtank.txt
$ git add fishtank.txt
$ git commit
```

7. In the commit message, write something such as `Feature cascading...` as a commit message subject. Then, in the body of the commit message, insert `jenkins 384895`. This is the important part, as the hook will use that number to look it up on the Jenkins issue tracker:

```
Feature: Cascading...
jenkins 384895
```

8. You should end up with the following output:

   ```
   Jenkins issue 384895 does not exist
   Please try again
   ```

9. This is what we expected. Now, verify whether the change has been committed or not with `git status`:

   ```
   $ git status
   On branch commit-msg-example
   Changes to be committed:
   (use "git reset HEAD <file>..." to unstage)
        modified:    fishtank.txt
   ```

10. Now, we will try to commit again; this time, we will be using the correct JIRA ID:

    ```
    $ git commit
    ```

11. Key in a commit message like the previous one; this time, make sure the Jenkins issue ID is one that exists. You can use `51444`:

    ```
    Feature: Cascading...
    jenkins 51444
    ```

12. Saving the commit message should result in an output as follows. We can clean it some more by removing the title HTML tags:

    ```
    <title>[#JENKINS-51444] Maven Parser creates errors during
    affectedFilesResolving - Jenkins JIRA</title>
    [commit-msg-example 3d39ca3] Feature: Cascading...
    1 file changed, 2 insertions(+)
    ```

13. As you can see, we can get information to output. We could also add this information to the commit message itself. Then, we can change and insert this as the `else` clause in the script:

    ```
    TITLE=$(curl
    https://issues.jenkins-ci.org/browse/JENKINS-${JIRA_ID} | grep -E
    "<title>.*</title>")
    TITLE=$(echo ${TITLE} | sed 's/^<title>//' | sed 's/<\/title>$//')
    echo "${TITLE}" >> $1
    echo "Jenkins issue ${JIRA_ID}"
    echo "${TITLE}"
    exit 0
    ```

[156]

14. To test this, we will create a commit again, and, in the message, we need to specify the JIRA ID that exists:

    ```
    $ echo "Shrimps and mosquitos" >> fishtank.txt
    $ git add fishtank.txt
    $ git commit
    After saving the commit message editor you will get an output similar like this.
    Jenkins issue 51444
    [JENKINS-51444] Maven Parser creates errors during affectedFilesResolving - Jenkins JIRA
    [commit-msg-example 6fa2cb4] Feature: Cascading...
    1 file changed, 1 insertion(+)
    ```

15. To verify whether we got the information in the message, we will use `git log -1` again:

    ```
    $ git log -1
    commit 6fa2cb47989e12b05cd2689aa92244cb244426fc
    Author: John Doe <john.doe@example.com>
    Date:   Thu Mar 6 09:46:18 2014 +0100
        Feature: Cascading...
        jenkins 51444
        [#JENKINS-51444] Maven Parser creates errors during affectedFilesResolving - Jenkins JIRA
    ```

As expected, we have the information at the end of the commit. In these examples, we are just discarding the commit message if the JIRA ID does not exist. This is a little harsh to the developer. So, you can combine this with the `prepare-commit-msg` hook. If `commit-msg` halts the commit process, then save the message temporarily so that the `prepare-commit-msg` hook can use that message when the developer tries again.

Preventing the push of specific commits

The pre-push hooks are triggered whenever you use the push command and the script execution happens before the push. So, we can prevent a push if we find a reason to reject it.

One reason could be that you have a commit with the `nopush` text in the commit message.

Getting ready

To use the Git pre-push, we need to have a remote repository. We will be cloning `jgit` again, as follows:

```
$ git clone https://git.eclipse.org/r/jgit/jgit chapter7.1
Cloning into 'chapter7.1'...
  remote: Counting objects: 2429, done
  remote: Finding sources: 100% (534/534)
  remote: Total 45639 (delta 145), reused 45578 (delta 145)
  Receiving objects: 100% (45639/45639), 10.44 MiB | 2.07 MiB/s, done.
  Resolving deltas: 100% (24528/24528), done.
  Checking connectivity... done.
  Checking out files: 100% (1576/1576), done.
```

How to do it...

We want to be able to push to a remote branch but, unfortunately, Git will try to authenticate through HTTPS for the `jgit` repository before the hooks are executed. Because of this, we will create a local clone from the `chapter7.1` directory, as follows. This will make our remote a local folder:

```
$ git clone --branch master ./chapter7.1/ chapter7.2
Cloning into ' chapter7.2'...
done.
Checking out files: 100% (1576/1576), done.
$ cd chapter7.2
$ git branch
* master
```

We are cloning the `chapter7.1` directory in a folder named `chapter7.2`, and will check the `master` branch when the clone has finished.

What we now want to do is to create a commit with a commit message that has `nopush` as part of it. By adding this word to the commit message, the code in the hook will automatically stop the push. We will be doing this on top of a branch. So, to start with, you should check out a `prepushHook` branch that tracks the `origin/master` branch and then creates a commit.

We will try to push it to the remote when we have the pre-push commit in place, as follows:

1. Start by creating a new branch named `prepushHook`, which tracks `origin/master`:

    ```
    $ git checkout -b prepushHook  --track origin/master
    Branch prepushHook set up to track remote branch master from
    origin.
    Switched to a new branch 'prepushHook'
    ```

2. Now, we use `reset` to go back to an earlier commit. It is not important how far back we go. So, we have just selected a random commit as follows:

    ```
    $ git reset --hard 2e0d178
    HEAD is now at 2e0d178 Add recursive variant of Config.getNames()
    methods
    ```

3. Now we can create a commit. We will do a simple inline replace with `sed`, and then add `pom.xml` and commit it:

    ```
    $ sed -i '' 's/2.9.1/3.0.0/g' pom.xml
    $ git add pom.xml
    $ git commit -m "Please nopush"
    [prepushHook 69d571e] Please nopush
    1 file changed, 1 insertion(+), 1 deletion(-)
    ```

4. To verify whether we have the commit with the text, run `git log -1`:

    ```
    $ git log -1
    commit 1269d14fe0c32971ea33c95126a69ba6c0d52bbf
    Author: John Doe <john.doe@example.com>
    Date:   Thu Mar 6 23:07:54 2014 +0100
        Please nopush
    ```

5. We have what we want in the commit message. Now, we just need to prepare the hook. We will start by copying the sample hook to the real name so that it will be executed on push:

    ```
    $ cp .git/hooks/pre-push.sample .git/hooks/pre-push
    ```

6. Edit the hook so that its code is as shown in the following snippet:

    ```
    #!/bin/bash
    echo "You are not allowed to push"
    exit 1
    ```

[159]

7. Now we are ready to push. We will be pushing our current branch HEAD to the master branch in the remote:

   ```
   $ git push origin HEAD:refs/heads/master
   You are not allowed to push
   error: failed to push some refs to '../chapter7.1/'
   ```

8. As expected, the hook is being executed, and the push is being denied by the hook. Now, we can implement the check we want to carry out. If we have the word nopush in any commit message, we want to exit. We can use git log --grep to search for commits with the keyword nopush in the commit message, as shown in the following command:

   ```
   $ git log --grep "nopush"
   commit 51201284a618c2def690c9358a07c1c27bba22d5
   Author: John Doe <john.doe@example.com>
   Date:   Thu Mar 6 23:07:54 2014 +0100
         Please nopush
   ```

9. We have our newly created commit with the keyword nopush. Now, we will perform a simple check for this in the hook and edit the pre-push hook so that it has the following text:

   ```
   #!/bin/bash
   COMMITS=$(git log --grep "nopush")
   if [ "$COMMITS" ]; then
     echo "You have commit(s) with nopush message"
     echo "aborting push"
     exit 1
   fi
   ```

10. Now we can try to push again to see what the result will be. We will try to push our HEAD to the master branch on the remote origin:

    ```
    $ git push origin HEAD:refs/heads/master
    You have commit(s) with nopush message
    aborting push
    error: failed to push some refs to
    '/Users/JohnDoe/repos/./chapter7.1/'
    ```

As expected, we are not allowed to push as we have the nopush message in the commit.

There's more...

Having a hook to prevent you from pushing commits that you don't want to push is very handy. You can specify any keywords you want. Words such as `reword`, `temp`, `nopush`, `temporary`, or `hack` can all be things you want to stop, but sometimes you want to get them through anyway.

What you can do is have a small checker that checks for specific words, then lists the commits, and asks if you want to push anyway.

If you change the script to the following snippet, the hook will try to find commits with the keyword `nopush` and list them. If you wish to push them in any case, you can answer the question and Git will push anyway:

```bash
#!/bin/bash
COMMITS=$(git log --grep "nopush" --format=format:%H)
if [ "$COMMITS" ]; then
   exitmaybe=1
fi
if [ $exitmaybe -eq 1 ]; then
while true
do
   clear
for commit in $COMMITS
do
   echo "$commit has no push in the message"
done
    echo "Are you sure you want to push the commit(s) "
      read -r REPLY <&1
      case $REPLY in
      [Yy]* ) break;;
      [Nn]* ) exit 1;;
    * ) echo "Please answer yes or no.";;
esac
done
fi
```

Try it with the `git push` command again, as shown in the following snippet:

```
$ git push origin HEAD:refs/heads/master
Commit 70fea355bac0c65fd51f4874d75e65b4a29ad763 has nopush in message
Are you sure you want to push the commit(s)
```

Type n and press *Enter*. Then, expect the push to be aborted with the following message:

```
error: failed to push some refs to '/Users/JohnDoe/repos/./chapter7.1/'
```

As predicted, it will not push. However, if you press y, Git will push to the remote. Try this now using the following command:

```
$ git push origin HEAD:refs/heads/master
054c5f78fdc82141e9d73e6b6955c38ff79c8b2e has no push in the message
Are you sure you want to push the commit(s)
y
To /Users/JohnDoe/repos/./chapter7.1/
 ! [rejected]        HEAD -> master (non-fast-forward)
error: failed to push some refs to 'c:/Users/Rasmus/repos/./chapter7.1/'
hint: Updates were rejected because a pushed branch tip is behind its remote
hint: counterpart. Check out this branch and integrate the remote changes
hint: (e.g. 'git pull ...') before pushing again.
hint: See the 'Note about fast-forwards' in 'git push --help' for details.
```

As predicted, the push will be tried, but, as you can see from the output, it is rejected by the remote. This is because we diverged, and the push was not working at the tip of the master branch.

So, with this hook, you can make your life a little easier by having the hook prevent you from accidentally pushing something you are not interested in being pushed. This example also considers commits that have been released; so, if you select a different keyword, then other commits—not only the locally created ones—will be taken into consideration by the script.

Configuring and using Git aliases

Git aliases, like Unix aliases, are short commands that can be configured on a global level or for each repository. It is a simple way of renaming some Git commands to use short abbreviations, for example, `git checkout` could be `git co`, and so on.

How to do it...

It's very simple and straightforward to create an alias. You simply need to configure it with `git config`.

What we will do is check a branch and then create its aliases one by one and execute them to view their output by performing the following steps:

1. So, we will start by checking a branch named `gitAlias`, which tracks the `origin/stable-3.2` branch:

   ```
   $ git checkout -b gitAlias --track origin/stable-3.2
   Branch gitAlias set up to track remote branch stable-3.2 from origin.
   Switched to a new branch 'gitAlias'
   ```

2. After this, we can start creating some aliases. We will start with the following one, which will simply just amend your commit:

   ```
   $ git config alias.amm 'commit --amend'
   ```

3. Executing this alias will open the commit message editor with the following message from the `HEAD` commit:

   ```
   $ git amm
   Prepare post 3.2.0 builds
   Change-Id: Ie2bfdee0c492e3d61d92acb04c5bef641f5f132f
   Signed-off-by: Matthias Sohn matthias.sohn@sap.com
   ```

4. As you can see, it can be very simple to speed up the process of your daily workflow with Git aliases. The following command will just work on the last 10 commits using `--oneline` as an option for `git log`:

   ```
   $ git config alias.lline 'log --oneline -10'
   ```

5. Using the alias will give you the following output:

   ```
   $ git lline
   314a19a Prepare post 3.2.0 builds
   699900c JGit v3.2.0.201312181205-r
   0ff691c Revert "Fix for core.autocrlf=input resulting in mo
   1def0a1 Fix for core.autocrlf=input resulting in modified f
   0ce61ca Canonicalize worktree path in BaseRepositoryBuilder
   be7942f Add missing @since tags for new public methods ig
   ea04d23 Don't use API exception in RebaseTodoLine
   3a063a0 Merge "Fix aborting rebase with detached head" into
   e90438c Fix aborting rebase with detached head
   2e0d178 Add recursive variant of Config.getNames() methods
   ```

6. You can also perform a simple checkout. Thus, instead of using the Git checkout, you can use `git co <branch>`. Configure it as follows:

   ```
   $ git config alias.co checkout
   ```

7. You will see that the aliases take arguments, just as the regular Git command does. Let's try the alias using the following command:

   ```
   $ git co master
   Switched to branch 'master'
   Your branch is up-to-date with 'origin/master'.
   $ git co gitAlias
   Switched to branch 'gitAlias'
   Your branch and 'origin/stable-3.2' have diverged,
   and have 1 and 1 different commit each, respectively.
     (use "git pull" to merge the remote branch into yours)
   ```

8. The command works as expected. You may wonder why we diverged after checking out the `gitAlias` branch again. Then, we diverged when we amended the `HEAD` commit. The next alias is creating a commit with everything that has not been committed in the work area, except for the untracked files:

   ```
   $ git config alias.ca 'commit -a -m "Quick commit"'
   ```

9. Before we can test the alias, we should create a file and modify it to show what it actually does. So, create a file as shown in the following command:

   ```
   $ echo "Sharks" > aquarium
   $ echo "New HEADERTEXT" > pom.xml
   ```

10. To verify what you want, run `git status`:

    ```
    Changes not staged for commit:
      (use "git add <file>..." to update what will be committed)
      (use "git checkout -- <file>..." to discard changes in working
    directory)
          modified:   pom.xml
      Untracked files:
          (use "git add <file>..." to include in what will be
    committed)
          aquarium
    no changes added to commit (use "git add" and/or "git commit -a")
    ```

11. Now, we can test the alias using the following command:

    ```
    $ git ca
    [gitAlias ef9739d] Quick commit
    1 file changed, 1 insertion(+), 606 deletions(-)
    rewrite pom.xml (100%)
    ```

12. To verify whether the `aquarium` file was part of the commit or not, use `git status`:

    ```
    Untracked files:
      (use "git add <file>..." to include in what will be committed)
      aquarium
      nothing added to commit but untracked files present (use "git add" to track)
    ```

13. You can also use `git log -1` to see the commit we just created:

    ```
    $ git log -1
    commit ef9739d0bffe354c75b82f3b785780f5e3832776
    Author: John Doe <john.doe@example.com>
    Date:   Thu Mar 13 00:01:49 2014 +0100
        Quick commit
    ```

14. The output is just as we expected. The next alias is a little different, as it will count the number of commits in the repository, and this can be done with the `wc` (`wordcount`) tool. However, since this is not a built-in Git tool, we have to use the exclamation mark and also specify Git:

    ```
    $ git config alias.count '!git log --all --oneline | wc -l'
    ```

15. Let's try it with the following command:

    ```
    $ git count
        3008
    ```

16. So, currently, we have `3008` commits in the repository. This also means you can execute external tools as if they were Git tools just by creating a Git alias; for instance, if you are using Windows, Mac, or Linux, you can create an alias as follows:

    ```
    $ git config alias.wa '!explorer .'  # Windows
    $ git config alias.wa '!open .'      # MacOS
    $ git config alias.wa '!xdg-open .'  # Linux
    ```

[165]

17. This alias will open up an Window Explorer at the path you are currently at. The next one shows what changed in the HEAD commit. It executes this with the --name-status option for git log:

```
$ git config alias.gl1 'log -1 --name-status'
```

18. Now try it using the following command:

```
$ git gl1
commit ef9739d0bffe354c75b82f3b785780f5e3832776
Author: John Doe <john.doe@example.com>
Date:   Thu Mar 13 00:01:49 2014 +0100
    Quick commit
    M       pom.xml
```

19. As you can see, it simply lists the commit and the files, including what happened to the files in the commit. As the aliases take arguments, we can actually reuse this functionality to list the information for another branch. Let's try it with the following command:

```
$ git gl1 origin/stable-2.1
commit 54c4eb69acf700fdf80304e9d0827d3ea13cbc6d
Author: Matthias Sohn <matthias.sohn@sap.com>
Date:   Wed Sep 19 09:00:33 2012 +0200
    Prepare for 2.1 maintenance changes
    Change-Id: I436f36a7c6dc86916eb4cde038b27f9fb183465a
    Signed-off-by: Matthias Sohn <matthias.sohn@sap.com>
M       org.eclipse.jgit.ant.test/META-INF/MANIFEST.MF
M       org.eclipse.jgit.ant.test/pom.xml
M       org.eclipse.jgit.ant/META-INF/MANIFEST.MF
M       org.eclipse.jgit.ant/pom.xml
M       org.eclipse.jgit.console/META-INF/MANIFEST.MF
M       org.eclipse.jgit.console/pom.xml
M       org.eclipse.jgit.http.server/META-INF/MANIFEST.MF
M       org.eclipse.jgit.http.server/pom.xml
... more output
```

As you can see, we get the expected output. So, for instance, if you have been using a specific set of options for git diff, then you can make it an alias to use it with ease.

How it works...

It is as simple as inserting text in the `config` file. So, you can try and open the `.git/config` configuration file, or you can list the configuration with `git config --list`:

```
$ git config --list | grep alias
alias.amm=commit --amend
alias.lline=log --oneline -10
alias.co=checkout
alias.ca=commit -a -m "Quick commit"
alias.count=!git log --all --oneline | wc -l
```

The `alias` feature is very strong, and the idea behind it is that you should use it to shorten those long one-liners that you often use. You can also use this feature to cut down those one-liners to shorter aliases so that you can use the command frequently and with more precision. If you have a long and complex Git comment as an alias, you will run it the same way every time, where keying a long command is bound to fail once in a while.

Configuring and using Git scripts

Yes, we have aliases, and aliases do what they do best – take short one-liners and convert them into short, useful Git commands. However, when it comes to longer scripts that are also a part of your process, and you would like to incorporate them into Git, you can simply name the script `git-scriptname`, and then use it as `git scriptname`.

How to do it...

There are a few things to remember. The script has to be in your path so that Git can use the script. Besides this, only imagination sets the boundaries:

1. Open your favorite editor and insert the following lines into the file:

   ```
   #!/bin/bash
   NUMBEROFCOMMITS=$(git log --all --oneline | wc -l)
   while :
   WHICHCOMMIT=$(( ( RANDOM % $NUMBEROFCOMMITS ) + 1 ))
   COMMITSUBJECT=$(git log --oneline --all -${WHICHCOMMIT} | tail -n1)
   COMMITSUBJECT_=$(echo "$COMMITSUBJECT" | cut -b1-60)
   do
       if [ $RANDOM -lt 14000 ]; then
           echo "${COMMITSUBJECT_} PASSED"
   ```

```
        elif [ $RANDOM -gt 15000 ]; then
            echo "${COMMITSUBJECT_} FAILED"
        fi
done
```

2. Save the file with the name `git-likeaboss`. This is a very simple script that will list random commit subjects with either passed or failed as the result. It will not stop until you press *Ctrl + C*:

```
$ git likeaboss
5ec4977 Create a MergeResult for deleted/modified   PASSED
fcc3349 Add reflog message to TagCommand            PASSED
591998c Do not allow non-ff-rebase if there are ed  PASSED
0d7dd66 Make sure not to overwrite untracked notfil PASSED
5218f7b Propagate IOException where possible where  FAILED
f5fe2dc Teach PackWriter how to reuse an existing s FAILED
```

3. Note that you can also tab complete these commands, and Git will take them into consideration when you slightly misspell commands, as follows:

```
$ git likeboss
git: 'likeboss' is not a git command. See 'git --help'.
Did you mean this?
    likeaboss
```

Obviously, this script, in itself, is not so useful in a day-to-day environment, but we hope you get the point we are trying to make. All scripts revolve around the software delivery chain and you can name them Git as they are part of Git. This makes it much easier to remember which of the scripts you have are available for your job.

> Both Git aliases and Git scripts will show up as Git commands when using tab completion. Type in `git <tab> <tab>` to see the list of possible Git commands.

Setting up and using a commit template

In this chapter, we have been using dynamic templates, but Git also has the option of a static commit template. A static template is essentially just a text file configured as a template. Using the template is very easy and straightforward.

Getting ready

First of all, we need a template. This has to be a text file that you know the location of. Create a file with the following content:

```
#subject no more than 74 characters please
#BugFix id in the following formats
#artf [123456]
#PCP [AN12354365478]
#Bug: 123456
#Descriptive text about what you have done
#Also why you have chosen to do in that way as
#this will make it easier for reviewers and other
#developers.
```

This is our take on a simple commit message template. You might find that there are other templates out there that prefer to have the bug in the title or at the bottom of the commit message. The reason for having this at the top is that people often tend not to read the important parts of the text! The important part here is the formatting of the references to systems outside Git. If we get these references correct, we can automatically update the defect system as well. Save the file as `~/committemplate`.

How to do it...

We will configure our newly created template, and then we will make a commit that will utilize the template.

To configure the template, we need to use `git config commit.template <pathtofile>` to set it, and, as soon as it is set, we can try to create a commit and see how it works:

1. Start by configuring the template as follows:

   ```
   $ git config commit.template  ~/committemplate
   ```

2. Now list the `config` file to see that it has been set:

   ```
   $ git config --list | grep template
   commit.template=/Users/JohnDoe/committemplate
   ```

3. As we predicted, the configuration was a success. The template, just like any other configuration, can be set at a global level using `git config --global`, or it can be set at a local repository level by leaving out the `--global` option. We configured our commit template for this repository only. Let's try and make a commit:

   ```
   $ git commit --allow-empty
   ```

4. Now, the commit message editor should open, and you should see our template in the commit message editor:

   ```
   #subject no more than 74 characters please
   #BugFix id in the following formats
   #artf [123456]
   #PCP [AN12354365478]
   #Bug: 123456
   #Descriptive text about what you have done
   #Also why you have chosen to do in that way as
   #this will make it easier for reviewers and other
   #developers.
   ```

It's really as simple as that.

In this chapter, we have seen how to prevent pushing when there are special words in commit messages. We have also seen how you can dynamically create a commit message with valid information for you or another developer when you are committing.
We went on to see how you can build functionality into your own Git by adding short scripts or aliases that are all executed using Git. Hopefully, this information will help you to work smarter instead of harder.

8
Recovering from Mistakes

In this chapter, we will cover the following recipes:

- Undo – Remove a commit completely
- Undo – Remove a commit and retain changes to files
- Undo – Remove a commit and retain changes in the staging area
- Undo – Working with a dirty area
- Redo – Recreate the latest commit with new changes
- Revert – Undo the changes introduced by a commit
- Reverting a merge
- Viewing past Git actions with git reflog
- Finding lost changes with git fsck

Introduction

It is possible to correct mistakes made in Git with git push context (without exposing them if the mistake is found before sharing or publishing the change). If the mistake has already been pushed, it is still possible to undo the changes made to the commit that introduced the mistake.

We will look at the `reflog` command and how we can use that and `git fsck` to recover lost information.

Recovering from Mistakes

There is no git undo command in core Git, one of the reasons being ambiguity on what needs to be undone, for example, and the last commit, the added file. If you want to undo the last commit, how should that be done? Should the changes introduced to the files by the commit be deleted? For instance, do you just roll back to the last known good commit, or should they be kept so that it could be changed for a better commit? Should the commit message simply be reworded? In this chapter, we'll explore the possibilities for undoing a commit in several ways, depending on what we want to achieve. We'll explore four ways to undo a commit:

- Undo everything, just remove the last commit as if it never happened
- Undo the commit and unstage the files; this takes us back to where we were before we started to add the files
- Undo the commit, but keep the files in the index or staging area so that we can just perform some minor modifications and then complete the commit
- Undo the commit with the dirty work area

The undo and redo commands in this chapter are performed on commits that are already published in the example repository. You should usually not perform the undo and redo commands on commits that are already published in a public repository, as you will be rewriting history. However, in the following recipes, we'll use an example repository and execute the operations on published commits so that everyone has the same experience.

Undo – Remove a commit completely

In this example, we'll learn how we can undo a commit as if it had never happened. We'll learn how we can use the reset command to effectively discard the commit and thereby reset our branch to the desired state.

Getting ready

In this example, we'll use the example of the `Git-Version-Control-Cookbook-Second-Edition_hello_world_cookbook` repository, clone the repository, and change our working directory to the cloned one:

```
$ git clone
https://github.com/PacktPublishing/Git-Version-Control-Cookbook-Second-
```

```
Edition_hello_world_cookbook.git
$ cd Git-Version-Control-Cookbook-Second-Edition_hello_world_cookbook.git
```

How to do it...

First, we'll try to undo the latest commit in the repository as though it never happened:

1. We'll make sure that our working directory is clean, no files are in the modified state, and nothing is added to the index:

    ```
    $ git status
    On branch master
    Your branch is up-to-date with 'origin/master'.

    nothing to commit, working directory clean
    ```

2. Also, check what is in our working tree:

    ```
    $ ls
    HelloWorld.java Makefile          hello_world.c
    ```

3. If all works well, we'll check the log to see the history of the repository. We'll use the `--oneline` switch to limit the output:

    ```
    $ git log --oneline
    3061dc6 Adds Java version of 'hello world'
    9c7532f Fixes compiler warnings
    5b5d692 Initial commit, K&R hello world
    ```

4. The most recent commit is the `3061dc6 Adds Java version of 'hello world'` commit. We will now undo the commit as though it never happened, and the history won't show it:

    ```
    $ git reset --hard HEAD^

    HEAD is now at 9c7532f Fixes compiler warnings
    ```

5. Check the log, status, and filesystem, so that you can see what actually happened:

    ```
    $ git log --oneline
    9c7532f Fixes compiler warnings
    5b5d692 Initial commit, K&R hello world

    $ git status
    On branch master
    ```

Recovering from Mistakes

```
Your branch is behind 'origin/master' by 1 commit, and can be fast-forwarded.
  (use "git pull" to update your local branch)
nothing to commit, working directory clean
$ ls
hello_world.c
```

6. The commit is now gone, along with all the changes it introduced (`Makefile` and `HelloWorld.java`).

> In the last output of the `git status` command, you can see that our master branch is one behind `origin/master`. This is similar to what we mentioned at the beginning of the chapter, because we are removing and undoing commits that are already published. Also, as mentioned, you should only perform the undo and redo (`git reset`) operations on commits that are not shared yet. Here, we only show it on the published commits to make the example easy to reproduce.

How it works...

Effectively, we are just changing the pointer of the master branch to point to the previous commit **HEAD**, which means the first parent of **HEAD**. Now, the branch will point to **9c7532f**, instead of the commit we removed, **35b29ae**. This is shown in the following diagram:

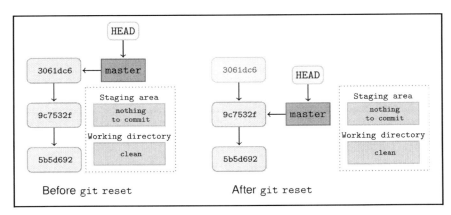

The preceding diagram also shows that the original **3061dc6** commit is still present in the repository, but new commits on the master branch will start from **9c7532f**; the **3061dc6** commit is called a dangling commit.

 You should only perform this undo operation on commits you haven't shared (pushed) yet, since when you create new commits following undo or reset, those commits form a new history that will diverge from the original history of the repository.

When the reset command is executed, Git looks at the commit pointed to by **HEAD** and finds the parent commit from this. The current branch, master, and the **HEAD** pointer, are then reset to the parent commit, as are the staging area and working tree.

Undo – Remove a commit and retain changes to files

Instead of performing the hard reset and thereby losing all the changes the commit introduced, the reset can be performed so that the changes are retained in the working directory.

Getting ready

We'll again use the example of the hello world repository. Make a fresh clone of the repository, or reset the master branch if you have already cloned one.

You can make a fresh clone as follows:

```
$ git clone https://github.com/PacktPublishing/Git-Version-Control-Cookbook-Second-Edition_hello_world_cookbook.git
$ cd Git-Version-Control-Cookbook-Second-Edition_hello_world_cookbook
```

You can reset the existing clone as follows:

```
$ git checkout master
$ git reset --hard origin/master

HEAD is now at 3061dc6 Adds Java version of 'hello world'
```

How to do it...

1. First, we'll check whether we have made any changes to files in the working tree (just for the clarity of the example) and the history of the repository:

    ```
    $ git status
    On branch master
    Your branch is up-to-date with 'origin/master'.

    nothing to commit, working directory clean

    $ git log --oneline
    3061dc6 Adds Java version of 'hello world'
    9c7532f Fixes compiler warnings
    5b5d692 Initial commit, K&R hello world
    ```

2. Now, we'll undo the commit and retain the changes introduced to the working tree:

    ```
    $ git reset --mixed HEAD^

    $ git log --oneline
    9c7532f Fixes compiler warnings
    5b5d692 Initial commit, K&R hello world

    $ git status
    On branch master
    Your branch is behind 'origin/master' by 1 commit, and can be fast-forwarded.
      (use "git pull" to update your local branch)

    Untracked files:
      (use "git add <file>..." to include in what will be committed)

        HelloWorld.java
        Makefile

    nothing added to commit but untracked files present (use "git add" to track)
    ```

We can see that our commit has been undone, but the changes to the file are preserved in the working tree, so more work can be done in order to create a proper commit.

How it works...

From the parent commit pointed to by the commit at **HEAD**, Git resets the branch pointer and **HEAD** to point to the parent commit. The staging area is reset, but the working tree is kept as it was before the reset, so the files affected by the undone commit will be in a modified state. This is illustrated in the following diagram:

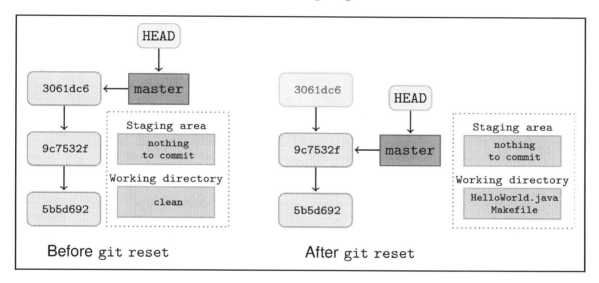

The --mixed option is the default behavior of git reset, so it can be omitted: git reset HEAD^

Undo – Remove a commit and retain changes in the staging area

Of course, it is also possible to undo the commit, but keep the changes to the files in the index or the staging area so that you are ready to recreate the commit with, for example, some minor modifications.

Getting ready

We'll still use the example of the hello world repository. Make a fresh clone of the repository, or reset the master branch if you have already cloned one.

Create a fresh clone as follows:

```
$ git clone
https://github.com/PacktPublishing/Git-Version-Control-Cookbook-Second-Edition_hello_world_cookbook.git
$ cd Git-Version-Control-Cookbook-Second-Edition_hello_world_cookbook
```

We can reset the existing clone as follows:

```
$ git checkout master
$ git reset --hard origin/master

HEAD is now at 3061dc6 Adds Java version of 'hello world'
```

How to do it...

1. Check whether we have any files in the modified state and check the log:

   ```
   $ git status
   On branch master
   Your branch is up-to-date with 'origin/master'.

   nothing to commit, working directory clean

   $ git log --oneline
   3061dc6 Adds Java version of 'hello world'
   9c7532f Fixes compiler warnings
   5b5d692 Initial commit, K&R hello world
   ```

2. Now, we can undo the commit, while retaining the changes in the index:

   ```
   $ git reset --soft HEAD^

   $ git log --oneline
   9c7532f Fixes compiler warnings
   5b5d692 Initial commit, K&R hello world

   $ git status
   On branch master

   Your branch is behind 'origin/master' by 1 commit, and can be fast-
   ```

```
               forwarded.

               (use "git pull" to update your local branch)

           Changes to be committed:

               (use "git reset HEAD <file>..." to unstage)

                 new file:    HelloWorld.java
                 new file:    Makefile
```

You can now make minor (or major) changes to the files you need, add them to the staging area, and create a new commit.

How it works...

Again, Git will reset the branch pointer and **HEAD** to point to the previous commit. However, with the `--soft` option, the index and working directories are not reset, that is, they have the same state as they had before we created the now undone commit.

The following diagram shows the Git state before and after the undo:

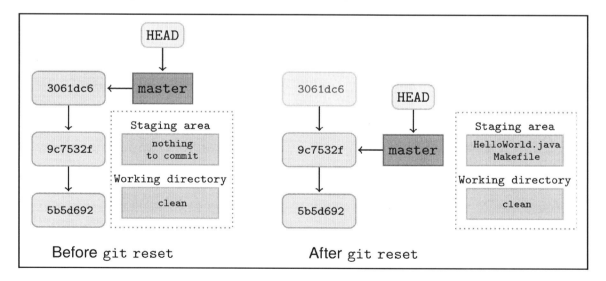

Undo – Working with a dirty area

In the previous examples, we assumed that the working tree was clean, that is, no tracked files were in the modified state. However, this is not always the case, and if a hard reset is carried out, the changes to the modified files will be lost. Fortunately, Git provides a smart way to quickly put stuff away so that it can be retrieved later using the `git stash` command.

Getting ready

Again, we'll use the example of the hello world repository. Make a fresh clone of the repository, or reset the master branch if you have already cloned one.

We can create the fresh clone as follows:

```
$ git clone https://github.com/PacktPublishing/Git-Version-Control-Cookbook-Second-Edition_hello_world_cookbook.git
$ cd Git-Version-Control-Cookbook-Second-Edition_hello_world_cookbook
```

We can reset the existing clone as follows:

```
$ git checkout master
$ git reset --hard origin/master

HEAD is now at 3061dc6 Adds Java version of 'hello world'
```

We'll also need to have some files in the working condition, so we'll change `hello_world.c` to the following:

```c
#include <stdio.h>

void say_hello(void) {
  printf("hello, worldn");
}

int main(void){
  say_hello();
  return 0;
}
```

How to do it...

In order to not accidentally delete any changes you have in your working tree when you are about to undo a commit, you can have a look at the current state of your working directory with `git status` command (as we already saw). If you have changes and you want to keep them, you can stash them away before undoing the commit and retrieve them afterward. Git provides a stash command that can put unfinished changes away, so it is easy to make quick context switches without losing work. The stash functionality is described further in Chapter 11, *Tips and Tricks*. For now, you can think of the stash command as a stack where you can put your changes and pop them later.

With the `hello_world.c` file in the working directory modified to the preceding state, we can try to do a hard reset on the HEAD commit, keeping our changes to the file by stashing them away before the reset and applying them again later:

1. First, check the history:

    ```
    $ git log --oneline
    3061dc6 Adds Java version of 'hello world'
    9c7532f Fixes compiler warnings
    5b5d692 Initial commit, K&R hello world
    ```

2. Then, check the status:

    ```
    $ git status
    On branch master
    Your branch is up-to-date with 'origin/master'.

    Changes not staged for commit:

      (use "git add <file>..." to update what will be committed)

      (use "git checkout -- <file>..." to discard changes in working directory)

        modified:   hello_world.c

    no changes added to commit (use "git add" and/or "git commit -a")
    ```

3. As expected, `hello_world.c` was in the modified state; so, stash it away, check the status, and perform the reset:

    ```
    $ git stash
    Saved working directory and index state WIP on master: 3061dc6 Adds Java version of 'hello world'
    ```

Recovering from Mistakes

```
            HEAD is now at 3061dc6 Adds Java version of 'hello world'

            $ git status
            On branch master
            Your branch is up-to-date with 'origin/master'.
            nothing to commit, working directory clean

            $ git reset --hard HEAD^
            HEAD is now at 9c7532f Fixes compiler warnings

            $ git log --oneline
            9c7532f Fixes compiler warnings
            5b5d692 Initial commit, K&R hello world
```

4. The reset is done, and we got rid of the commit we wanted. Let's resurrect the changes we stashed away and check the file:

```
            $ git stash pop
            On branch master
            Your branch is behind 'origin/master' by 1 commit, and can be fast-
            forwarded.

              (use "git pull" to update your local branch)

            Changes not staged for commit:
              (use "git add <file>..." to update what will be committed)
              (use "git checkout -- <file>..." to discard changes in working
            directory)
            modified:   hello_world.c
            no changes added to commit (use "git add" and/or "git commit -a")
            Dropped refs/stash@{0} (e56b68a1f5a0f72afcfd064ec13eefcda7a175ca)

            $ cat hello_world.c

            #include <stdio.h>
            void say_hello(void) {
              printf("hello, worldn");
            }
            int main(void){
              say_hello();
              return 0;
            }
```

So, the file is back to the state it was in before the reset, and we got rid of the unwanted commit.

How it works...

The reset command works as explained in the previous examples but, combined with the stash command, it forms a very useful tool that corrects mistakes even though you have already starting working on something else. The stash command works by saving the current state of your working directory and the staging area. Then, it reverts your working directory to a clean state.

Redo – Recreate the latest commit with new changes

As with undo, redo can mean a lot of things. In this context, redoing a commit will mean creating almost the same commit again with the same parent(s) as the previous commit, but with different content and/or different commit messages. This is quite useful if you've just created a commit, but have perhaps forgotten to add a necessary file to the staging area before you committed, or if you need to reword the commit message.

Getting ready

Again, we'll use the hello world repository. Make a fresh clone of the repository, or reset the master branch if you have already cloned one.

We can create a fresh clone as follows:

```
$ git https://github.com/PacktPublishing/Git-Version-Control-Cookbook-Second-Edition_hello_world_cookbook.git
$ cd Git-Version-Control-Cookbook-Second-Edition_hello_world_cookbook
```

We can reset an existing clone as follows:

```
$ git checkout master
$ git reset --hard origin/master

HEAD is now at 3061dc6 Adds Java version of 'hello world'
```

Recovering from Mistakes

How to do it...

Let's pretend we need to redo the latest commit because we need to reword the commit message to include a reference to the issue tracker.

1. Let's first take a look at the latest commit and make sure the working directory is clean:

    ```
    $ git log -1

    commit 3061dc6cf7aeb2f8cb3dee651290bfea85cb4392
    Author: John Doe <john.doe@example.com>
    Date:   Sun Mar 9 14:12:45 2014 +0100
        Adds Java version of 'hello world'
        Also includes a makefile

    $ git status
    On branch master
    Your branch is up-to-date with 'origin/master'.
    nothing to commit, working directory clean
    ```

2. Now, we can redo the commit and update the commit message with the git commit --amend command. This will bring up the default editor, and we can add a reference to the issue tracker in the commit message (Fixes: RD-31415):

    ```
    $ git commit --amend
    Adds Java version of 'hello world'
    Also includes a makefile
    Fixes: RD-31415

    # Please enter the commit message for your changes. Lines starting
    # with '#' will be ignored, and an empty message aborts the commit.
    #
    # Author:    John Doe <john.doe@example.com>
    #
    # On branch master
    # Your branch is up-to-date with 'origin/master'.
    #
    # Changes to be committed:
    #       new file:   HelloWorld.java
    #       new file:   Makefile
    #

    ~
    ~
    [master 75a41a2] Adds Java version of 'hello world'
     Author: John Doe <john.doe@example.com>
    ```

```
        2 files changed, 19 insertions(+)
        create mode 100644 HelloWorld.java
        create mode 100644 Makefile
```

3. Now, let's check the log again to see whether everything worked:

   ```
   $ git log -1

   commit 75a41a2f550325234a2f5f3ba41d35867910c09c
   Author:   John Doe <john.doe@example.com>
   Date: Sun Mar 9 14:12:45 2014 +0100    Adds Java version of 'hello
   world'   Also includes a makefile   Fixes: RD-31415
   ```

4. We can see that the commit message has changed, but we can't verify from the log output that the parent of the commit is the same as in the original commit, and so on, as we saw in the first commit we did. To check this, we can use the git cat-file command we learned about in Chapter 1, *Navigating Git*. First, let's see how the original commit looked:

   ```
   $ git cat-file -p 3061dc6

   tree d3abe70c50450a4d6d70f391fcbda1a4609d151f
   parent 9c7532f5e788b8805ffd419fcf2a071c78493b23

   author John Doe <john.doe@example.com> 1394370765 +0100
   committer John Doe <john.doe@example.com> 1394569447 +0100 Adds
   Java version of 'hello world' Also includes a makefile
   ```

   The parent commit is b8c39bb35c4c0b00b6cfb4e0f27354279fb28866, and the root tree is d3abe70c50450a4d6d70f391fcbda1a4609d151f.

5. Let's check the data from the new commit:

   ```
   $ git cat-file -p HEAD

   tree d3abe70c50450a4d6d70f391fcbda1a4609d151f
   parent 9c7532f5e788b8805ffd419fcf2a071c78493b23
   author John Doe <john.doe@example.com> 1394370765 +0100
   committer John Doe <john.doe@example.com> 1394655225 +0100

   Adds Java version of 'hello world'
   Also includes a makefile
   Fixes: RD-31415
   ```

Recovering from Mistakes

The parent is the same, that is, `9c7532f5e788b8805ffd419fcf2a071c78493b23` and the root tree is also the same, that is, `d3abe70c50450a4d6d70f391fcbda1a4609d151f`. This is what we expected as we only changed the commit message. If we had added some changes to the staging area and executed `git commit--amend`, we would have included those changes in the commit and the root-tree SHA1 ID would have been different, but the parent commit ID still the same.

How it works...

The `--amend` option to git commit is roughly equivalent to performing `git reset --soft HEAD^`, followed by fixing the files needed and adding those to the staging area. Then, we will run git commit reusing the commit message from the previous commit (`git commit -c ORIG_HEAD`).

There's more...

We can also use the `--amend` method to add missing files to our latest commit. Let's say you needed to add the `README.md` file to your latest commit in order to get the documentation up to date, but you have already created the commit, though you have not pushed it yet.

You then add the file to the index as you would while starting to craft a new commit. You can check with git status that only the `README.md` file is added:

```
$ git add README.md

$ git status
On branch master
Your branch and 'origin/master' have diverged,
and have 1 and 1 different commit each, respectively.
  (use "git pull" to merge the remote branch into yours)

Changes to be committed:
  (use "git reset HEAD <file>..." to unstage)

    new file:   README.md
```

Now, you can amend the latest commit with `git commit --amend`. The command will include files in the index in the new commit and you can, as with the last example, reword the commit message if needed. It is not needed in this example, so we'll pass the `--no-edit` option to the command:

```
$ git commit --amend --no-edit

[master f09457e] Adds Java version of 'hello world'
 Author: John Doe <john.doe@example.com>
 3 files changed, 20 insertions(+)
 create mode 100644 HelloWorld.java
 create mode 100644 Makefile
 create mode 100644 README.md
```

You can see from the output of the commit command that three files were changed and `README.md` was one of them.

> You can also reset the author information (name, email, and timestamp) with the commit `--amend` command. Just pass along the `--reset-author` option and Git will create a new timestamp and read author information from the configuration or environment, instead of the using information from the old commit object.

Revert – Undo the changes introduced by a commit

Revert can be used to undo a commit in history that has already been published (pushed), whereas this can't be done with the amend or reset options without rewriting history.

Revert works by applying the anti-patch introduced by the commit in question. A revert will, by default, create a new commit in history with a commit message that describes which commit has been reverted.

Getting ready

Again, we'll use the hello world repository. Make a fresh clone of the repository, or reset the master branch if you have already cloned one.

We can create a fresh clone as follows:

```
$ git clone
https://github.com/PacktPublishing/Git-Version-Control-Cookbook-Second-Edit
ion_hello_world_cookbook.git
$ cd Git-Version-Control-Cookbook-Second-Edition_hello_world_cookbook
```

We can reset the existing clone as follows:

```
$ cd Git-Version-Control-Cookbook-Second-Edition_hello_world_cookbook
$ git checkout master
$ git reset --hard origin/master
HEAD is now at 3061dc6 Adds Java version of 'hello world'
```

How to do it...

1. First, we'll list the commits in the repository:

   ```
   $ git log --oneline
   3061dc6 Adds Java version of 'hello world'
   9c7532f Fixes compiler warnings
   5b5d692 Initial commit, K&R hello world
   ```

2. We'll revert the second commit, `9c7532f`:

   ```
   $ git revert 9c7532f

   Revert "Fixes compiler warnings"
   This reverts commit 9c7532f5e788b8805ffd419fcf2a071c78493b23.

   # Please enter the commit message for your changes. Lines starting
   # with '#' will be ignored, and an empty message aborts the commit.
   # On branch master
   # Your branch is up-to-date with 'origin/master'.
   #
   # Changes to be committed:
   #       modified:   hello_world.c
   #
   ~
   ~
   ~
   "~/john.doe/packt/repos/Git-Version-Control-Cookbook-Second-
   Edition_hello_world_cookbook/.git/COMMIT_EDITMSG" 12L, 359C [master
   9b94515] Revert "Fixes compiler warnings"  1 file changed, 1
   insertion(+), 5 deletions(-)
   ```

3. When we check the log, we can see that a new commit has been made:

   ```
   $ git log --oneline
   9b94515 Revert "Fixes compiler warnings"
   3061dc6 Adds Java version of 'hello world'
   9c7532f Fixes compiler warnings
   5b5d692 Initial commit, K&R hello world
   ```

   We can take a closer look at the two commits with `git show` if we want a closer investigation of what happened.

How it works...

The `git revert` command applies the anti-patch of the commit in question to the current `HEAD` pointer. It will generate a new commit with the anti-patch and a commit message that describes the reverted commit(s).

There's more...

It's possible to revert more than one commit in a single revert, for example, `git revert master~6..master~2` will revert the commits from the sixth commit from the bottom in the master to the third commit from the bottom in the master (both included).

It is also possible not to create a commit while reverting; passing the `-n` option to `git revert` will apply the needed patched, but only to the working tree and the staging area.

Reverting a merge

Merge commits are a special case when it comes to revert. In order to be able to revert a merge commit, you'll have to specify which parent side of the merge you want to keep. However, when you revert a merge commit, you should keep in mind that though reverting will undo changes to files, it doesn't undo history. This means that when you revert a merge commit, you declare that you will not have any of the changes introduced by the merge in the target branch.

Recovering from Mistakes

The effect of this is that the subsequent merges from the other branch will only bring in changes of commits that are not ancestors of the reverted merge commit.

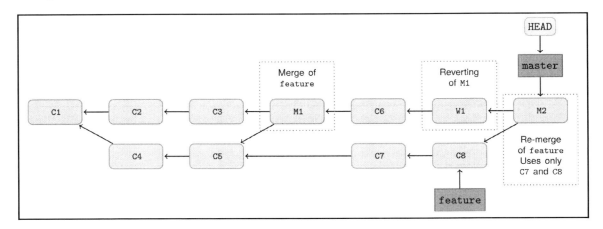

In this example, we will learn how to revert a merge commit, and we'll learn how we can merge the branch again, merging all of the changes by reverting to the reverted merge commit.

Getting ready

Again, we'll use the hello world repository. Make a fresh clone of the repository, or reset the master branch if you have already cloned one.

We can create a fresh clone as follows:

```
$ git clone https://github.com/PacktPublishing/Git-Version-Control-Cookbook-Second-Edition_hello_world_cookbook.git
$ cd Git-Version-Control-Cookbook-Second-Edition_hello_world_cookbook
```

We can reset the existing clone as follows:

```
$ cd Git-Version-Control-Cookbook-Second-Edition_hello_world_cookbook
$ git checkout master
$ git reset --hard origin/master

HEAD is now at 3061dc6 Adds Java version of 'hello world'
```

In this example, we also need to use some of the other branches in the repository, so we need to create them locally:

```
$ git branch -f feature/p-lang origin/feature/p-lang
Branch feature/p-lang set up to track remote branch feature/p-lang from origin.

$ git checkout develop
Switched to branch 'develop'
Your branch is up-to-date with 'origin/develop'.

$ git reset --hard origin/develop
HEAD is now at a95abc6 Adds Groovy hello world
```

How to do it...

On the develop branch, we have just checked that there is a merge commit that introduces hello world programs from languages that start with P.

Unfortunately, the Perl version doesn't run:

```
$ perl hello_world.pl

Can't find string terminator '"' anywhere before EOF at hello_world.pl line 3.
```

The following steps will help you revert a merge:

1. Let's take a look at the history, the latest five commits, and find the merge commit:

    ```
    $ git log --oneline --graph -5
    * a95abc6 Adds Groovy hello world
    *   5ae3beb Merge branch 'feature/p-lang' into develop
    |\
    | * 7b29bc3 php version added
    | * 9944417 Adds perl hello_world script
    * | ed9af38 Hello world shell script
    |/
    ```

Recovering from Mistakes

The commit we are looking for is `5ae3beb Merge branch 'feature/p-lang' into develop`; this adds the commits for hello world in Perl and PHP to the develop branch. We would like the fix of the Perl version to happen on the feature branch, and then merge it to develop when ready. In order to keep `develop` stable, we need to revert the merge commit that introduced the faulty Perl version. Before we perform the merge, let's just have a look at the content of HEAD:

```
$ git ls-tree --abbrev HEAD

100644 blob 28f40d8      helloWorld.groovy
100644 blob 881ef55      hello_world.c
100644 blob 5dd01c1      hello_world.php
100755 blob ae06973      hello_world.pl
100755 blob f3d7a14      hello_world.py
100755 blob 9f3f770      hello_world.sh
```

2. Revert the merge, keeping the history of the first parent:

```
$ git revert -m 1 5ae3beb

[develop e043b95] Revert "Merge branch 'feature/p-lang' into develop"

 2 files changed, 4 deletions(-)
 delete mode 100644 hello_world.php
 delete mode 100755 hello_world.pl
```

3. Let's have a look at the content of our new HEAD state:

```
$ git ls-tree --abbrev HEAD

100644 blob 28f40d8      helloWorld.groovy
100644 blob 881ef55      hello_world.c
100755 blob f3d7a14      hello_world.py
100755 blob 9f3f770      hello_world.sh
```

The Perl and PHP files introduced in the merge are gone, so the revert did its job.

How it works...

The revert command will take the patches introduced by the commit you want to revert and apply the reverse/anti-patch to the working tree. If all goes well, that is, there are no conflicts, a new commit will be made. While reverting a merge commit, only the changes introduced in the mainline (the -m option) will be kept, and all the changes introduced in the other side of the merge will be reverted.

There's more...

Though it is easy to revert a merge commit, you might run into issues if you later want to the branch again because the issues on the merge have not been fixed. While reverting the merge commit, you actually tell Git that you do not want any of the changes that the other branch introduced in this branch. So, when you try to merge in the branch again, you will only get the changes from the commits that are not ancestors of the reverted merge commit.

We will see this in action by trying to merge the `feature/p-lang` branch with the develop branch again:

```
$ git merge --no-edit feature/p-lang
CONFLICT (modify/delete): hello_world.pl deleted in HEAD and modified in feature/p-lang. Version feature/p-lang of hello_world.pl left in tree.
Automatic merge failed; fix conflicts and then commit the result.
```

We can solve the conflict just by adding `hello_world.pl`:

```
$ git add hello_world.pl

$ git commit
[develop 2804731] Merge branch 'feature/p-lang' into develop
```

Let's check the tree to see whether everything seems alright:

```
$ git ls-tree --abbrev HEAD

100644 blob 28f40d8    helloWorld.groovy
100644 blob 881ef55    hello_world.c
100755 blob 6611b8e    hello_world.pl
100755 blob f3d7a14    hello_world.py
100755 blob 9f3f770    hello_world.sh
```

The `hello_world.php` file is missing, but this makes sense as the change that introduced it was reverted in the reverted merge commit.

To perform a proper re-merge, we first have to revert the reverting merge commit; this might seem a bit weird, but it is the way to get the changes from before the revert back into our tree. Then, we can perform another merge of the branch, and we'll end up with all the changes introduced by the branch we're merging in. However, we first have to discard the merge commit we just made with a hard reset:

```
$ git reset --hard HEAD^
HEAD is now at c46deed Revert "Merge branch 'feature/p-lang' into develop"
```

Now, we can revert the reverting merge and re-merge the branch:

```
$ git revert HEAD

[develop 9950c9e] Revert "Revert "Merge branch 'feature/p-lang' into develop""
 2 files changed, 4 insertions(+)
 create mode 100644 hello_world.php
 create mode 100755 hello_world.pl

$ git merge feature/p-lang

Merge made by the 'recursive' strategy.
 hello_world.pl | 2 +-
 1 file changed, 1 insertion(+), 1 deletion(-)
```

Let's check the tree for the Perl and PHP files, and see whether the Perl file has been fixed:

```
$ git ls-tree --abbrev HEAD

100644 blob 28f40d8    helloWorld.groovy
100644 blob 881ef55    hello_world.c
100644 blob 5dd01c1    hello_world.php
100755 blob 6611b8e    hello_world.pl
100755 blob f3d7a14    hello_world.py
100755 blob 9f3f770    hello_world.sh

$ perl hello_world.pl
Hello, world!
```

See also

For more information on reverting merges, refer to the following articles:

- The *How To Revert a Faulty Merge* article at https://www.kernel.org/pub/software/scm/git/docs/howto/revert-a-faulty-merge.html
- The *Undoing Merges* article at http://git-scm.com/blog/2010/03/02/undoing-merges.html

Viewing past Git actions with git reflog

The `reflog` command stores information on updates to the tip of the branches in Git, where the normal `git log` command shows the ancestry chain from HEAD, and the `reflog` command shows what HEAD has pointed to in the repository. This is your history in the repository, which tells you how you have moved between branches, created your commits and resets, and so on. Basically, anything that makes HEAD point to something new is recorded in the `reflog`. This means that, by going through the `reflog` command, you can find lost commits that none of your branches or other commits point to. This makes the `reflog` command a good starting point for trying to find a lost commit.

Getting ready

Again, we'll use the hello world repository. If you make a fresh clone, make sure to run the scripts for this chapter so that there will be some entries in the `reflog` command.

The scripts can be found on the book's home page. If you just reset the master branch to `origin/master` after performing the recipes in this chapter, everything will be ready.

We can create a fresh clone as follows:

```
$ git clone https://github.com/PacktPublishing/Git-Version-Control-Cookbook-Second-Edition_hello_world_cookbook.git
$ cd Git-Version-Control-Cookbook-Second-Edition_hello_world_cookbook
```

Recovering from Mistakes

We can reset an existing clone as follows:

```
$ cd Git-Version-Control-Cookbook-Second-Edition_hello_world_cookbook
$ git checkout master
$ git reset --hard origin/master
HEAD is now at 3061dc6 Adds Java version of 'hello world'
```

How to do it...

1. Let's try to run the `reflog` command and limit ourselves to just the latest seven entries:

    ```
    $ git reflog -7

    3061dc6 HEAD@{0}: checkout: moving from develop to master
    d557284 HEAD@{1}: merge feature/p-lang: Merge made by the 'recursive' strategy.
    9950c9e HEAD@{2}: revert: Revert "Revert "Merge branch 'feature/p-lang' into develop""
    c46deed HEAD@{3}: reset: moving to HEAD^
    2804731 HEAD@{4}: commit (merge): Merge branch 'feature/p-lang' into develop
    c46deed HEAD@{5}: revert: Revert "Merge branch 'feature/p-lang' into develop"
    a95abc6 HEAD@{6}: checkout: moving from master to develop
    ```

    > In your repository, the commits will have different SHA-1 hashes due to the fact that the commits generated in the examples will have slightly different content, specifically your username and email address, but the order should be approximately the same.

    We can see the actions we performed in the last example by reverting, committing, and resetting. We can see the merge commit, `2804731`, that we abandoned. It didn't merge in all the changes we wanted it to due to the previous merge and its revert.

2. We can take a closer look at the commit with `git show`:

    ```
    $ git show 2804731
    commit 2804731c3abc4824cdab66dc7567bed4cddde0d3
    Merge: c46deed 32fa2cd
    Author: John Doe <john.doe@example.com>
    Date:   Thu Mar 13 23:20:21 2014 +0100

        Merge branch 'feature/p-lang' into develop
    ```

```
Conflicts:
        hello_world.pl
```

Indeed, this was the commit we chose to abandon in the previous example. We can also look at the tree of the commit, just as we did in the previous example, and check whether they are the same:

```
$ git ls-tree --abbrev 2804731

100644 blob 28f40d8    helloWorld.groovy
100644 blob 881ef55    hello_world.c
100755 blob 6611b8e    hello_world.pl
100755 blob f3d7a14    hello_world.py
100755 blob 9f3f770    hello_world.sh
```

From here, there are various ways to resurrect the changes. You can either check out the commit and create a branch; then, you'll have a pointer so that you can easily find it again. You can also check out specific files from the commit with `git checkout –path/to/file SHA-1`, or you can use the `git show` or `git cat-file` commands to view the files.

How it works...

For every movement of the HEAD pointer in the repository, Git stores the commit pointed to and the action for getting there. This can be commit, checkout, reset, revert, merge, rebase, and so on. The information is local to the repository and is not shared on pushes, fetches, and clones. Using the `reflog` command to find the lost commits is fairly easy if you know what you are searching for and the approximate time when you created the commit you are searching for. If you have a lot of reflog history, many commits, switching branches, and so on, it can be hard to search through the `reflog` command due to the amount of noise from the many updates to HEAD. The output of the `reflog` command can be a lot of options and, among them, there are options you can also pass on to the normal `git log` command.

Finding lost changes with git fsck

Another tool exists in Git that can help you find and recover lost commits and even blobs (files), which is `git fsck`. The `fsck` command tests the object database and verifies the SHA-1 ID of the objects and the connections they make. This command can also be used to find objects that are not reachable from any named reference, as it tests all the objects found in the database, which are in the `.git/objects` folder.

Getting ready

Again, we'll use the hello world repository. If you make a fresh clone, make sure to run the scripts for this chapter (`04_undo_dirty.sh`), so there will be some objects for `git fsck` to consider. The scripts can be found on the book's home page. If you just reset the master branch after performing the other recipes in the chapter, everything will be ready.

We can create the fresh clone as follows:

```
$ git clone https://github.com/PacktPublishing/Git-Version-Control-Cookbook-Second-Edition_hello_world_cookbook.git
$ cd Git-Version-Control-Cookbook-Second-Edition_hello_world_cookbook
```

We can reset an existing clone as follows:

```
$ cd Git-Version-Control-Cookbook-Second-Edition_hello_world_cookbook
$ git checkout master
$ git reset --hard origin/master
HEAD is now at 3061dc6 Adds Java version of 'hello world'
```

How to do it...

1. Let's look for the unreachable objects in the database:

    ```
    $ git fsck --unreachable
    
    Checking object directories: 100% (256/256), done.
    unreachable commit 147240ad0297f85c9ca3ed513906d4b75209e83d
    unreachable blob b16cf63ab66605f9505c17c5affd88b34c9150ce
    unreachable commit 4c3b1e10d8876cd507bcf2072c85cc474f7fb93b
    ```

Chapter 8

 The object's ID, the SHA-1 hash, will not be the same if you perform the example on your computer, as the committer, author, and timestamp will be different.

2. We found two commits and one blob. Let's take a closer look at each of them; the blob first:

    ```
    $ git show b16cf63ab66605f9505c17c5affd88b34c9150ce

    #include <stdio.h>
    void say_hello(void) {
      printf("hello, worldn");
    }

    int main(void){
      say_hello();
        return 0;
    }
    ```

    So, the blob is the `hello_world.c` file from the example, which stashes away your changes before resetting a commit. Here, we stashed away the file, performed a reset, and resurrected the file from the stash, but we never actually performed a commit. The stash command, however, did add the file to the database, so it could find it again, and the file will continue to be there until the garbage collection kicks in, or forever if it is referenced by a commit in the general history.

3. Let's look more closely at the two commits:

    ```
    $ git show 147240ad0297f85c9ca3ed513906d4b75209e83d

    commit 147240ad0297f85c9ca3ed513906d4b75209e83d
    Merge: 3061dc6 4c3b1e1
    Author: John Doe <john.doe@example.com>
    Date:   Thu Mar 13 23:19:37 2014 +0100
        WIP on master: 3061dc6 Adds Java version of 'hello world'

    diff --cc hello_world.c
    index 881ef55,881ef55..b16cf63
    --- a/hello_world.c
    +++ b/hello_world.c
    @@@ -1,7 -1,7 +1,10 @@@

      #include <stdio.h>
    ```

[199]

Recovering from Mistakes

```
--int main(void){
  ++void say_hello(void) {
    printf("hello, worldn");
++}

++int main(void){
  ++   say_hello();
  return 0;
--}
++}

$ git show 4c3b1e10d8876cd507bcf2072c85cc474f7fb93b

commit 4c3b1e10d8876cd507bcf2072c85cc474f7fb93b
Author: John Doe <john.doe@example.com>
Date:   Thu Mar 13 23:19:37 2014 +0100
    index on master: 3061dc6 Adds Java version of 'hello world'
```

Both of the commits are actually commits we made when we stashed away our changes in the previous example. The stash command creates a commit object with the content of the staging area, and a merge commit merging HEAD and the commit with the index with the content of the working directory (tracked files only). As we resurrected our stashed changes in the previous example, we no longer have any reference pointing at the preceding commits; therefore, they are found by `git fsck`.

How it works...

The `git fsck` command will test all the objects found in the `.git/objects` folder. When the `--unreachable` option is given, it will report the objects found that can't be reached from another reference; a reference can be a branch, a tag, a commit, a tree, the `reflog`, or changes that have been stashed away.

9
Repository Maintenance

In this chapter, we will cover the following recipes:

- Pruning remote branches
- Running garbage collection manually
- Turning off automatic garbage collection
- Splitting a repository
- Rewriting history – changing a single file
- Creating a backup of your repositories as mirror repositories
- A quick "how-to" submodule
- Subtree merging
- Submodule versus subtree merging

Introduction

In this chapter, we'll take a look at various tools used for repository maintenance. We'll look at how we can easily delete branches in the local repository that have been deleted from the remote repository. We'll also see how we can trigger garbage collection and how to turn it off. We'll take a look at how a repository can be split with the `filter-branch` command, and how the same command can be used to rewrite the history of a repository. Finally, we'll take a quick look at how to integrate other Git projects into a Git repository as subprojects, with either the submodule functionality or the subtree strategy.

Pruning remote branches

Often, the development of a software project tracked by Git happens on feature branches, and, as time goes by, an increasing number of feature branches are merged to the mainline. Usually, these feature branches are deleted in the main repository (the origin). However, branches are not automatically deleted from all clones while fetching and pulling request. Git must explicitly be told to delete branches from the local repository that have been deleted from the origin.

Getting ready

First, we'll set up two repositories and use one of them as a remote for the other. We will use the Git-Version-Control-Second-Edition_hello_world_flow_model repository, but first we'll clone a repository to a local bare repository:

```
$ git clone --bare
https://github.com/PacktPublishing/Git-Version-Control-Cookbook-Second-Edition_hello_world_flow_model.git hello_world_flow_model_remote
Cloning into bare repository 'hello_world_flow_model_remote'...
remote: Counting objects: 51, done.
remote: Total 51 (delta 0), reused 0 (delta 0), pack-reused 51
Unpacking objects: 100% (51/51), done.
```

Next, we'll clone the newly cloned repository to a local one with a working directory:

```
$ git clone hello_world_flow_model_remote hello_world_flow_model
```

Now, let's delete a couple of merged feature branches in the bare repository:

```
$ cd hello_world_flow_model_remote
$ git branch -D feature/continents
$ git branch -D feature/printing
$ git branch -D release/1.0
$ cd ..
```

Finally, change the directory to your working copy and make sure `develop` branch is checked out:

```
$ cd hello_world_flow_model
$ git checkout develop
$ git reset --hard origin/develop
```

How to do it...

1. Start by listing all of the branches using the following command:

   ```
   $ git branch -a
   * develop
     remotes/origin/HEAD -> origin/develop
     remotes/origin/develop
     remotes/origin/feature/cities
     remotes/origin/feature/continents
     remotes/origin/feature/printing
     remotes/origin/master
     remotes/origin/release/1.0
   ```

2. Let's try to fetch or pull and see whether anything happens, using the following command:

   ```
   $ git fetch
   $ git pull
   Already up to date.
   $ git branch -a

   * develop
     remotes/origin/HEAD -> origin/develop
     remotes/origin/develop
     remotes/origin/feature/cities
     remotes/origin/feature/continents
     remotes/origin/feature/printing
     remotes/origin/master
     remotes/origin/release/1.0
   ```

3. The branches are still there, even if they have been deleted in the remote repository. We need to tell Git explicitly to delete the branches that have also been deleted from the remote repository, using the following command:

   ```
   $ git fetch --prune
    x [deleted]         (none)       -> origin/feature/continents
    x [deleted]         (none)       -> origin/feature/printing
    x [deleted]         (none)       -> origin/release/1.0
   $ git branch -a
   * develop
     remotes/origin/HEAD -> origin/develop
     remotes/origin/develop
     remotes/origin/feature/cities
     remotes/origin/master
   ```

The branches have now also been deleted from our local repository.

How it works...

Git simply checks the remote-tracking branches under the remote or origin namespace and removes branches that are not found on the remote any more.

There's more...

There are several ways to remove the branches from Git that have been deleted from the master. It can be done while updating the local repository, as we saw with `git fetch --prune`, and also with `git pull --prune`. It can even be performed with the `git remote prune origin` command. This will also remove the branches from Git that are no longer available on the remote, but it will not update remote-tracking branches in the repository.

Running garbage collection manually

When using Git on a regular basis, you might notice that some commands sometimes trigger Git to perform garbage collection and pack loose objects into a pack file (Git's objects storage). The garbage collection and packing of loose objects can also be triggered manually by executing the `git gc` command. Triggering `git gc` is useful if you have a lot of loose objects. A loose object can, for example, be a blob, a tree, or a commit. As we saw in Chapter 1, *Navigating Git*, `blob-`, `tree-`, and `commit` objects are added to Git's database when we add files and create commits. These objects are first stored as unreachable objects in Git's object storage as single files inside the `.git/objects` folder. Eventually, or by manual request, Git packs the loose objects into pack files, which can reduce disk usage. A lot of objects can become loose after adding many files to Git, for example, when starting a new project or after frequent adds and commits. Running garbage collection will make sure that loose objects are packed, and objects not referred to by any reference or object will be deleted. The latter is useful when you have deleted some branches/commits and want to make sure that the objects referenced by them are also deleted.

Let's see how we can trigger garbage collection and remove some objects from the database.

Getting ready

First, we need a repository to perform the garbage collection on. We'll use the same repository as in the previous example:

```
$ git clone https://github.com/PacktPublishing/Git-Version-Control-Cookbook-Second-Edition_hello_world_flow_model.git
$ cd hello_world_flow_model
$ git checkout develop
$ git reset --hard origin/develop
```

How to do it...

1. First, we'll check the repository for unpacked objects; we can do this with the `count-objects` command:

   ```
   $ git count-objects
   51 objects, 204 kilobytes
   ```

2. We'll also check for unreachable objects, which are objects that can't be reached from any reference (tag, branch, or other object). The unreachable objects will be deleted when the garbage collection runs. We also check the size of the `.git` directory using the following command:

   ```
   $ git fsck --unreachable
   Checking object directories: 100% (256/256), done.

   $ du -sh .git

   292K    .git # Linux - 1K = 1024 bytes
   300K    .git # MacOS - 1K = 1000 bytes
   ```

3. There are no unreachable objects. This is because we just cloned and haven't actually worked in the repository. If we delete the origin remotely, the remote branches (`remotes/origin/*`) will be deleted, and we'll lose the reference to some of the objects in the repository; they'll be displayed as unreachable while running `fsck` and can be garbage collected:

   ```
   $ git remote rm origin
   $ git fsck --unreachable
   Checking object directories: 100% (256/256), done.
   unreachable commit 127c621039928c5d99e4221564091a5bf317dc27
   unreachable commit 472a3dd2fda0c15c9f7998a98f6140c4a3ce4816
   ```

```
unreachable blob e26174ff5c0a3436454d0833f921943f0fc78070
unreachable tree f03964e50809d5a0a9d35c208001b141ac36d997
unreachable commit f336166c7812337b83f4e62c269deca8ccfa3675
```

4. We can see that we have some unreachable objects due to the deletion of the remote. Let's try to trigger garbage collection manually:

```
$ git gc
Counting objects: 46, done.
Delta compression using up to 8 threads.
Compressing objects: 100% (44/44), done.
Writing objects: 100% (46/46), done.
Total 46 (delta 18), reused 0 (delta 0)
```

5. If we investigate the repository now, we will see the following:

```
$ git count-objects
5 objects, 20 kilobytes
$ git fsck --unreachable
Checking object directories: 100% (256/256), done.
Checking objects: 100% (46/46), done.
unreachable commit 127c621039928c5d99e4221564091a5bf317dc27
unreachable commit 472a3dd2fda0c15c9f7998a98f6140c4a3ce4816
unreachable blob e26174ff5c0a3436454d0833f921943f0fc78070
unreachable tree f03964e50809d5a0a9d35c208001b141ac36d997
unreachable commit f336166c7812337b83f4e62c269deca8ccfa3675
$ du -sh .git
120K    .git # Linux
124K    .git # MacOS
```

6. The object count is smaller. Git has packed the objects to the pack file stored in the `.git/objects/pack` folder. The size of the repository is also smaller, as Git compresses and optimizes the objects in the pack file. However, there are still some unreachable objects left. This is because objects will only be deleted if they are older than what is specified in the `gc.pruneexpire` configuration option, which defaults to two weeks (`config value: 2.weeks.ago`). We can override the default or configured option by running the `--prune=now` option:

```
$ git gc --prune=now
Counting objects: 46, done.
Delta compression using up to 8 threads.
Compressing objects: 100% (26/26), done.
Writing objects: 100% (46/46), done.
Total 46 (delta 18), reused 46 (delta 18)
```

7. Investigating the repository gives the following output:

```
$ git count-objects
0 objects, 0 kilobytes
$ git fsck --unreachable
Checking object directories: 100% (256/256), done.
Checking objects: 100% (46/46), done.
$ du -sh .git
100K    .git # Linux
104K    .git # MacOS
```

The unreachable objects have been deleted, there are no loose objects, and the repository size is smaller now that the objects have been deleted.

How it works...

The `git gc` command optimizes the repository by compressing file revisions and deleting objects that there are no references to. The objects can be commits, and so on. On an abandoned (deleted) branch, blobs from invocations of git add, commits discarded/redone with `git commit --amend`, or other commands can leave objects behind. Objects are, by default, already compressed with `zlib` when they are created and, when moved into the pack file, Git makes sure to only store the necessary changes. For example, if you change only a single line in a large file, storing the entire file in the pack file again would waste a bit of space. Instead, Git stores the latest file as a whole in the pack file and only the delta for the older version. This is pretty smart, as you are more likely to require the latest version of the file, and Git doesn't have to do delta calculations for this. This might seem like a contradiction to the information from Chapter 1, *Navigating Git*, where we learned that Git stores snapshots and not deltas. However, remember how the snapshot is made. Git hashes all of the file content in blobs, makes `tree` and `commit` objects, and the commit object describes the full tree state with the `root-tree sha-1` hash. Storing objects inside the pack-files has no effect on the computation of the tree state. When you check out an earlier version of commit, Git makes sure the sha-1 hashes match the branch, commit, or tag you requested.

Turning off automatic garbage collection

The automatic triggering of garbage collection can be turned off so that it will not run unless manually triggered. This can be useful if you are searching the repository for a lost commit/file and want to make sure that it is not being garbage collected while searching (running Git commands).

Getting ready

We'll use the `Git-Version-Control-Cookbook-Second-Edition_hello_world_flow_model` repository again for this example:

```
$ git clone https://github.com/PacktPublishing/Git-Version-Control-Cookbook-Second-Edition_hello_world_flow_model.git
Cloning into 'Git-Version-Control-Cookbook-Second-Edition_hello_world_flow_model'...
remote: Reusing existing pack: 51, done.
remote: Total 51 (delta 0), reused 0 (delta 0)
Unpacking objects: 100% (51/51), done.
Checking connectivity... done.
$ cd Git-Version-Control-Cookbook-Second-Edition_hello_world_flow_model
$ git checkout develop
Already on 'develop'
Your branch is up-to-date with 'origin/develop'.
$ git reset --hard origin/develop
HEAD is now at 2269dcf Merge branch 'release/1.0' into develop
```

How to do it...

1. To switch off automatic garbage collection from being triggered, we need to set the `gc.auto` configuration to 0. First, we'll check the existing setting, and then we can set it and verify the configuration using the following commands:

    ```
    $ git config gc.auto # exit code is 1 when not set
    $ echo $?
    1
    $ git config gc.auto 0
    $ git config gc.auto
    0
    ```

2. Now we can try to run `git gc` with the `--auto` flag, as it will be called when normally triggered from an other command:

   ```
   $ git gc --auto
   ```

3. As expected, nothing happens, as the configuration disables automatic garbage collection. We can still trigger it manually though (without the `--auto` flag):

   ```
   $ git gc
   Counting objects: 51, done.
   Delta compression using up to 8 threads.
   Compressing objects: 100% (49/49), done.
   Writing objects: 100% (51/51), done.
   Total 51 (delta 23), reused 0 (delta 0)
   ```

Splitting a repository

Sometimes, a project tracked with Git is not one logical project, but consists of several projects. This may be fully intentional and there is nothing wrong with that, but there can also be cases where projects tracked in the same Git repository really should belong to two different repositories. You can imagine a project where the code base grows and, at some point in time, one of the subprojects could have value as an independent project. This can be achieved by splitting the subfolders and/or files that contain the project that should have its own repository with the full history of commits touching the files and/or folders.

Getting ready

In this example, we'll use the JGit repository, so we'll have some history to filter through. The subfolders we split into are not really projects, but serve well as an example for this exercise.

1. First, clone the JGit repository and create local branches of the remote ones using the following command:

   ```
   $ git clone https://git.eclipse.org/r/jgit/jgit
   Cloning into 'jgit'...
   remote: Counting objects: 98, done
   remote: Total 95247 (delta 0), reused 95247 (delta 0)
   Receiving objects: 100% (95247/95247), 41.25 MiB | 1.91 MiB/s, done.
   Resolving deltas: 100% (41334/41334), done.
   $ cd jgit
   ```

```
$ git checkout master
Already on 'master'
Your branch is up-to-date with 'origin/master'.
```

2. Save the name of the current branch in a variable named `current`:

```
$ current=$(git rev-parse --symbolic-full-name --abbrev-ref HEAD)
```

3. In the following step, we create local branches from all the remote branches in the repository:

```
$ for br in $(git branch -a | grep -v $current | grep remotes | grep -v HEAD);
  do
    git branch ${br##*/} $br;
  done

Branch stable-0.10 set up to track remote branch stable-0.10 from origin.
Branch stable-0.11 set up to track remote branch stable-0.11 from origin.
Branch stable-0.12 set up to track remote branch stable-0.12 from origin.
...
```

First, we filter the branches. From all the branches (`git branch -a`), we exclude branches that match the `$current` variable somewhere in the name (`grep -v $current`). Then, we include only the branches that match the remote (`grep remotes`). Finally, we exclude all branches with HEAD (`grep -v HEAD`). For each of the branches (`$br`), we create a local branch with the name given after the last "/" in the full name of the branch (`git branch ${br##*/} $br`). For example, the branch `remotes/origin/stable-0.10` becomes the local branch `stable-0.10`.

4. Now, we'll prepare a short script that will delete everything apart from the input to the shell script from the Git index. Save the following to the `clean-tree` file in the folder that contains the JGit repository (not the repository itself):

```
#!/bin/bash
# Clean the tree for unwanted dirs and files
# $1 Files and dirs to keep

clean-tree () {
  # Remove everything but $1 from the git index/staging area
  for f in $(git ls-files | grep -v -E "$1" | grep -o -E "^[^/\"]+" | sort -u); do
```

```
        git rm -rq --cached --ignore-unmatch $f
    done
}

clean-tree $1
```

The short script filters all the files currently in the staging area (`git ls-files`), excluding the ones that match the input (`grep -v -E "$1"`). It lists only the first part of their `name/path` up to the first "/" (`grep -o -E "^[^/\"]"`), and finally sorts them by unique entries (`sort -u`). The entries in the remaining list (`$f`) are removed from the staging of Git (`git rm -rq --cached --ignore-unmatch $f`). The `--cached` option tells Git to remove them from the staging area and `--ignore-unmatched` tells Git not to fail if the file does not exist in the staging area. The `-rq` option is recursive and quiet respectively.

> The staging area contains all the files tracked by Git in the last snapshot (commit) and files (modified or new) you have added with `git add`. However, you only see differences between the latest commit and the staging area when you run `git status`, along with differences between the working tree and the staging area.

5. Make the file executable using the following command:

   ```
   $ chmod +x clean-tree
   ```

6. Now we are ready to split out a subpart of the repository.

How to do it...

1. First, we'll decide which folders and files to keep in the new repository; we'll delete everything from the repository except those files. We'll store the files and folders to be kept in a string separated by | so that we can feed it to `grep` as a regular expression, as shown in the following command:

   ```
   keep="org.eclipse.jgit.http|LICENSE|.gitignore|README.md|.gitattributes"
   ```

2. Now we are ready to start the conversion of the repository. We'll use the `git filter-branch` command, which can rewrite the entire history of the repository; just what we need for this task.

Repository Maintenance

Always remember to make sure you have a backup of the repository you are about to run `git filter-branch` on, in case something goes wrong.

3. We'll use the `--index-filter` option to filter the branch. The option allows us to rewrite the index or staging area just before each commit is recorded, and we'll do this with the `clean-tree` script we created previously. We'll also preserve tags using `cat` as the `tag-name-filter`. We'll perform the rewrite on all branches and remember to use the absolute path to the clean-tree script:

```
$ git filter-branch --prune-empty  --index-filter
"\"/absolute/path/to/clean-tree\" \"$keep\"" --tag-name-filter cat
-- --all
...
Rewrite 720734983bae056955bec3b36cc7e3847a0bb46a (13/3051)
Rewrite 6e1571d5b9269ec79eadad0dbd5916508a4fee82 (23/3051)
Rewrite 2bfe561f269afdd7f4772f8ebf34e5e25884942b (37/3051)
Rewrite 2086fdaedd5e71621470865c34ad075d2668af99 (60/3051)
...
```

4. The rewrite takes a bit of time, as all commits need to be processed. Once the rewrite is done, we can see that everything is deleted, except the files and folders we wanted to keep:

```
$ git ls-tree --abbrev HEAD
100644 blob f57840b7e .gitattributes
100644 blob 3679a3365 .gitignore
100644 blob 1b85c6466 LICENSE
100644 blob 54133e1d3 README.md
040000 tree 2edd8e193 org.eclipse.jgit.http.apache
040000 tree cda583881 org.eclipse.jgit.http.server
040000 tree daace995c org.eclipse.jgit.http.test
```

5. The cleanup isn't done just yet. `git filter-branch` saves all the original references, branches and tags, under the `refs/original` namespace in the repository. After verification, the new history looks good, and we can get rid of the original `refs`, as these point to objects that are not in our current history and take up a lot of disk space. We'll delete all the original refs and run the garbage collector to clear the repository of old objects:

```
$ du -sh .git
  53M   .git # MacOS
```

[212]

6. Delete original references, `refs/original`, and remove old objects with `git gc`, as shown in the following command:

   ```
   $ git for-each-ref --format="%(refname)" refs/original/ | xargs -n 1 git update-ref -d
   $ git reflog expire --expire=now --all
   $ git gc --prune=now
   Counting objects: 96863, done.
   Delta compression using up to 4 threads.
   Compressing objects: 100% (28811/28811), done.
   Writing objects: 100% (96863/96863), done.
   Total 96863 (delta 42589), reused 94395 (delta 41334)
   ```

7. Check the size of the repository after garbage collection:

   ```
   $ du -sh .git
   44M    .git  # MacOS
   ```

8. The repository is now clean of all old objects, the size has been reduced, and the history is preserved for the files and directories we listed to keep.

How it works...

The `git filter-branch` command has different filter options depending on what needs to be done when rewriting the repository. In this example, where we are only removing files and folders from the repository; the `index-filter` is highly usable, as it allows us to rewrite the index just before recording a commit in the database without actually checking out the tree on disk, thereby saving a lot of disk I/O. The `clean-tree` script we prepared previously is then used to remove the unwanted files and folders from the index. First, we list the content of the index and filter the files and folders we want to keep. Then, we remove the remaining files and folders (`$f`) from the index with the following command:

```
git rm -rq --cached --ignore-unmatch $f
```

The `--cached` option tells Git to remove the index from files, and the `-rq` option tells it to remove `recursive (r)` option and be quiet (q). Finally, the `--ignore-unmatch` option is used so that `git rm` will not exit with an error if it tries to remove a file that is not in the index.

There's more...

There are many more filters for `git filter-branch`; the most common ones and their use cases are as follows:

- `env-filter`: This filter is used to modify the environment where commits are recorded. This is particularly useful when rewriting author and committer information.
- `tree-filter`: The `tree-filter` is used to rewrite the tree. This is useful if you need to add or modify files in the tree, for example, to remove sensitive data from a repository.
- `msg-filter`: This filter is used to update the commit message.
- `subdirectory-filter`: This filter can be used if you want to extract a single subdirectory to a new repository and keep the history of that subdirectory. The subdirectory will be the root of the new repository.

Rewriting history – changing a single file

In this example, we'll see how we can use Git `filter-branch` to remove sensitive data from a file throughout the repository history.

Getting ready

For simplicity, we'll use a very simple example repository. It contains a few files. One of them is .credentials, which contains a username and password. Start by cloning the repository and changing the directory, as shown in the following command:

```
$ git clone https://github.com/PacktPublishing/Git-Version-Control-Cookbook-Second-Edition_Remove-Credentials.git
$ cd Git-Version-Control-Cookbook-Second-Edition_Remove-Credentials
```

Before proceeding, you can take a look at the content of the repository using `ls` and examine the history with `git log`.

How to do it...

1. As we need to modify a file when rewriting the history of this repository, we'll use the `tree-filter` option to filter the branch. The `.credentials` file looks as follows:

   ```
   username = foobar
   password = verysecret
   ```

2. All we need to do is remove everything after the equals sign on each line of the file. We can use the following `sed` command to do this:

   ```
   sed -i '' -e 's/^\(.*=\).*$/\1/'
   ```

3. We can now run the filter branch with the following command:

   ```
   $ git filter-branch --prune-empty  --tree-filter "test -f .credentials && sed -i '' -e 's/^\(.*=\).*$/\1/' .credentials || true" -- --all
   ```

4. If we look at the file now, we can see that the username and password are gone:

   ```
   $ cat .credentials
   username =
   password =
   ```

5. As we saw in the previous example, we still need to clean up after `filter-branch`, by deleting original references, expiring the `reflog`, and triggering garbage collection. But, at this point, you can compare the content and commit history of the repository.

How it works...

For each commit in the repository, Git will check the content of that commit and run `tree-filter`. If the filter fails with a non-zero exit code, `filter-branch` will fail. Therefore, it is important to remember to handle cases where `tree-filter` might fail. This is the reason why the previous `tree-filter` checks whether the `.credentials` file exists, runs the `sed` command if it does, and otherwise returns true to continue the `filter-branch`.

Creating a backup of your repositories as mirror repositories

Even though Git is distributed and every clone is essentially a backup, there are some tricks that can be useful when backing up Git repositories. A normal Git repository has a working copy of the files it tracks and the full history of the repository in the .git folder of that repository. The repositories on the server, the ones you push to and pull from, will usually be bare repositories. A bare repository is a repository without a working copy. Roughly, it is just the .git folder of a normal repository. A mirror repository is almost the same as a bare repository, except it fetches all the references under refs/*, whereas a bare repository only fetches the references that fall under refs/heads/*. We'll now take a closer look at a normal, a bare, and a mirror clone of the JGit repository.

Getting ready

We'll start by creating three clones of the JGit repository: a normal, a bare, and a mirror clone. When we create the first clone, we can use that as a reference repository for the other clones. In this way, we can share the objects in the database, and we don't have to transfer the same data three times:

```
$ git clone https://git.eclipse.org/r/jgit/jgit
$ git clone --reference jgit --bare https://git.eclipse.org/r/jgit/jgit
$ git clone --mirror --reference jgit https://git.eclipse.org/r/jgit/jgit jgit.mirror
```

How to do it...

1. One of the differences between a normal repository and a bare or mirror one is that there are no remote branches in a bare repository. All the branches are created locally. We can see this in the three repositories by listing the branches with the git branch command as follows:

    ```
    $ cd jgit
    $ git branch
    * master
    $ cd ../jgit.git # or cd ../jgit.mirror
    $ git branch
    * master
      stable-0.10
      stable-0.11
    ```

```
stable-0.12
...
```

2. To see the difference between the bare and mirror repositories, we need to list the different refspecs fetches and the different refs namespaces. List the fetch refspec of origin in the mirror repository (jgit.mirror):

   ```
   $ cd ../jgit.mirror
   $ git config remote.origin.fetch
   +refs/*:refs/*
   ```

3. List the different refs namespaces in the mirror repository:

   ```
   $ git show-ref | cut -f2 -d " " | cut -f1,2 -d / | sort -u
   refs/cache-automerge
   refs/changes
   refs/heads
   refs/meta
   refs/notes
   refs/tags
   ```

4. There is no explicit refspec fetch in the configuration for origin in the bare repository (jgit.git). When no configuration entry is found, Git uses the default refspec fetch, as it does in a normal repository. We can check the remote URL of origin using the following command:

   ```
   $ cd ../jgit.git
   $ git config remote.origin.url
   https://git.eclipse.org/r/jgit/jgit
   ```

5. List the different refs namespaces in the bare repository using the following command and see the difference:

   ```
   $ git show-ref | cut -f2 -d " " | cut -f1,2 -d / | sort -u
   refs/heads
   refs/tags
   ```

6. Finally, we can list the refspec fetch and refs namespaces for the normal repository (jgit):

   ```
   $ cd ../jgit
   $ git config remote.origin.fetch
   +refs/heads/*:refs/remotes/origin/*
   $ git show-ref | cut -f2 -d " " | cut -f1,2 -d / | sort -u
   refs/heads
   refs/remotes
   refs/tags
   ```

7. The mirror repository has four ref namespaces not found in either the normal or the bare repositories: `refs-cache-automerge`, `changes`, `meta`, and `notes`. The normal repository is the only one that has the `refs/remote` namespace.

How it works...

The normal and bare repositories are pretty similar, only the mirror one sticks out. This is due to the `refspec` fetch on the mirror repository, `+refs/*:refs/*`, which will fetch all `refs` from the remote and not just `refs/heads/*` and `refs/tags/*` as a normal repository (and a `bare` repository) does. The many different `ref` namespaces on the JGit repository is because the JGit repository is managed by Gerrit Code Review. It uses different namespaces for repository-specific content, such as change branches for all commits submitted for code review, and metadata on code review score.

The `mirror` repositories are ideal when you would like a quick way to back up a Git repository. It ensures that you have everything included without the need for additional access than the Git access to the machine that hosts the Git repository.

There's more...

The repositories on GitHub store extra information in some refs namespaces. If a repository has had a pull request made, the pull request will be recorded in the `refs/pull/*` namespace. Let's look at this in the following example:

```
$ git clone --mirror git@github.com:jenkinsci/extreme-feedback-plugin.git
$ cd extreme-feedback-plugin.git
$ git show-ref | cut -f2 -d " " | cut -f1,2 -d / | sort -u
refs/heads
refs/meta
refs/pull
refs/tags
```

A quick "how-to" submodule

When working on a software project, you sometimes find yourself in a situation where you need to use another project as a part of your project. This other project can be anything, from another project you are developing to a third-party library. You want to keep projects separate, even though you need to use one project for the other. Git has a mechanism for this kind of project dependency, called submodules. The basic idea is that you can clone another Git repository into your project as a subdirectory, but keep the commits from the two repositories separate, as shown in the following diagram:

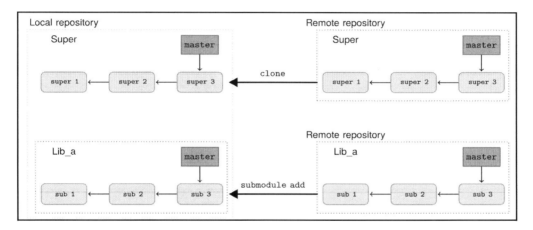

Getting ready

We'll start by cloning an example repository to be used as the super project:

```
$ git clone https://github.com/PacktPublishing/Git-Version-Control-Cookbook-Second-Edition_Super.git
$ cd Git-Version-Control-Cookbook-Second-Edition_Super
```

How to do it...

1. We'll add a subproject, lib_a, to the super project as a Git submodule:

    ```
    $ git submodule add
    https://github.com/PacktPublishing/Git-Version-Control-Cookbook-Sec
    ond-Edition_lib_a.git lib_a
    Cloning into 'lib_a'...
    remote: Counting objects: 18, done.
    remote: Compressing objects: 100% (14/14), done.
    remote: Total 18 (delta 4), reused 17 (delta 3)
    Receiving objects: 100% (18/18), done.
    Resolving deltas: 100% (4/4), done.
    Checking connectivity... done.
    ```

2. Let's check git status using the following command:

    ```
    $ git status
    On branch master
    Your branch is up-to-date with 'origin/master'.

    Changes to be committed:
      (use "git reset HEAD <file>..." to unstage)

        new file:   .gitmodules
        new file:   lib_a
    ```

3. We can take a closer look at the two files in the Git index; .gitmodules is a regular file, so we can use cat:

    ```
    $ cat .gitmodules
    [submodule "lib_a"]
      path = lib_a
      url =
    https://github.com/PacktPublishing/Git-Version-Control-Cookbook-Sec
    ond-Edition_lib_a.git
    $ git diff --cached lib_a
    diff --git a/lib_a b/lib_a
    new file mode 160000
    index 0000000..0d96e7c
    --- /dev/null
    +++ b/lib_a
    @@ -0,0 +1 @@
    +Subproject commit 0d96e7cfc4d4db64002e63af0f7325d33bdaf84f
    ```

The `.gitmodules` file, as above, contains information about all the submodules registered in the repository. The `lib_a` file stores which commit the submodule's HEAD is pointing to when added to the super project. Whenever the submodule is updated with new commits (created locally or fetched), the super project will show the submodule as having changed while running `git status`. If the changes to the submodule can be accepted, the submodule revision in the super project is updated by adding the submodule file and committing this to the super project.

4. We'll update the submodule, `lib_a`, to the latest change on the develop branch using the following command:

```
$ cd lib_a
$ git checkout develop
Branch develop set up to track remote branch develop from origin by rebasing.
Switched to a new branch 'develop'
$ cd ..
$ git status
On branch master
Your branch is ahead of 'origin/master' by 1 commit.
  (use "git push" to publish your local commits)

Changes not staged for commit:
  (use "git add <file>..." to update what will be committed)
  (use "git checkout -- <file>..." to discard changes in working directory)

    modified:   lib_a (new commits)

no changes added to commit (use "git add" and/or "git commit -a")
```

5. Let's just check whether there are any updates to the submodule:

```
$ git submodule update
Submodule path 'lib_a': checked out '0d96e7cfc4d4db64002e63af0f7325d33bdaf84f'
```

6. Oops! Now we actually reset our submodule to the state described in the file for that submodule. We need to switch to the submodule again, check develop, and this time create a commit in the super repository:

```
$ cd lib_a
$ git status
HEAD detached at 0d96e7c
nothing to commit, working directory clean
```

Repository Maintenance

```
$ git checkout develop
Previous HEAD position was 0d96e7c... Fixes book title in README
Switched to branch 'develop'
Your branch is up-to-date with 'origin/develop'.
$ cd ..
$ git status
On branch master
Your branch is ahead of 'origin/master' by 1 commit.
  (use "git push" to publish your local commits)

Changes not staged for commit:
  (use "git add <file>..." to update what will be committed)
  (use "git checkout -- <file>..." to discard changes in working
directory)

    modified:   lib_a (new commits)

no changes added to commit (use "git add" and/or "git commit -a")
$ git add lib_a
$ git commit -m 'Updated lib_a to newest version'
[master 4d371bb] Updated lib_a to newest version
 2 files changed, 4 insertions(+)
 create mode 100644 .gitmodules
 create mode 160000 lib_a
```

Notice that, by default, the submodule is in a detached head state, which means that HEAD is pointing directly to a commit instead of a branch. You can still edit the submodule and record commits; however, if you perform a submodule update in the super repository without first committing a new submodule state, your changes can be hard to find. Always remember to check out or create a branch while switching to a submodule to work on. If so, you can just check out the branch again and get your changes back. Since Git Version 1.8.2, it has been possible to make submodules track a branch rather than a single commit. Git 1.8.2 was released on March 13, 2013, and you can check your version by running git --version.

7. To make Git track the branch of a submodule rather than a specific commit, we need to record the name of the branch we want to track. This is done in the .gitmodules file for the submodule; here, we'll use the stable branch:

```
$ git config -f .gitmodules submodule.lib_a.branch stable
$ cat .gitmodules
[submodule "lib_a"]
  path = lib_a
```

```
        url = 
https://github.com/PacktPublishing/Git-Version-Control-Cookbook-Sec
ond-Edition_lib_a.git
        branch = stable
```

8. We can now add and commit the submodule, and then try to update it using the following command:

```
$ git add .gitmodules
$ git commit -m 'Make lib_a module track its stable branch'
[master bf9b9ba] Make lib_a module track its stable branch
 1 file changed, 1 insertion(+)
$ git submodule update --remote
Submodule path 'lib_a': checked out
'8176a16db21a48a0969e18a51f2c2fb1869418fb'
$ git status
On branch master
Your branch is ahead of 'origin/master' by 2 commits.
  (use "git push" to publish your local commits)

Changes not staged for commit:
  (use "git add <file>..." to update what will be committed)
  (use "git checkout -- <file>..." to discard changes in working
directory)

    modified:   lib_a (new commits)

no changes added to commit (use "git add" and/or "git commit -a")
```

The submodule is still in the detached HEAD state. However, when updating the submodule with `git submodule update --remote`, changes from the submodule's remote repository will be fetched and the submodule will be updated to the latest commit on the branch it is tracking. We still need to record a commit to the super repository, specifying the state of the submodule.

There's more...

When you are cloning a repository that contains one or more submodules, you need to explicitly fetch them after the clone. We can try this with our newly created submodule repository:

```
$ git clone super super_clone
Cloning into 'super_clone'...
done.
```

Now, initialize and update the submodules:

```
$ cd super_clone
$ git submodule init
Submodule 'lib_a' (https://github.com/PacktPublishing/Git-Version-Control-Cookbook-Second-Edition_lib_a.git) registered for path 'lib_a'
$ git submodule update --remote
Cloning into 'lib_a'...
remote: Counting objects: 18, done.
remote: Compressing objects: 100% (14/14), done.
remote: Total 18 (delta 4), reused 17 (delta 3)
Receiving objects: 100% (18/18), done.
Resolving deltas: 100% (4/4), done.
Checking connectivity... done.
Submodule path 'lib_a': checked out '8176a16db21a48a0969e18a51f2c2fb1869418fb'
```

The repository is ready for development!

> When cloning the repository, the submodules can be initialized and updated directly after the clone if the `--recursive` or `--recurse-submodules` option is given.

Subtree merging

An alternative to submodules is subtree merging. Subtree merging is a strategy that can be used when performing merges with Git. The strategy is useful when merging a branch (or, as we'll see in this recipe, another project) into a subdirectory of a Git repository instead of the root directory. When using the subtree merge strategy, the history of the subproject is joined with the history of the super project, while the subproject's history can be kept clean, except for commits intended to go upstream.

Getting ready

We'll use the same repositories as in the last recipe, and we'll reclone the super project to get rid of the submodule setup:

```
$ git clone https://github.com/PacktPublishing/Git-Version-Control-Cookbook-Second-Edition_Super.git
$ cd Git-Version-Control-Cookbook-Second-Edition_Super
```

How to do it...

1. We'll add the subproject as a new remote and fetch the history:

   ```
   $ git remote add lib_a https://github.com/PacktPublishing/Git-Version-Control-Cookbook-Second-Edition_lib_a.git
   $ git fetch lib_a
   warning: no common commits
   remote: Reusing existing pack: 18, done.
   remote: Total 18 (delta 0), reused 0 (delta 0)
   Unpacking objects: 100% (18/18), done.
   From https://github.com/PacktPublishing/Git-Version-Control-Cookbook-Second-Edition_lib_a.git
    * [new branch]      develop    -> lib_a/develop
    * [new branch]      master     -> lib_a/master
    * [new branch]      stable     -> lib_a/stable
   ```

2. We can now create a local branch, `lib_a_master`, which points to the same commit as the master branch in lib a (`lib_a/master`):

   ```
   $ git checkout -b lib_a_master lib_a/master
   Branch lib_a_master set up to track remote branch master from lib_a by rebasing.
   Switched to a new branch 'lib_a_master'
   ```

3. We can check the content of our working tree using the following command:

   ```
   $ ls
   README.md   a.txt
   ```

4. If we switch back to the `master` branch, we should see the content of the super repository in our directory:

```
$ git checkout master
Switched to branch 'master'
Your branch is up-to-date with 'origin/master'.
$ ls
README.md  super.txt
```

5. Git changes branches and populates the working directory as normal, even though the branches are originally from two different repositories. Now, we want to merge the history from `lib_a` into a subdirectory. First, we prepare a merge commit by merging with the `ours` strategy and make sure the commit isn't completed (we need to bring in all the files):

```
$ git merge -s ours --no-commit --allow-unrelated-histories
lib_a_master
Automatic merge went well; stopped before committing as requested
```

In short, what the `ours` strategy tells Git to do is the following: merge in this branch, but keep the resulting tree the same as the tree on the tip of this branch. So, the branch is merged, but all the changes it introduced are discarded. In our previous command line, we also passed the `--no-commit` option. This option stops Git from completing the merge, but leaves the repository in a merging state. We can now add the content of the `lib_a` repository to the `lib_a` folder in the repository root. We do this with `git read-tree` to make sure the two trees are exactly the same, as follows:

```
$ git read-tree --prefix=lib_a/ -u lib_a_master
```

6. Our current directory structure looks as follows:

```
$ tree
.
|-- README.md
|-- lib_a
|   |-- README.md
|   '-- a.txt
'-- super.txt
```

7. It is time to conclude the merge commit we started using the following command:

```
$ git commit -m 'Initial add of lib_a project'
[master 5066b7b] Initial add of lib_a project
```

Now, the subproject is added. Next, we'll see how we can update the super project with new commits from the subproject and how to copy commits made in the super project to the subproject.

8. We need to add and commit a few changes to the super project using the following command:

   ```
   $ echo "Lib_a included!" >> super.txt
   $ git add super.txt
   $ git commit -m "Update super.txt"
   [master 83ef9a4] Update super.txt
    1 file changed, 1 insertion(+)
   ```

9. Changes are made to the subproject and committed in the super project:

   ```
   $ echo "The b file in lib_a" >> lib_a/b.txt
   $ git add lib_a/b.txt
   $ git commit -m "[LIB_A] Enhance lib_a with b.txt"
   [master debe836] [LIB_A] Enhance lib_a with b.txt
    1 file changed, 1 insertion(+)
    create mode 100644 lib_a/b.txt
   ```

   The current history looks like the following screenshot:

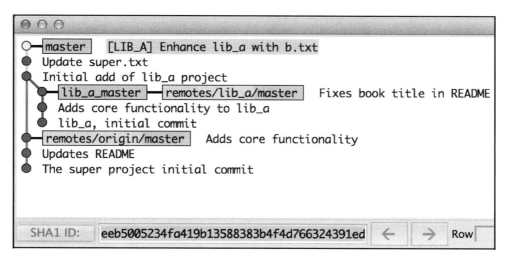

The merge can be seen in the preceding screenshot, and also the two root commits of the repository: the original root commit and the root from `lib_a`.

Repository Maintenance

10. Now, we will learn how to integrate new commits into the super repository made in the subproject, `lib_a`. Normally, we would do this by checking out the `lib_a_master` branch and performing pull on it to get the latest commit from the remote repository. However, as we are working with example repositories in this recipe, no new commits are available on the master branch. Instead, we'll use the `develop` and `stable` branches from `lib_a`. We'll now integrate commits from the develop branch into `lib_a`. We do this directly using the `lib_a/develop` reference in the repository as follows:

```
$ git merge -m '[LIB_A] Update lib_a project to latest state' -s subtree lib_a/develop
Merge made by the 'subtree' strategy.
 lib_a/a.txt | 2 ++
 1 file changed, 2 insertions(+)
```

Our master branch has now been updated with the commits from `lib_a/develop`, as shown in the following screenshot:

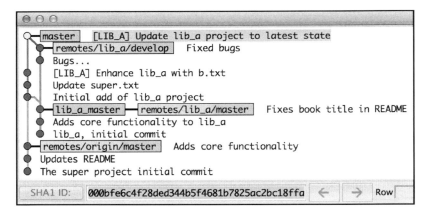

11. Now, it is time to add the commits we made in the `lib_a` directory back to the `lib_a` project. First, we'll change the `lib_a_master` branch and merge that with `lib_a/develop` to be as up-to-date as possible:

```
$ git checkout lib_a_master
$ git merge lib_a/develop
Updating 0d96e7c..ab47aca
Fast-forward
 a.txt | 2 ++
 1 file changed, 2 insertions(+)
```

12. We are now ready to merge changes from the super project with the subproject. In order to not merge the history of the super project with the subproject, we'll use the `--squash` option. This option stops Git from completing the merge and, unlike the previous case, where we also stopped a merge from recording a commit, it does not leave the repository in a merging state. The state of the working directory and staging area are, however, set as though a real merge has happened:

    ```
    $ git merge --squash -s subtree --no-commit master
    Squash commit -- not updating HEAD
    Automatic merge went well; stopped before committing as requested
    ```

13. Now, we can record a commit with all the changes made in `lib_a` from the super project:

    ```
    $ git commit -m 'Enhance lib_a with b.txt'
    [lib_a_master 01e45f7] Enhance lib_a with b.txt
     1 file changed, 1 insertion(+)
     create mode 100644 b.txt
    ```

    The history for the `lib_a` repository is seen in the following screenshot:

    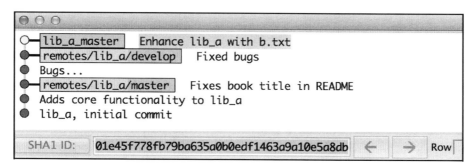

14. We can integrate more changes from `lib_a/stable` into the super project, but first we'll update the `lib_a_master` branch so that we can integrate them from here:

    ```
    $ git merge lib_a/stable
    Merge made by the 'recursive' strategy.
     a.txt | 2 ++
     1 file changed, 2 insertions(+)
    ```

[229]

A new commit was added to the subproject, as shown in the following screenshot:

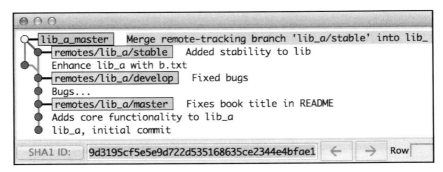

15. The last task is to integrate the new commit on `lib_a_master` into the `master` branch in the super repository. This is done as in the previous case, using the `subtree strategy` option to `git merge`:

```
$ git checkout master
$ git merge -s subtree -m '[LIB_A] Update to latest state of lib_a' lib_a_master
Merge made by the 'subtree' strategy.
 lib_a/a.txt | 2 ++
 1 file changed, 2 insertions(+)
```

The resulting history is shown in the following screenshot:

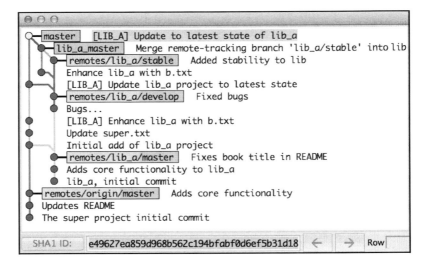

How it works...

When using the subtree strategy, Git finds out which subtree in your repository the branch you are trying to merge fits into. This is why we added the content of the `lib_a` repository with the `read-tree` command, to make sure we got the exact same SHA-1 ID for the `lib_a` directory in the super project as the root tree in the `lib_a` project. In the following example, the SHA-1 is found in the first command.

We can verify this by finding the SHA-1 of the `lib_a` tree in the super project in the commit that we merged the subproject with:

```
$ git log -1 | head -1 | awk '{print $2}'
0f10e563c6824402d30380c9f8fbf87769e64e8a
$ git ls-tree 0f10e563c6824402d30380c9f8fbf87769e64e8a 100644 blob
456a5df638694a699fff7a7ff31a496630b12d01 README.md 040000 tree
7d66ad11cb22c6d101c7ac9c309f7dce25231394 lib_a 100644 blob
c552dead26fdba634c91d35708f1cfc2c4b2a100 super.txt
```

The ID of the root tree at `lib_a/master` can be found out by using the following command:

```
$ git cat-file -p lib_a/master
tree 7d66ad11cb22c6d101c7ac9c309f7dce25231394
parent a7d76d9114941b9d35dd58e42f33ed7e32a9c134
author John Doe <john.doe@example.com> 1396553189 +0200
committer John Doe <john.doe@example.com> 1396553189 +0200

Fixes book title in README
```

See also

Another way of using subtree merging is with the `git subtree` command. This is not enabled by default in many Git installations, but has been distributed with Git since 1.7.11. You can see how to install and use it at the following links:

- For installation, go to
  https://github.com/git/git/blob/master/contrib/subtree/INSTALL
- To understand how to use a subtree, go to
  https://github.com/git/git/blob/master/contrib/subtree/git-subtree.txt

If you are a Homebrew or an Ubuntu user, their basic packages have support for subtrees. For Fedora, you must install additional packages.

Submodule versus subtree merging

There is no easy answer to the question of whether or not to use submodules or subtree merging for a project. When choosing submodules, a lot of extra pressure is put on the developers working on the project, as they need to make sure they keep the submodules and the super project in sync. When choosing to add a project by subtree merging, little to no extra complexity is added for developers. The repository maintainer, however, needs to make sure the subproject is up-to-date and that commits are added back to the subproject. Both methods work and are in use, and it is probably just a matter of getting used to either method. A completely different solution is to use the build system of the super project to fetch the necessary dependencies, as for example, Maven or Gradle does.

10
Patching and Offline Sharing

In this chapter, we will cover the following recipes:

- Creating patches
- Creating patches from branches
- Applying patches
- Sending patches
- Creating Git bundles
- Using a Git bundle
- Creating archives from a tree

Introduction

With the distributed nature of Git and the many existing hosting options available for it, it's very easy to share history between machines when they are connected through a network. In cases where the machines that need to share history are not connected or can't use the supported transport mechanisms, Git provides other methods to share history.

Git provides an easy way to format patches from existing history, sending them in an email and applying them to another repository. Git also has a bundle concept, where a bundle that contains only part of the history of a repository can be used as a remote for another repository. Finally, Git provides a simple and easy way to create an archive for a snapshot of the folder/subfolder structure of a given reference.

With the different methods provided by Git, it is easy to share history between repositories, especially where the normal push/pull methods are not available.

Patching and Offline Sharing

Creating patches

In this recipe, we'll learn how to make patches out of commits. Patches can be sent via email for quick sharing or can be copied to sneakernet devices (USB sticks, memory cards, external hard disk drives, and so on) if they need to be applied to an offline computer or suchlike. Patches can be useful methods to review code, as the reviewer can apply a patch to their repository, investigate the difference, and check the program. If the reviewer decides that the patch is good, they can publish (`push`) it to a public repository, given that the reviewer is the maintainer of the repository. If the reviewer rejects the patch, they can simply reset their branch to the original state and inform the author of the patch that more work is needed before it can be accepted.

Getting ready

In this example, we'll clone and use a new repository. The repository is just an example repository for Git commands and only contains some example commits:

```
$ git clone https://github.com/PacktPublishing/Git-Version-Control-Cookbook-Second-Edition_offline-sharing.git
$ cd Git-Version-Control-Cookbook-Second-Edition_offline-sharing
$ git checkout master
```

How to do it...

Let's see the history of the repository, as shown by `gitk`:

```
$ git log --graph --all --oneline
* 4bc2b08 (master) Calculate pi with more digits
| * 971ac91 (doc) Adds Documentation folder
| * 2a0c8d6 Add build information
| * 9d00fcc Update readme
| | * 583225a (HEAD -> develop) Adds functionality to prime-test a range of numbers
| | * f6c5713 Adds Makefile for easy building
| | * d00ffc0 Move print functionality of is_prime
| |/
|/|
* | 6e46ff8 Adds checker for prime number
|/
* 8bddff2 Adds math, pi calculation
* 6de7cef Offline sharing, patch, bundle and archive
```

There are three branches in the repository: master, develop, and doc. All of them differ from the others by one or more commits. On the master branch, we can now create a patch file for the latest commit on the master branch and store it in the latest-commit folder, as shown in the following command:

```
$ git format-patch -1 -o latest-commit
latest-commit/0001-Calculate-pi-with-more-digits.patch
```

If we look at the file created by the patch command, we will see the following:

```
$ cat latest-commit/0001-Calculate-pi-with-more-digits.patch

From 4bc2b08517141c2b84ae76ccaab3a380c19de8a6 Mon Sep 17 00:00:00 2001
From: John Doe <john.doe@example.com>
Date: Thu, 10 Apr 2014 09:19:29 +0200
Subject: [PATCH] Calculate pi with more digits

Dik T. Winter style

Build: gcc -Wall another_pi.c -o pi
Run: ./pi
---
 another_pi.c | 21 ++++++++++++++++++++++
 1 file changed, 21 insertions(+)
 create mode 100644 another_pi.c

$ diff --git a/another_pi.c b/another_pi.c
new file mode 100644
index 0000000..86df41b
--- /dev/null
+++ b/another_pi.c
@@ -0,0 +1,21 @@
+/* Pi with 800 digits
+ * Dik T. Winter style, but modified sligthly
+ * https://crypto.stanford.edu/pbc/notes/pi/code.html
+ */
+ #include <stdio.h>
+
+void another_pi (void) {
+  printf("800 digits of pi:\n");
+  int a=10000, b=0, c=2800, d=0, e=0, f[2801], g=0;
+  for ( ;b-c; )f[b++]=a/5;
+  for (;d=0,g=c*2;c-=14,printf("%.4d",e+d/a),e=d%a)
+  for (b=c; d+=f[b]*a, f[b]=d%--g,d/=g--,--b; d*=b);
+
+  printf("\n");
+}
```

```
+
+int main (void){
+ another_pi();
+
+ return 0;
+}
--
2.14.0
```

The previous snippet is the contents of the produced patch file. It contains a header much like an email with the `From`, `Date`, and `Subject` fields, a body with the commit message, and, after the three dashes (`---`), the actual patch, followed finally by two dashes (`--`), and the Git version used to generate the patch. The patch generated by `git format-patch` is in the **UNIX** mailbox format, but with a magic fixed timestamp to identify that it comes from `git format-patch` rather than a real mailbox. You can see the timestamp in the first line after the `sha-1` ID **Mon Sep 17 00:00:00 2001**.

How it works...

When generating the patch, Git will `diff` the commit at `HEAD` with its parent commit and use this `diff` as the patch. The `-1` option tells Git to only generate patches for the last commit, and `-o latest-commit` tells Git to store the patch in the `latest-commit` folder. The folder will be created if it does not already exist.

There's more...

If you want to create patches for several commits, say the last three commits, you just pass on `-3` to `git format-patch` instead of `-1`.

Format the latest three commits as patches in the `latest-commits` folder:

```
$ git format-patch -3 -o latest-commits
latest-commits/0001-Adds-math-pi-calculation.patch
latest-commits/0002-Adds-checker-for-prime-number.patch
latest-commits/0003-Calculate-pi-with-more-digits.patch

$ ls -1 latest-commits
0001-Adds-math-pi-calculation.patch
0002-Adds-checker-for-prime-number.patch
0003-Calculate-pi-with-more-digits.patch
```

Creating patches from branches

Instead of counting the number of commits you need to make patches for, you can create patches by specifying the target branch when running the `format-patch` command.

Getting ready

We'll use the same repository as in the previous example:

```
$ git clone https://github.com/PacktPublishing/Git-Version-Control-Cookbook-Second-Edition_offline-sharing.git
$ cd Git-Version-Control-Cookbook-Second-Edition_offline-sharing
```

Make sure we have the `develop` branch checked out:

```
$ git checkout develop
```

How to do it...

We'll pretend that we have been working on the `develop` branch and have made some commits. Now, we need to format patches for all those commits so that we can send them to the repository maintainer or carry them to another machine.

Let's see the commits on `develop`, not on `master`:

```
$ git log --oneline master..develop
583225a (HEAD -> develop) Adds functionality to prime-test a range of numbers
f6c5713 Adds Makefile for easy building
d00ffc0 Move print functionality of is_prime
```

Now, instead of running `git format-patch -3` to get patches made for these three commits, we'll tell Git to create patches for all of the commits that are not on the `master` branch:

```
$ git format-patch -o not-on-master master
not-on-master/0001-Move-print-functionality-of-is_prime.patch
not-on-master/0002-Adds-Makefile-for-easy-building.patch
not-on-master/0003-Adds-functionality-to-prime-test-a-range-of-numbers.patch
```

How it works...

Git makes a list of commits from `develop` that are not on the `master` branch, much like we did before creating the patches, and makes patches for these. We can check the contents of the `not-on-master`folder, which we specified as the output folder (`-o`) and verify that it contains the patches as expected:

```
$ ls -1 not-on-master
0001-Move-print-functionality-of-is_prime.patch
0002-Adds-Makefile-for-easy-building.patch
0003-Adds-functionality-to-prime-test-a-range-of-numbers.patch
```

There's more...

The `git format-patch` command has many options besides the `-<n>` option to specify the number of commits in order to create patches for the `-o <dir>` for the target directory. Some useful options are as follows:

- `-s, --signoff`: Adds a `Signed-off-by` line to the commit message in the patch file with the name of the committer. This is often required when mailing patches to the repository maintainers. This line is required for patches to be accepted when they are sent to the Linux kernel mailing list and the Git mailing list.
- `-n, --numbered`: Numbers the patch in the subject line as `[PATCH n/m]`.
- `--suffix=.<sfx>`: Sets the suffix of the patch; it can be empty and does not have to start with a dot.
- `-q, --quiet`: Suppresses the printing of patch filenames when generating patches.
- `--stdout`: Prints all commits to the standard output instead of creating files.

Applying patches

Now we know how to create patches from commits, it's time to learn how to apply them.

Getting ready

We'll use the repository from the previous examples, along with the generated patches, as follows:

```
$ cd Git-Version-Control-Cookbook-Second-Edition_offline-sharing
$ git checkout master
$ ls -1a
.
..
.git
Makefile
README.md
another_pi.c
latest-commit
math.c
not-on-master
```

How to do it...

First, we'll check out the `develop` branch and apply the patch generated from the `master` branch (`0001-Calculate-pi-with-more-digits.patch`) in the first example.

We use the Git `am` command to apply the patches; `am` is short for `apply from mailbox`:

```
$ git checkout develop
Your branch is up-to-date with 'origin/develop'.
$ git am latest-commit/0001-Calculate-pi-with-more-digits.patch
Applying: Adds functionality to prime-test a range of numbers
error: patch failed: math.c:47
error: math.c: patch does not apply
Patch failed at 0001 Adds functionality to prime-test a range of numbers
The copy of the patch that failed is found in: .git/rebase-apply/patch
When you have resolved this problem, run "git am --continue".
If you prefer to skip this patch, run "git am --skip" instead.
To restore the original branch and stop patching, run "git am --abort".
```

We can resolve the conflict in line 47 (an empty line to be removed) and continue:

```
$ git add math.c
$ git am --continue
Applying: Adds functionality to prime-test a range of numbers
```

We can also apply the `master` branch to the series of patches that was generated from the `develop` branch, as follows:

```
$ git checkout master
Switched to branch 'master'
Your branch is up-to-date with 'origin/master'.
$ git am not-on-master/*
Applying: Move print functionality of is_prime
```

Patching and Offline Sharing

```
Applying: Adds Makefile for easy building
Applying: Adds functionality to prime-test a range of numbers
```

How it works...

The `git am` command takes the mailbox file specified in the input and applies the patch in the file to the files needed. Then, a commit is recorded using the commit message and author information from the patch. The committer identity of the commit will be the identity of the person performing the `git am` command. We can see the author and committer information with `git log`, but we need to pass the `--pretty=fuller` option to also view the committer information:

```
$ git log -1 --pretty=fuller
commit 45e49d0c4fcd44b73e11d61e025a62ab2655e42d (HEAD -> master)
Author:     John Doe <john.doe@example.com>
AuthorDate: Wed Apr 9 21:50:18 2014 +0200
Commit:     John Doe <john.doe@example.com>
CommitDate: Sun Jun 3 21:58:46 2018 +0200

    Adds functionality to prime-test a range of numbers
```

There's more...

The `git am` command applies the patches in the files specified and records the commits in the repository. However, if you only want to apply the patch to the working tree or the staging area and not record a commit, you can use the `git apply` command.

We can try to apply the patch from the `master` branch to the `develop` branch once again; we just need to reset the `develop` branch first:

```
$ git checkout develop
Switched to branch 'develop'
Your branch is ahead of 'origin/develop' by 1 commit.
  (use "git push" to publish your local commits)
$ git reset --hard origin/develop
HEAD is now at c131c8b Adds functionality to prime-test a range of numbers
$ git apply latest-commit/0001-Calculate-pi-with-more-digits.patch
```

We can check the state of the repository with the `status` command:

```
$ git status
On branch develop
Your branch is up-to-date with 'origin/develop'.
```

[240]

```
Untracked files:
  (use "git add <file>..." to include in what will be committed)
    another_pi.c
    latest-commit/
    not-on-master/
nothing added to commit but untracked files present (use "git add" to
track)
```

We successfully applied the patch to the working tree. We can also apply it to the staging area and the working tree using the `--index` option, or only to the staging area using the `--cached` option.

Sending patches

In the previous example, you saw how to create and apply patches. You can, of course, attach these patch files directly to an email, but Git provides a way to send patches directly as emails with the `git send-email` command. The command requires some setting up, but how you do that is heavily dependent on your general mail and SMTP configuration. A general guide can be found in the Git help pages or by visiting: http://git-scm.com/docs/git-send-email.

Getting ready

We'll set up the same repository as in the previous example:

```
$ git clone https://github.com/PacktPublishing/Git-Version-Control-Cookbook-Second-Edition_offline-sharing.git
$ cd Git-Version-Control-Cookbook-Second-Edition_offline-sharing
```

How to do it...

First, we'll send the same patch as the one we created in the first example. We'll send it to ourselves using the email address we specified in our Git configuration. Let's create the patch again with `git format-patch` and send it with `git send-email`:

```
$ git format-patch -1 -o latest-commit
latest-commit/0001-Calculate-pi-with-more-digits.patch
```

Save the email address from the Git configuration to a variable as follows:

```
$ emailaddr=$(git config user.email)
```

Send the patch using the email address in both the `--to` and `--from` fields:

```
$ git send-email --to $emailaddr --from $emailaddr latest-commit/0001-Calculate-pi-with-more-digits.patch
latest-commit/0001-Calculate-pi-with-more-digits.patch
(mbox) Adding cc: John Doe <john.doe@example.com> from line 'From: John Doe <john.doe@example.com>'
  OK. Log says:
  Server: smtp.gmail.com
  MAIL FROM:<john.doe@example.com>
  RCPT TO:<john.doe@example.com>
  From: john.doe@example.com
  To: john.doe.example.com
  Subject: [PATCH] Calculate pi with more digits
  Date: Mon, 14 Apr 2014 09:00:11 +0200
  Message-Id: <1397458811-13755-1-git-send-email-john.doe@example.com>
  X-Mailer: git-send-email 1.9.1
```

Checking your email will reveal a new email in your inbox.

How it works...

As we saw in the previous examples, `git format-patch` creates the patch files in the Unix mbox format, so only a little extra effort is required to allow Git to send the patch as an email. When sending emails with `git send-email`, make sure your **Mail User Agent** (**MUA**) does not break the lines in the patch files, replace tabs with spaces, and so on. You can test this easily by sending a patch to yourself and checking whether it can be applied cleanly to your repository.

There's more...

The `send-email` command can, of course, be used to send more than one patch at a time. If a directory is specified instead of a single patch file, all the patches in that directory will be sent. We don't even have to generate the patch files before sending them; we can just specify the same range of revisions we want to send as we would have specified for the `format-patch` command. Then, Git will create the patches on the fly and send them. When we send a series of patches this way, it is good practice to create a cover letter with a bit of explanation about the patch series that follows. A cover letter can be created by passing `--cover-letter` to the `send-email` command. We'll try sending patches for the commits on `develop`, since it is branched from `master` (the same patches as in the second example), as follows:

```
$ git checkout develop
Switched to branch 'develop'
Your branch is up-to-date with 'origin/develop'.
$ git send-email --to john.doe@example.com --from
 john.doe@example.com --cover-letter --annotate origin/master
   /tmp/path/for/patches/0000-cover-letter.patch
   /tmp/path/for/patches/0001-Move-print-functionality-of-is_prime.patch
   /tmp/path/for/patches/0002-Adds-Makefile-for-easy-building.patch
   /tmp/path/for/patches/0003-Adds-functionality-to-prime-test-a-range-of-numbers.patch
    (mbox) Adding cc: John Doe <john.doe@example.com> from line 'From: John Doe <john.doe@example.com>'
   OK. Log says:
   Server: smtp.gmail.com
   MAIL FROM:<john.doe@example.com>
   RCPT TO:<john.doe@exmample.com>
   From: john.doe@example.com
   To: john.doe@example.com
   Subject: [PATCH 0/3] Cover Letter describing the patch series
   Date: Sat, 14 Jun 2014 23:35:14 +0200
   Message-Id: <1397459884-13953-1-git-send-email-john.doe@example.com>
   X-Mailer: git-send-email 1.9.1
   ...
```

We can check our email inbox and see the four emails we sent: the cover letter and the three patches.

Before sending the patches, the cover letter is filled out and, by default, has [PATCH 0/3] (if sending three patches) in the subject line. A cover letter with only the default template subject and body won't be sent as default. In the scripts that come with this chapter, the `git send-email` command invokes the `--force` and `--confirm=never` options. This was done for script automation to force Git to send the mails even though the cover letter has not been changed from the default. You can try to remove these options, put in the `--annotate` option, and run the scripts again. You should then be able to edit the cover letter and emails that contain the patches before sending them.

Creating Git bundles

Another method for sharing repository history between repositories is to use the `git bundle` command. A Git bundle is a series of commits that can work as a remote repository, but without having the full history of a repository included in the bundle.

Getting ready

We'll use a fresh clone of the `offline-sharing` repository, as follows:

```
$ git clone https://github.com/PacktPublishing/Git-Version-Control-Cookbook-Second-Edition_offline-sharing.git
$ cd Git-Version-Control-Cookbook-Second-Edition_offline-sharing
$ git checkout master
```

How to do it...

First, we'll create a root bundle, as shown in the following command, so that the history in the bundle forms a complete history and the initial commit is also included:

```
$ git bundle create myrepo.bundle master
Counting objects: 12, done.
Delta compression using up to 8 threads.
Compressing objects: 100% (11/11), done.
Writing objects: 100% (12/12), 1.88 KiB | 0 bytes/s, done.
Total 12 (delta 1), reused 0 (delta 0)
```

We can verify the bundle content with `git bundle verify`:

```
$ git bundle verify myrepo.bundle
The bundle contains this ref:
1e42a2dfa3a377d412efd27a77b973c75935c62a refs/heads/master
The bundle records a complete history.
myrepo.bundle is okay
```

To make it easy to remember which commit we included as the latest commit in the bundle, we create a `tag` that points to this commit; the commit is also pointed to by the `master` branch:

```
$ git tag bundleForOtherRepo master
```

We have created the root bundle that contains the initial commits of the repository history. We can now create a second bundle that contains the history from the tag we just created to the tip of the `develop` branch. Note that, in the following command, we use the same name for the bundle file, `myrepo.bundle`, and this will overwrite the old bundle file:

```
$ git bundle create myrepo.bundle bundleForOtherRepo..develop
Counting objects: 12, done.
Delta compression using up to 8 threads.
Compressing objects: 100% (9/9), done.
Writing objects: 100% (9/9), 1.47 KiB | 0 bytes/s, done.
Total 9 (delta 2), reused 0 (delta 0)
```

It might seem strange to overwrite the bundle file just after creating it, but there is some sense in giving bundle files the same name. As you will also see in the next recipe, when using a bundle file, you add it to your repository as a remote, the URL being the file path of the bundle. The first time you do this is with the root bundle file and the URL. The file path of the bundle file will be stored as the URL of the remote repository. So, the next time you need to update the repository, you just overwrite the bundle file and perform `fetch` from the repository.

If we verify the bundle, we can see which commit needs to exist in the target repository before the bundle can be used:

```
$ git bundle verify myrepo.bundle
The bundle contains this ref:
c131c8bb2bf8254e46c013bfb33f4a61f9d4b40e refs/heads/develop
The bundle requires this ref:
ead7de45a504ee19cece26daf45d0184296f3fec
myrepo.bundle is okay
```

We can check the history and see that the `ead7de4` commit is where `develop` is branched off, so it makes sense that this commit is the basis for the bundle we have just created:

```
$ gitk master develop
```

The previous command gives the following output:

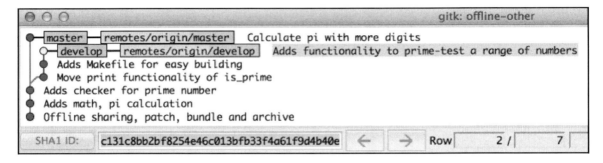

How it works...

The `bundle` command creates a binary file with the history of the specified commit range included. When creating the bundle as a range of commits that do not include the initial commit in the repository (for example, `bundleForOtherRepo..develop`), it's important to make sure that the range matches the history in the repository in which the bundle is going to be used.

Using a Git bundle

In the last example, we saw how we could create bundles from the existing history, which contains a specified range of history. Now, we'll learn how to use these bundles either to create a new repository or to add a history to an existing one.

Getting ready

We'll use the same repository and methods as in the last example to create bundles, but we'll recreate them in this example to be able to use them one at a time. First, we'll prepare the repository and the first bundle, as shown in the following commands:

```
$ rm -rf offline-sharing
$ git clone https://github.com/PacktPublishing/Git-Version-Control-Cookbook-Second-Edition_offline-sharing.git
$ cd Git-Version-Control-Cookbook-Second-Edition_offline-sharing
$ git checkout master
Branch master set up to track remote branch master from origin by rebasing.
Switched to a new branch 'master'
$ git bundle create myrepo.bundle master
Counting objects: 12, done.
Delta compression using up to 8 threads.
Compressing objects: 100% (11/11), done.
Writing objects: 100% (12/12), 1.88 KiB | 0 bytes/s, done. Total 12 (delta 1), reused 0 (delta 0)
$ git tag bundleForOtherRepo master
```

How to do it...

Now, let's create a new repository from the bundle file we just created. We can do that with the `git clone` command and by specifying the URL to the remote repository as the path to the bundle. We'll see how to do that in the following code snippet:

```
$ cd ..
$ git clone -b master Git-Version-Control-Cookbook-Second-Edition_offline-sharing/myrepo.bundle offline-other
Cloning into 'offline-other'...
Receiving objects: 100% (12/12), done.
Resolving deltas: 100% (1/1), done.
Checking connectivity... done.
```

The new repository is created in the `offline-other` folder. Let's check the history of that repository by using the following command:

```
$ cd offline-other
$ git log --oneline --decorate --all
1e42a2d (HEAD, origin/master, master) Calculate pi with more digits
ead7de4 Adds checker for prime number
337bfd0 Adds math, pi calculation
7229805 Offline sharing, patch, bundle and archive
```

Patching and Offline Sharing

The repository contains, as expected, all the history of the `master` branch in the original repository. We can now create a second bundle, the same as in the previous example, that contains history from the tag we created (`bundleForOtherRepo`) to the tip of the `develop` branch:

```
$ cd ..
$ cd Git-Version-Cookbook-Second-Edition_offline-sharing
$ git bundle create myrepo.bundle bundleForOtherRepo..develop
Counting objects: 12, done.
Delta compression using up to 8 threads.
Compressing objects: 100% (9/9), done.
Writing objects: 100% (9/9), 1.47 KiB | 0 bytes/s, done.
Total 9 (delta 2), reused 0 (delta 0)
$ git bundle verify myrepo.bundle
The bundle contains this ref:
c131c8bb2bf8254e46c013bfb33f4a61f9d4b40e refs/heads/develop
The bundle requires this ref:
ead7de45a504ee19cece26daf45d0184296f3fec
myrepo.bundle is okay
```

As we also saw in the previous example, the bundle requires the `ead7de45a504ee19cece26daf45d0184296f3fec` commit to already exist in the repository we'll use with the bundle. Let's check the repository we created from the first bundle for this commit by using the following command:

```
$ cd ..
$ cd offline-other
$ git show -s ead7de45a504ee19cece26daf45d0184296f3fec
  commit ead7de45a504ee19cece26daf45d0184296f3fec
  Author: John Doe <john.doe@example.com>
  Date:   Wed Apr 9 21:28:51 2014 +0200
  Adds checker for prime number
```

The commit exists. Now we can use the new bundle file as it has the same filename and path as the first bundle we created. We can just use `git fetch` in the `offline-other` repository as follows:

```
$ git fetch
  Receiving objects: 100% (9/9), done.
  Resolving deltas: 100% (2/2), done.
  From /path/to/repo/offline-sharing/myrepo.bundle
   * [new branch]      develop    -> origin/develop
```

We can now `checkout develop`, and verify that the history for the `develop` and `master` branches matches the one in the original repository:

```
$ git checkout develop
```

[248]

```
  Branch develop set up to track remote branch develop from origin by
rebasing.
  Switched to a new branch 'develop'
$ gitk --all
```

The previous command gives the following output:

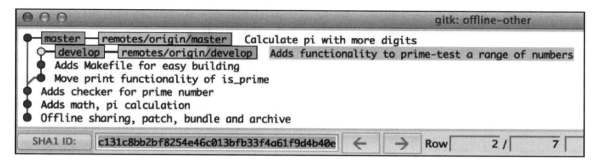

There's more...

The bundle is useful for updating the history of repositories on machines where the normal transport mechanisms can't be used due to missing network connections between the machines, firewall rules, and so on. There are, of course, other methods than the Git bundle for transporting history to remote machines. A bare repository on a USB stick could also be used, or even plain patches can be applied to a repository. The advantage of the Git bundle is that you don't have to write the entire history to a bare repository each time you need to update a remote, but only the part of history that is missing.

Creating archives from a tree

Sometimes, it's useful to have a snapshot of the directory structure, as specified by a particular commit, but without the corresponding history. This can, of course, be done by checking the particular commit followed by deleting/omitting the .git folder when creating an archive. But with Git, there is a better way to do this, which is built in so it is possible to create an archive from a particular commit or reference. When using Git to create the archive, you also make sure that the archive only contains the files tracked by Git and not any untracked files or folders you might have in your working directory.

Getting ready

We'll use the same `offline-sharing` repository as was used in the previous examples in this chapter:

```
$ git clone https://github.com/PacktPublishing/Git-Version-Control-Cookbook-Second-Edition_offline-sharing.git
$ cd Git-Version-Control-Cookbook-Second-Edition_offline-sharing
```

How to do it...

We'll start by creating an archive of the directory structure on the latest commit on the `master` branch. The `offline-sharing` repository is checked out on the `develop` branch by default, so we'll use the reference `origin/master` to specify the ref for the archive:

```
$ git archive --prefix=offline/ -o offline.zip origin/master
```

The `--prefix` option prepends the specified prefix to each file in the archive, effectively adding an `offline` directory as a root directory for the files in the repository, and the `-o` option tells Git to create the archive in the `offline.zip` file, which of course, is compressed in the ZIP format. We can investigate the ZIP archive to check whether the files contain the following:

```
$ unzip -l offline.zip
  Archive:  offline.zip
  1e42a2dfa3a377d412efd27a77b973c75935c62a
    Length      Date    Time    Name
   ---------  ---------- -----   ----
         0   04-10-14 09:19   offline/
       162   04-10-14 09:19   offline/README.md
       485   04-10-14 09:19   offline/another_pi.c
       672   04-10-14 09:19   offline/math.c
   ---------                  -------
      1319                    4 files
```

If we look in the Git repository in the `origin/master` commit, we can see that the files are the same; the `-l` option tells Git to specify each file's size, as follows:

```
$ git ls-tree -l origin/master
100644 blob c79cad47938a25888a699142ab3cdf764dc99193 162    README.md
100644 blob 86df41b3a8bbfb588e57c7b27742cf312ab3a12a 485    another_pi.c
100644 blob d393b41eb14561e583f1b049db716e35cef326c3 672    math.c
```

There's more...

The `archive` command can also be used to create an archive for a subdirectory of the repository. We can use this on the `doc` branch of the repository to ZIP the content of the `Documentation` folder:

```
$ git archive --prefix=docs/ -o docs.zip origin/doc:Documentation
```

Again, we can list the contents of the ZIP file and the `Documentation` tree at `origin/doc`, as follows:

```
$ unzip -l docs.zip
  Archive:  docs.zip
    Length      Date    Time    Name
    --------    ----    ----    ----
         0   04-13-14  21:14   docs/
        99   04-13-14  21:14   docs/README.md
       152   04-13-14  21:14   docs/build.md
    --------                   -------
       251                     3 files
$ git ls-tree -l origin/doc:Documentation
100644 blob b65b4fc78c0e39b3ff8ea549b7430654d413159f 99    README.md
100644 blob f91777f3e600db73c3ee7b05ea1b7d42efde8881 152   build.md
```

There are other format options besides the ZIP format for the archive, for example, `tar`, `tar.gz`, and so on. The format can be specified with the `--format=<format>` option or as a suffix to the output filename with the `-o` option. The following two commands will produce the same output file:

```
$ git archive --format=tar.gz HEAD > offline.tar.gz
$ git archive -o offline.tar.gz HEAD
```

Patching and Offline Sharing

The Git archive command behaves a bit differently if a commit/tag ID or a tree ID is passed as an identifier. If a commit or tag ID is given, the ID will be stored in a global extended pax header for the TAR format, and as a file comment for the ZIP format. If only the tree ID is given, no extra information will be stored. You can actually see this in the previous examples, where the first ID was given a branch as a reference. As the branch points to a commit, the ID of this commit was written as a comment on the file and we can actually see it in the output of the archive listing:

```
$ unzip -l offline.zip
  Archive:  offline.zip
  1e42a2dfa3a377d412efd27a77b973c75935c62a
    Length      Date    Time    Name
   --------    ----    ----    ----
         0   04-10-14  09:19   offline/
       162   04-10-14  09:19   offline/README.md
       485   04-10-14  09:19   offline/another_pi.c
       672   04-10-14  09:19   offline/math.c
   --------                    -------
      1319                     4 files
```

In the second example, we also passed a branch as a reference, but furthermore, we specified the `Documentation` folder as the subfolder we wanted to create an archive from. This corresponds to passing the ID of the tree to the archive command; hence, no extra information will be stored in the archive.

11
Tips and Tricks

In this chapter, we will cover the following recipes:

- Using git stash
- Saving and applying stashes
- Debugging with git bisect
- Using the blame command
- Coloring the UI in the prompt
- Autocompletion
- Bash prompt with status information
- More aliases
- Interactive add
- Interactive add with Git gui
- Ignoring files
- Showing and cleaning ignored files

Introduction

In this chapter, you will find some tips and tricks that can be useful in everyday Git work; from stashing away your changes when you get interrupted while doing an important task, to efficient bug hunting with `bisect` and `blame`, to finding color and status information in your prompt. We'll also look at aliases, how you can create clean commits by selecting which lines should be included in the commit and, finally, how you can ignore files.

Using git stash

In this example, we'll explore the `git stash` command and learn how we can use it to quickly `stash` away uncommitted changes and retrieve them again. This can be useful when you are interrupted while doing an urgent task and you are not yet ready to commit the work you currently have in your working directory. With the `git stash` command, you can save the state of your current working directory with/without a staging area and restore the working tree to a clean state.

Getting ready

In this example, we'll use the `Git-Version-Control-Cookbook-Second-Edition_tips_and_tricks` repository. We'll use the `master` branch, but before we are ready to try the `stash` command, we need to create some changes in the working directory and the staging area, as follows:

```
$ git clone https://github.com/PacktPublishing/Git-Version-Control-Cookbook-Second-Edition_tips_and_tricks.git
$ cd Git-Version-Control-Cookbook-Second-Edition_tips_and_tricks
$ git checkout master
```

Make some changes to `foo` and add them to the staging area, as follows:

```
$ echo "Just another unfinished line" >> foo
$ git add foo
```

Make some changes to `bar` and create a new file:

```
$ echo "Another line" >> bar
$ echo "Some content" > new_file
$ git status
On branch master
Your branch is up-to-date with 'origin/master'.
  Changes to be committed:
    (use "git reset HEAD <file>..." to unstage)
       modified:   foo
  Changes not staged for commit:
    (use "git add <file>..." to update what will be committed)
    (use "git checkout -- <file>..." to discard changes in working directory)
       modified:   bar
  Untracked files:
    (use "git add <file>..." to include in what will be committed)
```

```
        new_file
```

We can see that we have one file added to the staging area, `foo`, one modified file, `bar`, and an untracked file in the work area as well, `new_file`.

How to do it...

With the preceding state of our repository, we can stash away the changes so that we can work on something else. The basic command will put away changes from the staging area and changes made to tracked files. It leaves untracked files in the working directory:

```
$ git stash
Saved working directory and index state WIP on master: d611f06 Update foo
and bar
$ git status
On branch master
Your branch is up-to-date with 'origin/master'.
  Untracked files:
    (use "git add <file>..." to include in what will be committed)
      new_file
nothing added to commit but untracked files present (use "git add" to
track)
```

We can now work on something else and create and commit those changes. We'll change the first line of the `foo` file and create a commit with this change:

```
# MacOS (BSD sed):
$ sed -i '' 's/First line/This is the very first line of the foo file/' foo
# Linux (GNU sed):
$ sed 's/First line/This is the very first line of the foo file/' foo
$ git add foo $ git commit -m "Update foo" [master fa4b595] Update foo 1
file changed, 1 insertion(+), 1 deletion(-)
```

We can see the current work we have stashed away with the `git stash list` command:

```
$ git stash list
stash@{0}: WIP on master: b6dabd7 Update foo and bar
```

To get the changes we stashed away back, we can pop them from the `stash` stack, as follows:

```
$ git status
On branch master
Your branch is ahead of 'origin/master' by 1 commit.
  (use "git push" to publish your local commits)
Untracked files:
    (use "git add <file>..." to include in what will be committed)
    new_file
nothing added to commit but untracked files present (use "git add" to track)
$ git stash pop
Auto-merging foo
On branch master
Your branch is ahead of 'origin/master' by 1 commit.
  (use "git push" to publish your local commits)
Changes not staged for commit:
    (use "git add <file>..." to update what will be committed)
    (use "git checkout -- <file>..." to discard changes in working directory)
        modified:   bar
        modified:   foo
Untracked files:
    (use "git add <file>..." to include in what will be committed)
    new_file
no changes added to commit (use "git add" and/or "git commit -a")
Dropped refs/stash@{0} (733703568b7dcf2a0d5e4db5957d351417bcd793)
```

Now, the stashed changes are available again in the working repository and the `stash` entry has been deleted. Note that the changes are applied only to the working directory, although one of the files was staged when we created the `stash`.

How it works...

We have created two commits: one for the index and one for the work area. In `gitk`, we can see the commits that `stash` creates to put the changes away (`gitk stash`), as shown in the following screenshot:

Chapter 11

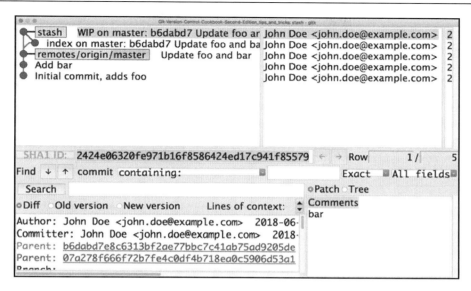

We can also see the state of the branches after we created the commit (`gitk --reflog`), as shown in the following screenshot:

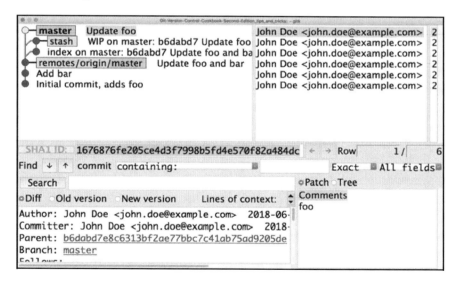

Tips and Tricks

Git actually creates two commits under the refs/stash namespace. One commit contains the contents of the staging area. This commit is called index on master. The other commit is the work in progress in the working directory, WIP on master. When Git puts away changes by creating commits, it can use its normal resolution methods to apply the stashed changes back to the working directory. This means that if a conflict arises when applying the stash, you need it to be solved in the usual way.

There's more...

In the preceding example, we saw only the very basic usage of the stash command, putting away changes to untracked files and changes added to the staging area. It is also possible to include untracked files in the stash command. This can be done with the --include-untracked option. We can add foo to the staging area; firstly, to have the same state as when we created the stash earlier and then to create a stash that includes untracked files:

```
$ git add foo
$ git stash --include-untracked
Saved working directory and index state WIP on master: 691808e Update foo
$ git status
On branch master
Your branch is ahead of 'origin/master' by 1 commit.
  (use "git push" to publish your local commits)
nothing to commit, working directory clean
```

Now, we can see that new_file has disappeared from the working directory. It's included in the stash, and we can check this with Gitk. It will show up as another commit of untracked files:

```
$ gitk master stash
```

Gitk shows the stash with its untracked files:

Chapter 11

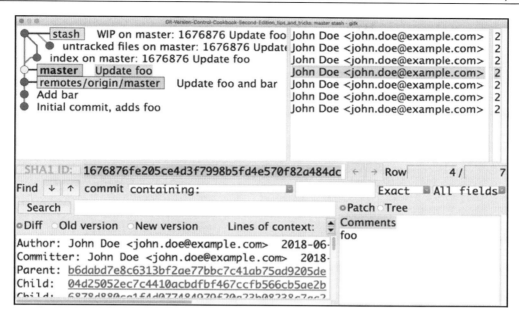

We can also make sure that the changes we added to the staging area are added back to the staging area after we apply the stash, so we end up with the exact same state as before we stashed our changes away:

```
$ git stash pop --index
On branch master
Your branch is ahead of 'origin/master' by 1 commit.
  (use "git push" to publish your local commits)
  Changes to be committed:
    (use "git reset HEAD <file>..." to unstage)
      modified:   foo
  Changes not staged for commit:
    (use "git add <file>..." to update what will be committed)
    (use "git checkout -- <file>..." to discard changes in working directory)
      modified:   bar
  Untracked files:
    (use "git add <file>..." to include in what will be committed)
      new_file
Dropped refs/stash@{0} (ff331af57406948619b0671dab8b4f39da1e8fa2)
```

[259]

It's also possible to put away only the changes in the working directory, while keeping the changes in the staging area. We can do this either for only the tracked files or by stashing away untracked files (`--include-untracked`), as follows:

```
$ git stash --keep-index --include-untracked
Saved working directory and index state WIP on master: 00dd8f8 Update foo
HEAD is now at 00dd8f8 Update foo
$ git status
On branch master
Your branch is ahead of 'origin/master' by 1 commit.
  (use "git push" to publish your local commits)
  Changes to be committed:
    (use "git reset HEAD <file>..." to unstage)
      modified:   foo
```

Saving and applying stashes

When stashing away work, we can easily have more than one state stashed away at a time. However, the default names for stashed away changes aren't always helpful. In this example, we'll see how we can save stashes and name them so that it is easy to identify them again when listing the content of the stash. We'll also learn how to apply a stash without deleting it from the stash list.

Getting ready

We'll use the same repository as in the previous example, continuing from the state we left it in:

```
$ cd Git-Version-Control-Cookbook-Second-Edition_tips_and_tricks
$ git status
On branch master
Your branch is ahead of 'origin/master' by 1 commit.
  (use "git push" to publish your local commits)
  Changes to be committed:
    (use "git reset HEAD <file>..." to unstage)
      modified:   foo
$ git stash list
stash@{0}: WIP on master: 4447f69 Update foo
```

How to do it...

To save the current state to a stash with a description we can remember at a later point in time, use the following command:

```
$ git stash save 'Updates to foo'
Saved working directory and index state On master: Updates to foo
```

Our `stash` list now looks like the following:

```
$ git stash list
stash@{0}: On master: Updates to foo
stash@{1}: WIP on master: 2302181 Update foo
```

We can change `bar` and create a new `stash`:

```
$ echo "Another change" >> bar
$ git stash save 'Made another change to bar'
Saved working directory and index state On master: Made another change to bar
$ git stash list
stash@{0}: On master: Made another change to bar
stash@{1}: On master: Updates to foo
stash@{2}: WIP on master: 2302181 Update foo
```

We can apply the stashes back to the working tree (and staging area with the `--index` option) without deleting them from the `stash` list:

```
$ git stash apply 'stash@{1}'
On branch master
Your branch is ahead of 'origin/master' by 1 commit.
  (use "git push" to publish your local commits)
Changes not staged for commit:
  (use "git add <file>..." to update what will be committed)
  (use "git checkout -- <file>..." to discard changes in working directory)
        modified:   foo
no changes added to commit (use "git add" and/or "git commit -a")
$ git stash apply --quiet 'stash@{0}'
$ git stash list
stash@{0}: On master: Made another change to bar
stash@{1}: On master: Updates to foo
stash@{2}: WIP on master: 2302181 Update foo
```

The stashes are still in the `stash` list, and they can be applied in any order and referred to with the `stash@{stash-no}` syntax. The `--quiet` option suppresses the status output after the stashes have been applied.

There's more...

For stashes applied with `git stash apply`, the `stash` needs to be deleted with `git stash drop`:

```
$ git stash drop 'stash@{1}'
Dropped stash@{1} (e634b347d04c13fc0a0d155a3c5893a1d3841fcd)
$ git stash list
stash@{0}: On master: Made another change to bar
stash@{1}: WIP on master: 1676cdb Update foo
```

Keeping the stashes in the `stash` list by using `stash apply` and explicitly deleting them with `git stash drop` has some advantages over just using `stash pop`. When using the `pop` option, the stashes in the list are automatically deleted if they can be successfully applied. But if it fails and triggers the conflict resolution mode, the stash applied is not dropped from the list and continues to exist on the `stash` stack. This might later lead to accidentally using the wrong `stash` because it was thought to have been removed. By consistently using `git stash apply` and `git stash drop`, you can avoid this scenario.

> The `git stash` command can also be used to apply debug information to an application. Let's pretend you have been bug hunting and have added a lot of debug statements to your code in order to track down a bug. Instead of deleting all those debug statements, you can save them as a Git stash:
> `$ git stash save "Debug info stash"`
> Then, if you need debug statements later, you can just apply the stash and you'll be ready to debug.

Debugging with git bisect

The `git bisect` command is an excellent tool to find which commit caused a bug in the repository. The tool is particularly useful if you are looking at a long list of commits that may contain the bug. The `bisect` command performs a binary search through the commit history to find the commit that introduced the bug as fast as possible. The binary search method, or bisection method, as it is also called, is a search method where an algorithm finds the position of a key in a sorted array. In each step of the algorithm, the key is compared to the middle value of the array and if they match, the position is returned. Otherwise, the algorithm repeats its search in the subarray to the right or left of the middle value, depending on whether the middle value was greater or less than the key. In the Git context, the list of commits in the history makes up for the array of values to be tested, and the key can be a test if the code can be compiled successfully at the given commit. The binary search algorithm has a performance of $O(\log n)$.

Getting ready

We'll use the same repository as seen in the last example, but from a clean state:

```
$ git clone https://github.com/PacktPublishing/Git-Version-Control-Cookbook-Second-Edition_tips_and_tricks.git
$ cd Git-Version-Control-Cookbook-Second-Edition_tips_and_tricks
$ git checkout bug_hunting
```

The `bug_hunting` branch contains 23 commits, since it branched off from the `master` branch. We know that the tip of the `bug_hunting` branch contains the bug and that it was introduced in a commit, since it branched off from `master`. The bug was introduced in the following commit:

```
commit 83c22a39955ec10ac1a2a5e7e69fe7ca354129af
Author: HAL 9000 <John.Doe@example.com>
Date:   Tue May 13 09:53:45 2014 +0200
Bugs...
```

Tips and Tricks

The bug is clearly visible in the map.txt file, in the middle of Australia. The following snippet of the file shows the bug:

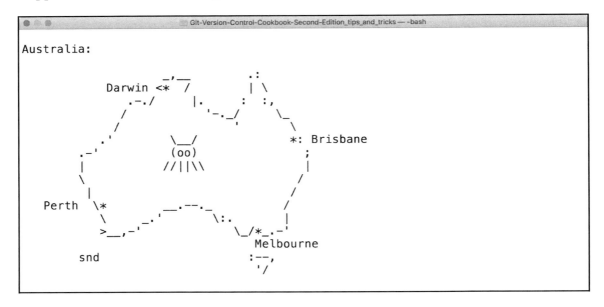

Now, all we need is some way to reproduce/detect the bug so that we can test the different commits. This could, for example, simply be to compile the code, run tests, and so on.

For this example, we'll create a test script to check for bugs in the code (a simple grep for oo should do it in this example; see for yourself if you can find the bug in the map.txt file):

```
$ echo "! grep -q oo map.txt" > ../test.sh
$ chmod +x ../test.sh
```

It's better to create this test script outside the repository to prevent interactions between checkouts, compilation, and so on in the repository.

How to do it...

To begin bisecting, we simply type the following:

```
$ git bisect start
```

To mark the current commit (HEAD -> bug_hunting) as bad, we type the following:

```
$ git bisect bad
```

We also want to mark the last known good commit (master) as good:

```
$ git bisect good master
Bisecting: 11 revisions left to test after this (roughly 4 steps)
[9d2cd13d4574429dd0dcfeeb90c47a2d43a9b6ef] Build map part 11
```

This time, something happened. Git did a checkout of 9d2cd13, which it wants us to test and mark as either good or bad. It also tells us there are 11 revisions to test after this, and it can be done in approximately four steps. This is how the bisecting algorithm works: every time a commit is marked as good or bad, Git will checkout the one between the commit that has just been marked and the current commit of opposite value. In this way, Git quickly narrows down the number of commits to check. It also knows that there are approximately four steps, and this makes sense since, with 11 revisions left, the maximum number of tries is $log_2(11) = 3.46$ before the faulty commit is found.

We can test with the test.sh script we created previously, and based on the return value, mark the commit as good or bad:

```
$ ../test.sh; test $? -eq 0 && git bisect good || git bisect bad
# git bisect good
Bisecting: 5 revisions left to test after this (roughly 3 steps)
[c45cb51752a4fe41f52d40e0b2873350b95a9d7c] Build map part 16
```

The test marks the commit as good and Git checks out the next commit to be marked, until we hit the commit that introduces the bug:

```
$ ../test.sh; test $? -eq 0 && git bisect good || git bisect bad
# git bisect bad
Bisecting: 2 revisions left to test after this (roughly 2 steps)
[83c22a39955ec10ac1a2a5e7e69fe7ca354129af] Bugs...
$ ../test.sh; test $? -eq 0 && git bisect good || git bisect bad
# git bisect bad
Bisecting: 0 revisions left to test after this (roughly 1 step)
[670ab8c42a6cb1c730c7c4aa0cc26e5cc31c9254] Build map part 13
$ ../test.sh; test $? -eq 0 && git bisect good || git bisect bad
# git bisect good
83c22a39955ec10ac1a2a5e7e69fe7ca354129afis the first bad commit
```

```
commit 83c22a39955ec10ac1a2a5e7e69fe7ca354129af
Author: HAL 9000 <aske.olsson@switch-gears.dk>
Date:   Tue May 13 09:53:45 2014 +0200
    Bugs...
:100644 100644 8a13f6bd858aefb70ea0a7d8f601701339c28bb0
1afeaaa370a2e4656551a6d44053ee0ce5c3a237 M map.txt
```

After four steps, Git has identified the `83c22a3` commit as the first bad commit. We can end the `bisect` session and take a closer look at the commit:

```
$ git bisect reset
Previous HEAD position was 670ab8c... Build map part 13
Switched to branch 'bug_hunting'
Your branch is up-to-date with 'origin/bug_hunting'.
$ git show 83c22a39955ec10ac1a2a5e7e69fe7ca354129af
commit 83c22a39955ec10ac1a2a5e7e69fe7ca354129af
Author: HAL 9000 <john.doe@example.com>
Date:   Tue May 13 09:53:45 2014 +0200
    Bugs...
diff --git a/map.txt b/map.txt
index 8a13f6b..1afeaaa 100644
--- a/map.txt
+++ b/map.txt
@@ -34,6 +34,6 @@ Australia:
                       .-./         |.     :     :,
                     /              '-._/       _
                   /                    '
 -             .'                                   *: Brisbane
 -           .-'                                    ;
 -           |                                      |
 +             .'         __/                       *: Brisbane
 +           .-'         (oo)                       ;
 +           |           //|\                       |
```

Clearly, a bug was introduced with this commit.

The following annotated screenshot shows the steps taken by the `bisect` session:

Chapter 11

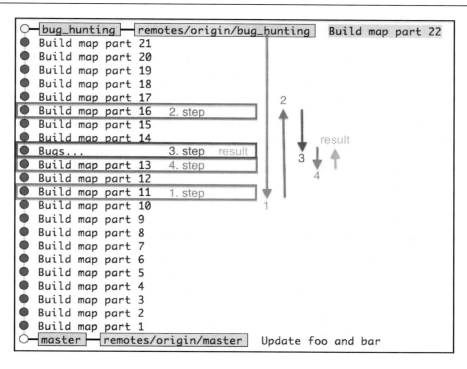

Note that the bisection algorithm actually hits the faulty commit in the third step, but it needs to look further to make sure that the commit isn't just a child commit of the faulty commit, and is in fact the commit that introduced the bug.

There's more...

Instead of running all the bisecting steps manually, it's possible to do it automatically by passing Git a script, makefile, or test to run on each commit. The script needs to exit with a **zero-status** to mark a commit as good and a **non-zero** status to mark it as bad. We can use the test.sh script we created at the beginning of this chapter for this. First, we set up the good and bad commits:

```
$ git bisect start HEAD master
Bisecting: 11 revisions left to test after this (roughly 4 steps)
[9d2cd13d4574429dd0dcfeeb90c47a2d43a9b6ef] Build map part 11
```

Then, we tell Git to run the `test.sh` script and automatically mark the commits:

```
$ git bisect run ../test.sh running ../test.sh Bisecting: 5 revisions left
to test after this (roughly 3 steps)
[c45cb51752a4fe41f52d40e0b2873350b95a9d7c] Build map part 16 running
../test.sh Bisecting: 2 revisions left to test after this (roughly 2 steps)
[83c22a39955ec10ac1a2a5e7e69fe7ca354129af] Bugs... running ../test.sh
Bisecting: 0 revisions left to test after this (roughly 1 step)
[670ab8c42a6cb1c730c7c4aa0cc26e5cc31c9254] Build map part 13 running
../test.sh 83c22a39955ec10ac1a2a5e7e69fe7ca354129afis the first bad commit
commit 83c22a39955ec10ac1a2a5e7e69fe7ca354129af Author: HAL 9000
<john.doe@example.com> Date: Tue May 13 09:53:45 2014 +0200   Bugs...
:100644 100644 8a13f6bd858aefb70ea0a7d8f601701339c28bb0
1afeaaa370a2e4656551a6d44053ee0ce5c3a237 M map.txt bisect run success
```

Git found the same commit and we can now exit the bisecting session:

```
$ git bisect reset
Previous HEAD position was 670ab8c... Build map part 13
Switched to branch 'bug_hunting'
```

Using the blame command

The `bisect` command is good when you don't know where in your code there is a bug, but you can test for it and thereby find the commit that introduced it. If you already know where in the code the bug is but want to find the commit that introduced it, you can use `git blame`. The `blame` command will annotate every line in the file with the commit that most recently touched that line, making it easy to find the commit ID and then the full context of the commit.

Getting ready

We'll use the same repository and branch as in the bisect example:

```
$ git clone
https://github.com/PacktPublishing/Git-Version-Control-Cookbook-Second-Edition_tips_and_tricks.git
$ cd Git-Version-Control-Cookbook-Second-Edition_tips_and_tricks
$ git checkout bug_hunting
```

How to do it...

We know that the bug is in map.txt on lines 37-39. To annotate each line in the file with the commit ID and author, we'll run git blame on the file. We can further limit the search to specific lines with the -L <from>,<to> option, as shown in the following screenshot:

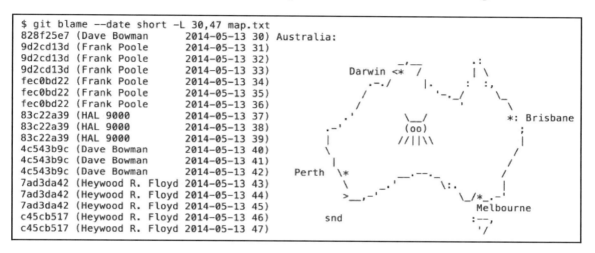

From the output, it can clearly be seen that the commit with the ID 83c22a39 by HAL 9000 introduced the bug.

There's more...

The blame command can be used even if the file has been refactored and the code has been moved around. With the -M option, the blame command can detect lines that have been moved within the file, and with the -C option, Git can detect lines that were moved or copied from other files in the same commit. If the -C option is used three times -CCC, the blame command will find lines that were copied from other files in any commit.

Coloring the UI in the prompt

By default, Git has no colors when displaying information in the terminal. However, displaying colors is a feature of Git that is only a configuration away.

Getting ready

We'll use the `Git-Version-Control-Cookbook-Second-Edition_tips_and_tricks` repository:

```
$ git clone
https://github.com/PacktPublishing/Git-Version-Control-Cookbook-Second-Edition_tips_and_tricks.git
$ cd Git-Version-Control-Cookbook-Second-Edition_tips_and_tricks
```

How to do it...

First, we'll edit and add `foo`:

```
$ echo "And another line" >> foo
$ git add foo
```

Change `foo` some more, but don't add it to the staging area:

```
$ echo "Last line ...so far" >> foo
```

Create a new file called `test`:

```
$ touch test
```

The `git status` command will show us the status:

```
$ git status
On branch master
Your branch is up-to-date with 'origin/master'.
  Changes to be committed:
    (use "git reset HEAD <file>..." to unstage)
      modified:   foo
  Changes not staged for commit:
    (use "git add <file>..." to update what will be committed)
    (use "git checkout -- <file>..." to discard changes in working directory)
      modified:   foo
  Untracked files:
    (use "git add <file>..." to include in what will be committed)
      test
```

We can set the `color.ui` configuration to `auto` or `true` to get color in the UI when required:

```
$ git config --global color.ui true
```

```
$ git status
On branch master
Your branch is up-to-date with 'origin/master'.
Changes to be committed:
  (use "git reset HEAD <file>..." to unstage)
    modified:   foo

Changes not staged for commit:
  (use "git add <file>..." to update what will be committed)
    (use "git checkout -- <file>..." to discard changes in working directory)
      modified:   foo
Untracked files:
  (use "git add <file>..." to include in what will be committed)
  test
```

There's more...

The `color.ui` configuration works with a long range of Git commands, `diff`, `log`, and `branch` included. The following is an example of `git log` when setting `color.ui` to `true`:

```
$ git log --oneline --decorate --graph
* c111003 (HEAD -> master, origin/master, origin/HEAD) Update foo and bar
* 270e97b Add bar
* 43fd490 Initial commit, adds foo
```

Autocompletion

Git comes with built-in support for the autocompletion of Git commands for the `bash` and `zsh` shells. If you use either of these shells, you can enable the autocompletion feature and let the `<tab>` option help you complete commands.

Getting ready

Generally, the autocompletion feature is distributed with the Git installation, but it is not enabled by default on all platforms or distributions. To enable it, we need to find the `git-completion.bash` file distributed/installed with the Git installation.

Linux

For Linux users, the location may vary depending on the distribution. Generally, the file can be found at /etc/bash_completion.d/git-completion.bash.

Mac

For Mac users, it can generally be found at /Library/Developer/CommandLineTools/usr/share/git-core/git-completion.bash.

If you installed Git from Homebrew, it can be found at /usr/local/Cellar/git/2.15.0/etc/bash_completion.d/git-completion.bash.

Windows

With the **Msysgit** installation on Windows, the completion functions are already enabled in the Git Bash shell it bundles.

If you can't find the file on your system, you can obtain the latest version from https://github.com/git/git/blob/master/contrib/completion/git-completion.bash and install it in your home directory.

How to do it...

To enable the completion feature, you need to run the source command on the completion file, which you can do by adding the following lines to your .bashrc or .zshrc file, depending on your shell and the location of the Git completion file:

```
if [ -f /etc/bash_completion.d/git-completion.bash ]; then
    source /etc/bash_completion.d/git-completion.bash
fi
```

How it works...

Now you are ready to try this. Switch to an existing Git repository, for example, cookbook-tips-tricks, and type the following commands:

```
$ git che<tab><tab>
checkout        cherry          cherry-pick
```

You can add another `c<tab>` and the command will autocomplete to `checkout`. But the autocompletion feature doesn't only complete commands; it can also help you complete branch names, and so on. This means that you can continue with the checkout and write `mas<tab>`. You should be able to see the output completed to the `master` branch, unless you are in a repository where there are several branches starting with `mas`.

There's more...

The completion feature also works with options. This is quite useful if you can't remember the exact option but you may remember some of it, for example, when using `git branch`:

```
git branch --<tab><tab>
--abbrev=              --merged           --set-upstream-to=
--color                --no-abbrev        --track
--contains             --no-color         --unset-upstream
--edit-description     --no-merged        --verbose
--list                 --no-track
```

Bash prompt with status information

Another cool feature Git provides is having the prompt display status information if the current working directory is a Git repository.

Getting ready

For the status information prompt to work, we also need to source another file, `git-prompt.sh`, which is usually distributed with the Git installation and located in the same directory as the completion file.

How to do it...

In your `.bashrc` or `.zshrc` file, add the following code snippet, again depending on your shell and the location of the `git-prompt.sh` file:

```
if [ -f /etc/bash_completion.d/git-prompt.sh ]; then
    source /etc/bash_completion.d/git-prompt.sh
fi
```

How it works...

To make use of the Command Prompt, we must change the `PS1` variable; usually this is set to something like the following:

```
PS1='\u@\h:\w$ '
```

The preceding command shows the current user, an @ sign, the hostname, the current working directory relative to the user's home directory, and finally, the $ character:

```
john.doe@yggdrasil:~/cookbook-tips-tricks$
```

We can change this to add a branch name after the working directory by adding `$(__git_ps1 " (%s)")` to the `PS1` variable:

```
PS1='\u@\h:\w$(__git_ps1 " (%s)") $ '
```

Our prompt will now look like this:

```
john.doe@yggdrasil:~/cookbook-tips-tricks (master) $
```

It is also possible to show the state of the working tree, the index, and so on. We can enable these features by exporting some environment variables in the `.bashrc` file that `git-prompt.sh` picks up.

The following environment variables can be set:

Variable	Value	Effect
GIT_PS1_SHOWDIRTYSTATE	Nonempty	Shows * for unstaged changes and + for staged changes.
GIT_PS1_SHOWSTASHSTATE	Nonempty	Shows the $ character if something is stashed.
GIT_PS1_SHOWUNTRACKEDFILES	Nonempty	Shows the % character if there are untracked files in the repository.
GIT_PS1_SHOWUPSTREAM	auto verbose name legacy Git svn	Auto shows whether you are behind (<) or ahead (>) of the upstream branch. A <> value is displayed if the branch is diverged and = if it is up to date. Verbose shows the number of commits behind/ahead. Name shows the upstream name. Legacy is verbose for old versions of Git. Git compares `HEAD` to `@{upstream}`. SVN compares `HEAD` to `svn upstream`.

[274]

`GIT_PS1_DESCRIBE_STYLE`	contains branch describe default	Displays extra information when on a detached `HEAD`. Contains is relative to a newer annotated tag (`v1.6.3.2~35`). Branch is relative to a newer tag or branch (`master~4`). Describe is relative to an older annotated tag (`v1.6.3.1-13-gdd42c2f`). Default is the tag that matches exactly.

Let's try to set some of the variables in the `~/.bashrc` file:

```
export GIT_PS1_SHOWUPSTREAM=auto
export GIT_PS1_SHOWDIRTYSTATE=enabled
PS1='u@h:w$(__git_ps1 " (%s)") $ '
```

Let's see the `~/.bashrc` file in action:

```
john.doe@yggdrasil:~ $ cd tips_and_tricks/
john.doe@yggdrasil:~/tips_and_tricks (master=) $ touch test
john.doe@yggdrasil:~/tips_and_tricks (master=) $ git add test
john.doe@yggdrasil:~/tips_and_tricks (master +=) $ echo "Testing" > test
john.doe@yggdrasil:~/tips_and_tricks (master *+=) $ git commit -m "test"
[master 5c66d65] test
 1 file changed, 0 insertions(+), 0 deletions(-)
 create mode 100644 test
john.doe@yggdrasil:~/tips_and_tricks (master *>) $
```

When using the `__git_ps1` option, Git will also display information when merging, rebasing, bisecting, and so on. This is very useful and a lot of `git status` commands suddenly become unnecessary, as you have the information right there in the prompt.

There's more...

What is a terminal without some colors these days? The `git-prompt.sh` script also supports this. All we need to do is set the `GIT_PS1_SHOWCOLORHINTS` variable to a nonempty value and, instead of using `PS1`, we need to use `PROMPT_COMMAND`. Let's change `~/.bashrc`:

```
export GIT_PS1_SHOWUPSTREAM=auto
export GIT_PS1_SHOWDIRTYSTATE=enabled
export GIT_PS1_SHOWCOLORHINTS=enabled
PROMPT_COMMAND='__git_ps1 "\u@\h:\w" "\$ "'
```

If we redo the same scenario as the previous one, we get the following:

```
jd@yggdrasil:~/Packt/Git-Version-Control-Cookbook-Second-Edition_tips_and_tricks (master=)$ touch test
jd@yggdrasil:~/Packt/Git-Version-Control-Cookbook-Second-Edition_tips_and_tricks (master=)$ git add test
jd@yggdrasil:~/Packt/Git-Version-Control-Cookbook-Second-Edition_tips_and_tricks (master +=)$ echo "Testing" > test
jd@yggdrasil:~/Packt/Git-Version-Control-Cookbook-Second-Edition_tips_and_tricks (master *+=)$ git commit -m "test"
[master 09a97ad] test
 1 file changed, 0 insertions(+), 0 deletions(-)
 create mode 100644 test
jd@yggdrasil:~/Packt/Git-Version-Control-Cookbook-Second-Edition_tips_and_tricks (master *>)$
```

See also

If you are using `zsh` or just want to try something new with many features, such as completion, Git support, and so on, you should take a look at the `oh-my-zsh` framework, available for `zsh` at: https://github.com/robbyrussell/oh-my-zsh.

More aliases

In Chapter 2, *Configuration*, we saw how we can create aliases and looked at a few examples of them. In this section, we will look at some more examples of useful aliases.

Getting ready

We will have to clone the `cookbook-tips-tricks` repository and check out the `aliases` branch:

```
$ git clone https://github.com/PacktPublishing/Git-Version-Control-Cookbook-Second-Edition_tips_and_tricks.git
$ cd Git-Version-Control-Cookbook-Second-Edition_tips_and_tricks
$ git checkout aliases
```

How to do it...

Here, we'll see some examples of aliases, with a short description of each of them and an example of how to use them. The aliases are just made for the local repository; use `--global` to make them available for all the repositories.

1. Let's begin with an alias to show the current branch only:

   ```
   $ git config alias.b "rev-parse --abbrev-ref HEAD"
   $ git b
   aliases
   ```

2. To show a compact graph history view with colors, the following alias will save you many keystrokes:

   ```
   $ git config alias.graph "log --graph --pretty=format:'%Cred%h%Creset -%C(yellow)%d%Creset %s %Cgreen(%cr) %C(bold blue)<%an>%Creset' --abbrev-commit --date=relative"
   $ git graph origin/conflict aliases
   ```

   The following screenshot shows you a typical output, where commits are colored red, committers are colored blue, and so on:

   ```
   * 23c230c - (origin/conflict) Spaceship upgrade (11 days ago) <John Doe>
   * d51acd7 - Adds spaceship (11 days ago) <John Doe>
   * b5f195d - Adds directory structure (11 days ago) <John Doe>
   * a274c0b - Update foo and bar (11 days ago) <John Doe>
   * 455f8fb - Add bar (11 days ago) <John Doe>
   * 4f49d8f - Initial commit, adds foo (11 days ago) <John Doe>
   * 75e6d44 - (HEAD -> aliases, origin/aliases) Better spaceship design (11 days ago) <John Doe>
   * a4293e2 - Adds spaceship (11 days ago) <John Doe>
   * 76824a9 - Adds directory structure (11 days ago) <John Doe>
   * ef58221 - Update foo and bar (11 days ago) <John Doe>
   * 43fac3e - Add bar (11 days ago) <John Doe>
   * 8b0e66e - Initial commit, adds foo (11 days ago) <John Doe>
   ```

3. When resolving a conflicted merge, it can be useful to get a list of the conflicted/unmerged files:

   ```
   $ git config alias.unmerged '!git ls-files --unmerged | cut -f2 | sort -u'
   ```

4. We can see the previous alias in action by merging the `origin/conflict` branch:

   ```
   $ git merge origin/conflict
   Auto-merging spaceship.txt
   CONFLICT (content): Merge conflict in spaceship.txt
   Automatic merge failed; fix conflicts and then commit the result.
   ```

5. First, check the output of `git status`:

   ```
   $ git status
   On branch aliases
   Your branch is up-to-date with 'origin/aliases'.
   You have unmerged paths.
     (fix conflicts and run "git commit")
     Unmerged paths:
       (use "git add <file>..." to mark resolution)
         both modified:      spaceship.txt
   no changes added to commit (use "git add" and/or "git commit -a")
   ```

6. We see the unmerged path mentioned in the output. Let's use the `unmerged` alias to get a simple list of unmerged files:

   ```
   $ git unmerged
   spaceship.txt
   ```

7. You can abort the merge as follows:

   ```
   $ git merge --abort
   ```

8. During a work day, you will type `git status` many times. Adding a shorthand status can be helpful:

   ```
   $ git config alias.st "status"
   $ git st
   On branch aliases
   Your branch is up-to-date with 'origin/aliases'.
   nothing to commit, working directory clean
   ```

9. An even shorter status with branch and file information can be defined as follows:

   ```
   $ git config alias.s 'status -sb'
   ```

10. To try it out, first modify `foo` and create an untracked `test` file:

    ```
    $ touch test
    $ echo testing >> foo
    ```

11. Next, try your new `s` alias:

    ```
    $ git s
    ## aliases...origin/aliases
    M foo
    ?? test
    ```

12. Often, you'll just want to show the latest commit with some stats:

    ```
    $ git config alias.l1 "log -1 --shortstat"
    $ git l1
      commit a43eaa9b461e811eeb0f18cce67e4465888da333
      Author: John Doe <john.doe@example.com>
      Date:   Wed May 14 22:46:32 2014 +0200
        Better spaceship design
     1 file changed, 9 insertions(+), 9 deletions(-)
    ```

13. But sometimes, you need a bit more context. The following alias is the same as the previous but for the five latest commits (the output is not shown):

    ```
    $ git config alias.l5 "log -5 --decorate --shortstat"
    ```

14. A commit listing with statistics on the changed files in color can be displayed using the following alias:

    ```
    $ git config alias.ll 'log --pretty=format:"%C(yellow)%h%Creset %s
    %Cgreen(%cr)  %C(bold blue)<%an>%Creset %Cred%d%Creset" --numstat'
    $ git ll -5
    ```

As the next screenshot shows, committers are colored blue, their age in green, and so on:

```
b6dabd7 Update foo and bar (4 years, 2 months ago) <John Doe> (HEAD -> master, origin/master, origin/HEAD)
7       0       bar
7       0       foo

4afd2b8 Add bar (4 years, 2 months ago) <John Doe>
1       0       bar

7601046 Initial commit, adds foo (4 years, 2 months ago) <John Doe>
3       0       foo
✓ ~/Packt/Git-Version-Control-Cookbook-Second-Edition_tips_and_tricks [master|✓]
21:59 $
```

15. If you work in many repositories, remember that the `upstream/tracking` branch can be difficult. The following alias is shorthand for showing this:

    ```
    $ git config alias.upstream "rev-parse --symbolic-full-name --abbrev-ref=strict HEAD@{u}"
    $ git upstream
    origin/aliases
    ```

16. You can show the details of ID/SHA-1 (commit, tag, tree, blob) with the `details` alias. Not that you save many keystrokes, but `details` is easier to remember:

    ```
    $ git config alias.details "cat-file -p"
    $ git details HEAD
    tree bdfdaacbb29934b239db814e599342159c4390dd
    parent 8fc1819f157f2c3c25eb973c2a2a412ef3d5517a
    author John Doe <john.doe@example.com> 1400100392 +0200
    committer John Doe <john.doe@example.com> 1400100392 +0200
    Better spaceship design
    ```

17. A repository will grow, and the directory tree will become large. You can show the number of `cd-ups` and, `../`, needed to go to the repository root using the following alias, which can be useful in shell scripts:

    ```
    $ git config alias.root "rev-parse --show-cdup"
    $ cd sub/directory/example
    $ pwd
    /path/to/cookbook-tips-tricks/sub/directory/example
    $ git root
    ../../../
    $ cd $(git root)
    ```

```
$ pwd
/path/to/cookbook-tips-tricks
```

18. The path of the repository on the filesystem can easily be viewed with the following alias:

    ```
    $ git config alias.path "rev-parse --show-toplevel"
    $ git path
    /path/to/cookbook-tips-tricks
    ```

19. If we need to abandon whatever changes we have in the index, working tree, and also possibly the commits, and reset the working tree to a known state (commit ID) but we don't want to touch the untracked files, all we need is a `ref` to a state of the repository to be restored, for example, HEAD:

    ```
    $ git config alias.abandon "reset --hard"
    $ echo "new stuff" >> foo
    $ git add foo
    $ echo "other stuff" >> bar
    $ git s
    ## aliases...origin/aliases
    M  bar
    M  foo
    ?? test
    $ git abandon HEAD
    $ git s
    ## aliases...origin/aliases
    ?? test
    ```

Interactive add

The exposed staging area Git offers sometimes leads to confusion, especially when adding a file, changing it a bit, and then adding the file again to be able to commit the changes made after the first add. While it can seem a bit cumbersome to add the file after every little change, it is also a big advantage that you can stage and unstage changes. With the `git add` command, it's even possible to only add some changes to a file in the staging area. This comes in handy, especially if you make a lot of changes to a file and, for example, want to split the changes into bug fixes, refactoring, and features. This example will show how you can easily do this.

Getting ready

Again, we'll use the `Git-Version-Control-Cookbook-Second-Edition_tips_and_tricks` repository. Clone it and check out the interactive branch:

```
$ git clone https://github.com/PacktPublishing/Git-Version-Control-Cookbook-Second-Edition_tips_and_tricks.git
$ cd Git-Version-Control-Cookbook-Second-Edition_tips_and_tricks
$ git checkout interactive
```

How to do it...

First, we need some changes to be added; we do this by resetting the latest commit:

```
$ git reset 'HEAD^'
Unstaged changes after reset:
M       liberty.txt
```

Now we have a modified file. To start the interactive add, we can either run the `git add -i` or `git add -p` filename. The `-i` option brings up an interface where all the different files in the modified state can be added interactively one at a time. The `add -p/--patch` option is simpler and just gives you the option to add parts of the file specified:

```
$ git add -p liberty.txt
diff --git a/liberty.txt b/liberty.txt
index 8350a2c..9638930 100644
--- a/liberty.txt
+++ b/liberty.txt
@@ -8,6 +8,13 @@
        WW) ,WWW)
        7W),WWWW'
        'WWWWWW'
+           9---W)
+       ,,--WPL=YXW===
+       (P),CY:,I/X'F9P
+       WUT===---/===9)
+       -HP+----Y(C=9W)
+        '9Y3'-'-OWPT-
+         'WWLUIECW
        (:7L7C7'
        ,P---=YWFL
        Y-=:9)UW:L
Stage this hunk [y,n,q,a,d,/,j,J,g,e,?]?
```

Git asks you whether you want to stage the previous change (the hunk), but also shows quite a lot of options, which can be expanded a little bit if you type ?:

```
Stage this hunk [y,n,q,a,d,/,j,J,g,e,?]?
y - stage this hunk
n - do not stage this hunk
q - quit; do not stage this hunk nor any of the remaining ones
a - stage this hunk and all later hunks in the file
d - do not stage this hunk nor any of the later hunks in the file
g - select a hunk to go to
/ - search for a hunk matching the given regex
j - leave this hunk undecided, see next undecided hunk
J - leave this hunk undecided, see next hunk
k - leave this hunk undecided, see previous undecided hunk
K - leave this hunk undecided, see previous hunk
s - split the current hunk into smaller hunks
e - manually edit the current hunk
? - print help
```

There are a lot of options, but with the help text, they are quite self-explanatory. Let's add the current hunk, y, and look at the next one:

```
Stage this hunk [y,n,q,a,d,/,j,J,g,e,?]? y
@@ -17,16 +24,17 @@
         7WYW))PW W
         7WH)),WC)
         7L--/XY)
+DEBUG: Don't include this line...
         9+-,KY7)
         W9-Y3+7)
         W'=9WI7)
         ,W    '-YY)
-        W     ::W
-        ,T    :X)
-        ()    '9W   'L.                       ,-
-        (C    =:9   '9L                       ,T
-        ()    ,,-7)  7WL                      ,F'
-        ()    ,T9)    '9WL                    ,YF
+        W     ::W                       ,
+        ,T    :X)                 ()
+        ()    '9W   'L.           ()          ,-
+        (C    =:9   '9L           ()          ,T
+        ()    ,,-7)  7WL          WW          ,F'
+        ()    ,T9)    '9WL        --          ,YF
         ()    '-/(W           -==+PE9P7===O)          -,
         'W,  ,   T+/WX=L-. ,WP+()+3L3,),=WL   --==-T-
         7)   -,YW '-=9WPL+PT--  ':--L/=9WP=-'
Stage this hunk [y,n,q,a,d,/,K,j,J,g,s,e,?]?
```

Tips and Tricks

Whoa! It looks like there is a debug line there that we should not add. Let's split the hunk, s:

```
Stage this hunk [y,n,q,a,d,/,K,j,J,g,s,e,?]? s
Split into 2 hunks.
@@ -17,7 +24,8 @@
         7WYW))PW W
         7WH)),WC)
         7L--/XY)
+DEBUG: Don't include this line...
         9+-,KY7)
         W9-Y3+7)
         W'=9WI7)
    ,W    '-YY)
Stage this hunk [y,n,q,a,d,/,K,j,J,g,e,?]?
```

We don't want the output to be staged, use n, but we'll stage the next hunk and all the hunks later, in the a file:

```
Stage this hunk [y,n,q,a,d,/,K,j,J,g,e,?]? n
@@ -20,13 +28,13 @@
         9+-,KY7)
         W9-Y3+7)
         W'=9WI7)
    ,W    '-YY)
-        W     ::W
-       ,T     :X)
-       ()    '9W    'L.                      ,-
-       (C    =:9    '9L                     ,T
-       ()   ,,-7)   7WL                    ,F'
-       ()   , T9)  '9WL                    ,YF
+        W     ::W
+       ,T     :X)              ()
+       ()    '9W    'L.        ()           ,-
+       (C    =:9    '9L        ()          ,T
+       ()   ,,-7)   7WL        WW          ,F'
+       ()   , T9)  '9WL        --          ,YF
         ()   '-/(W       -==+PE9P7===O)           -,
        'W, ,   T+/WX=L-. ,WP+()+3L3,),=WL   --==-T-
         7)    -,YW '-=9WPL+PT--  ':--L/=9WP=-'
Stage this hunk [y,n,q,a,d,/,K,j,J,g,e,?]? a
```

Let's see the current status and the difference between the working directory and staging area:

```
$ git status
On branch interactive
Your branch is behind 'origin/interactive' by 1 commit, and can be fast-
```

```
            forwarded.
          (use "git pull" to update your local branch)
        Changes to be committed:
          (use "git reset HEAD <file>..." to unstage)
              modified:   liberty.txt
        Changes not staged for commit:
          (use "git add <file>..." to update what will be committed)
          (use "git checkout -- <file>..." to discard changes in working directory)
              modified:   liberty.txt
        $ git diff
        diff --git a/liberty.txt b/liberty.txt
        index 035083e..9638930 100644
        --- a/liberty.txt
        +++ b/liberty.txt
        @@ -24,6 +24,7 @@
                 7WYW))PW W
                 7WH)),WC)
                 7L--/XY)
        +DEBUG: Don't include this line...
                 9+-,KY7)
                 W9-Y3+7)
                 W'=9WI7)
```

Perfect! We got all the changes staged except the debug line, so the result can be committed:

```
        $ git commit -m 'Statue of liberty completed'
        [interactive 1ccb885] Statue of liberty completed
        1 file changed, 36 insertions(+), 29 deletions(-)
```

There's more...

As mentioned earlier, it's also possible to use `git add -i` to interactively add files. If we do this after resetting our branch, we will get the following menu:

```
        $ git add -i
              staged      unstaged path
        1:    unchanged     +37/-29 liberty.txt
        *** Commands ***
        1: status     2: update     3: revert    4: add untracked
        5: patch      6: diff       7: quit      8: help
        What now>
```

Tips and Tricks

The eight options pretty much do what they say. We can choose the patch option to get into the patch menu, as we saw previously, but first we have to choose which files to add patches for:

```
What now> p
           staged     unstaged path
1:      unchanged        +37/-29 liberty.txt
Patch update>> 1
           staged     unstaged path
* 1:      unchanged        +37/-29 liberty.txt
Patch update>>
diff --git a/liberty.txt b/liberty.txt
index 8350a2c..9638930 100644
--- a/liberty.txt
+++ b/liberty.txt
...
```

Once we have chosen the files, we want to add patches so they get a * character in the menu. To begin patching, just click on `<return>`. When you're done, you'll return to the menu and can quit, review, revert, and so on.

Interactive add with Git gui

The interactive features of `git add` are really powerful for creating clean commits that only contain a single logical change, even though it was coded as a mix of feature adding and bug fixing. The downside of the interactive `git add` feature is that it is hard to get an overview of all the changes that exist in the file when only being showed one hunk at a time. To get a better overview of the changes and still be able to only add selected hunks (and even single lines), we can use `git gui`. Git GUI is normally distributed with the Git installation (MsysGit on Windows) and can be launched from the command line: `git gui`. If your distribution doesn't have Git GUI available, you can probably install it from the package manager called `git-gui`.

Getting ready

We'll use the same repository as in the last example and reset it to the same state so that we can perform the same adds with Git GUI:

```
$ git clone https://github.com/PacktPublishing/Git-Version-Control-Cookbook-Second-Edition_tips_and_tricks.git
$ cd Git-Version-Control-Cookbook-Second-Edition_tips_and_tricks
```

```
$ git checkout interactive
$ git reset HEAD^
```

How to do it...

Load Git GUI in the `Git-Version-Control-Cookbook-Second-Edition_tips_and_tricks` repository. Here, you can see the unstaged changes (files) at the top-left and the staged changes (files) underneath. The main window will display the unstaged changes in the current marked file. You can right-click on a hunk and see a context menu with options for staging and so on. The first hunk shown by Git GUI is much larger than what we saw before with `git add -p`. Choose **Show Less Context** to split the hunk, as shown in the following screenshot:

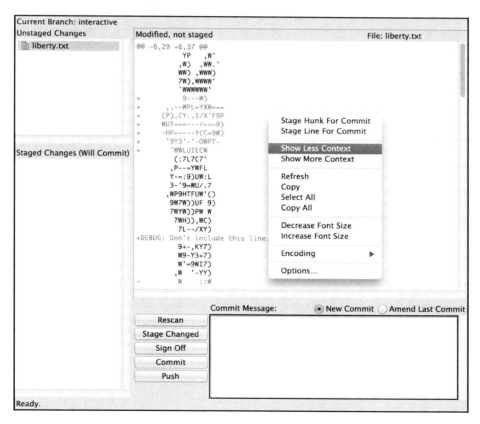

Tips and Tricks

Now, we get a smaller hunk like before, as shown in the following screenshot:

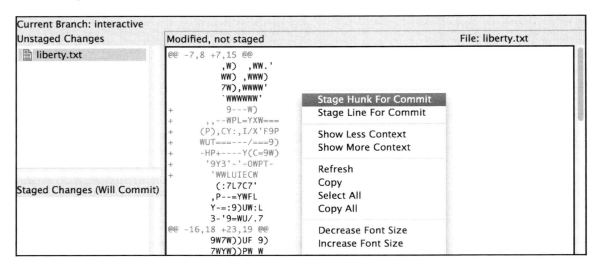

For the first hunk, we just choose to add **Stage Hunk For Commit**, and the next hunk moves to the top of the screen, as shown in the next screenshot:

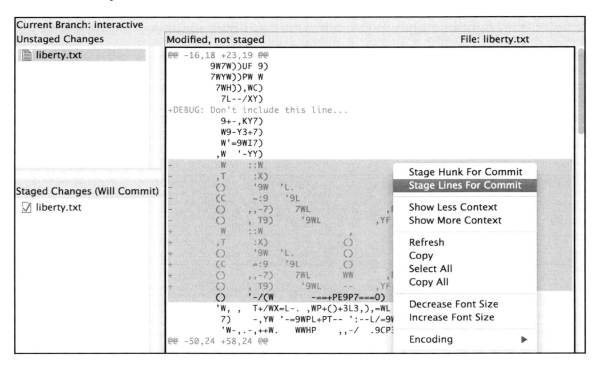

Here, we can select the lines we want to add, instead of performing another split, and stage those lines: **Stage Lines For Commit**. We can add the rest of the hunks except the one with the debug line. Now, we are ready to create a commit and we can do so from the Git GUI. We can just write the commit message in the field at the bottom of the screen and hit **Commit**, as shown in the next screenshot:

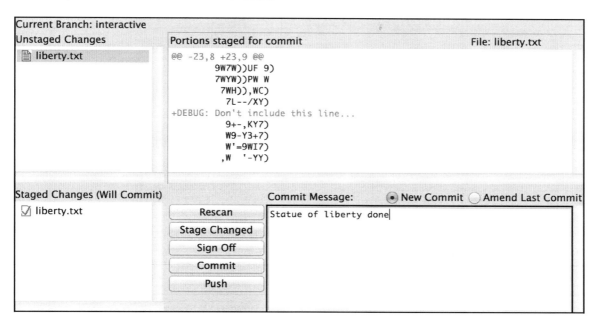

Ignoring files

For every repository, there are usually certain types of files you don't want tracked in the repository. The files can be configuration files, build output, or just backup files created by the editor when editing the file. To avoid these files showing up in the untracked files section of the `git status` output, it's possible to add them to a file called `.gitignore`. Entries in this file that match files in the working directory will not be considered by `git status`.

Tips and Tricks

Getting ready

Clone the `Git-Version-Control-Cookbook-Second-Edition_tips_and_tricks` repository and check out the `ignore` branch:

```
$ git clone https://github.com/PacktPublishing/Git-Version-Control-Cookbook-Second-Edition_tips_and_tricks.git
$ cd Git-Version-Control-Cookbook-Second-Edition_tips_and_tricks
$ git checkout ignore
```

How to do it...

1. First, we'll create some files and directories:

    ```
    $ echo "Testing" > test.txt
    $ echo "Testing" > test.txt.bak
    $ mkdir bin
    $ touch bin/foobar
    $ touch bin/frotz
    ```

2. Let's see the output of `git status`:

    ```
    $ git status
    On branch ignore
    Your branch is up-to-date with 'origin/ignore'.
     Untracked files:
        (use "git add <file>..." to include in what will be committed)
           test.txt
    nothing added to commit but untracked files present (use "git add" to track)
    ```

3. Only the `test.txt` file showed up in the output. This is because the rest of the files are ignored by Git. We can check the content of `.gitignore` to see how this happened:

    ```
    $ cat .gitignore
    *.config
    *.bak
    # Java files
    *.class
    bin/
    ```

Chapter 11

This means that `*.bak`, `*.class`, `*.config`, and everything in the `bin` directory are being ignored by Git.

4. If we try to add files in a path ignored by Git, for example `bin`, it will complain:

   ```
   $ git add bin/frotz
   The following paths are ignored by one of your .gitignore files:
   bin/frotz
   Use -f if you really want to add them.
   ```

   But, it also gives us the option to use `-f` if we really want to add it, which is `-f`:

   ```
   $ git add -f bin/frotz
   $ git status
   On branch ignore
     Your branch is up-to-date with 'origin/ignore'.
       Changes to be committed:
         (use "git reset HEAD <file>..." to unstage)
           new file:   bin/frotz
   Untracked files:
     (use "git add <file>..." to include in what will be committed)
   test.txt
   ```

5. If we ignore the `foo` file, which is already tracked, and modify it, it still shows up in the status, since tracked files are not ignored:

   ```
   $ echo "foo" >> .gitignore
   $ echo "more testing" >> foo
   $ git status
   On branch ignore
   Your branch is up-to-date with 'origin/ignore'.
     Changes to be committed:
       (use "git reset HEAD <file>..." to unstage)
         new file:   bin/frotz
     Changes not staged for commit:
       (use "git add <file>..." to update what will be committed)
       (use "git checkout -- <file>..." to discard changes in working directory)
           modified:   .gitignore
           modified:   foo
     Untracked files:
       (use "git add <file>..." to include in what will be committed)
     test.txt
   ```

[291]

6. Let's add and commit `foo`, `.gitignore`, and the contents of the current staging area:

```
$ git add foo .gitignore
$ git commit -m 'Add bin/frotz with force, foo & .gitignore'
[ignore fc60b44] Add bin/frotz with force, foo & .gitignore
3 files changed, 2 insertions(+)
create mode 100644 bin/frotz
```

There's more...

It's also possible to ignore files of a repository without the `.gitignore` files. You can put your ignored files in a global ignore file, for example `~/.gitignore_global`, and globally configure Git to also consider entries in this file to be ignored:

```
$ git config --global core.excludesfile ~/.gitignore_global
```

You can also do it per repository in the `.git/info/exclude` file. If you use either of these options, you won't be able to easily share the ignored file; they can't be added to the repository as they are stored outside it. Sharing `.gitignore` files is much easier; you just add and commit them to Git. But, let's see how the other options work:

```
$ echo "*.test" > .git/info/exclude
$ touch test.test
$ git status
On branch ignore
  Your branch is ahead of 'origin/ignore' by 1 commit.
    (use "git push" to publish your local commits)
  Untracked files:
    (use "git add <file>..." to include in what will be committed)
      test.txt
nothing added to commit but untracked files present (use "git add" to track)
$ ls
bar         bin         foo
test.test   test.txt    test.txt.bak
```

We can see that the `.test` file didn't show up in the `status` output and that the ignored files exist in the working directory.

See also

A wide range of files are commonly ignored, for example, to avoid accidentally adding text editor backup files, `*.swp`, `*~.`, and `*.bak` are commonly ignored. If you are working on a Java project, you might add `*.class`, `*.jar`, and `*.war` to your `.gitignore` and `*.o`, `*.elf`, and `*.lib` if you are working on a C project. GitHub has a repository dedicated to collect Git ignore files for different programming languages and editors/IDEs. You can find it at: https://github.com/github/gitignore.

Showing and cleaning ignored files

Ignoring files is useful for filtering noise from the output of `git status`. But sometimes, it's necessary to check which files are ignored. This example will show you how to do that.

Getting ready

We'll continue in the repository from the last example.

How to do it...

To show the files we have ignored, we can use the `clean` command. Normally, the `clean` command will remove the untracked files from the working directory, but it is possible to run this in dry-run mode, `-n`, which just shows what would happen:

```
$ git clean -Xnd
Would remove bin/foobar
Would remove test.test
Would remove test.txt.bak
```

The options used in the preceding command specify the following:

- `-n, --dry-run`: Only lists what will be removed
- `-X`: Removes only the files ignored by Git
- `-d`: Removes the untracked directories in addition to the untracked files

Tips and Tricks

The ignored files can also be listed with the `ls-files` command:

```
$ git ls-files -o -i --exclude-standard
bin/foobar
test.test
test.txt.bak
```

Where the `-o` option, `--others`, shows the untracked files, the `-i` option, `--ignored`, shows only the ignored files, and `--exclude-standard` uses the standard exclusion files `.git/info/exclude` and `.gitignore` in each directory, and the user's global exclusion file.

There's more...

If we need to remove the ignored files, we can of course use `git clean` to do this; instead of the dry-run option, we pass the force option, `-f`:

```
$ git clean -Xfd
Removing bin/foobar
Removing test.test
Removing test.txt.bak
```

To remove all the untracked files and not just the ignored files, use `git clean -xfd`. The lowercase `x` means we don't use the ignore rules, we just remove everything that is not tracked by Git.

12
Git Providers, Integrations, and Clients

In this chapter, we will cover the following recipes:

- Setting up an organization at GitHub
- Creating a repository at GitHub
- Adding templates for issues and pull requests
- Creating a GitHub API key
- Using GitHub to authenticate at Jenkins
- Triggering Jenkins builds
- Using Jenkinsfiles

Introduction

It is possible to host your own Git installation and maintain a central server for your organization. If you are a small company or an open source project, maintaining such an infrastructure can be a burden. But today, there exists a number of Git providers who can lift the burden.

GitHub is the best-known Git provider with 40 million users. Many high-profiled open source projects are hosted by GitHub. Once you have created an account at GitHub, you can explore the 85 million Git repositories currently hosted.

In modern software development, **continuous integration** (**CI**) is popular. The idea is that changes from developers are merged into the code base as soon as possible. Git's **pull requests** (**PRs**) are a way of doing so. Of course, GitHub provides a UI to create PRs and let's collaborators do code reviews. Part of a CI policy is also to run all tests automatically. Software like Jenkins can be configured to build and test for every commit.

Setting up an organization at GitHub

Whether you have a commercial product or an open source project, there is likely a company or a group of people behind it. GitHub supports such a structure by allowing users to create an organization.

An organization can have repositories associated and it has members. The advantage of using an organization is that members might come and go (developers will get a new job, and leave), but the repositories will be associated with the organization so there will be no need to transfer ownership of repositories.

As a user, you can be a member of multiple organizations. It is common to be a member of your employer's organization but also of a number of organizations behind open source projects.

Getting ready

You will need a user account at GitHub. For this recipe, we will use the GitHub user `johndoepackt`. Any user can create an organization.

If you don't have a GitHub account, it is time to create one. Once you have created your account and signed in, you are ready to go.

How to do it...

1. Creating an organization is a function under **Settings**. So, you need to find **Settings** in your GitHub account, as shown in the following screenshot:

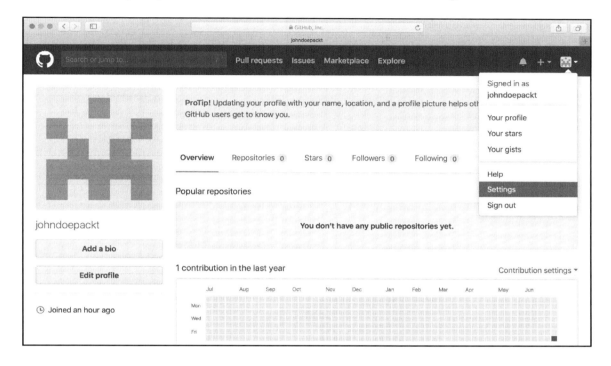

2. One menu item in **Settings** is **Organizations**. You can create an organization in two different ways. You can either turn your user into an organization or create a separate organization. We will create an organization and not turn the user into an organization, as shown in the next screenshot:

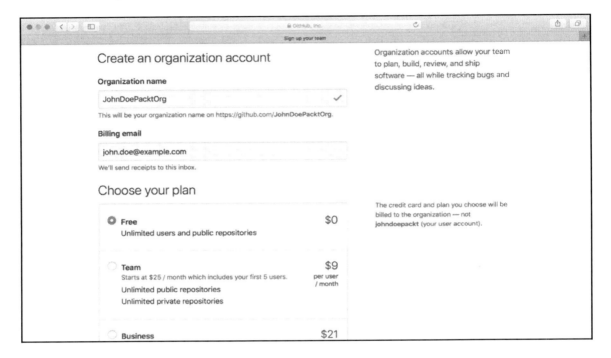

3. Once the organization is created, you can invite users to become members. It is also possible to add outside or external collaborators.

How it works...

Organizations at GitHub are a layer on top of Git. They can be seen as a way to provide access control to associated repositories.

When GitHub users explore the repositories associated with your organizations, they will be subject to the privileges you have set up. This means that you are in charge of what you allow others to see.

If you are a paying customer at GitHub, your organization can have private repositories. A private repository is only accessible by members of the organization. A company can have open source projects or examples as public repositories. But, by using a private repository, it is possible to have some company secrets.

There's more...

Each organization has a number of settings that you can tweak. In order to increase the security of your organization, you can require that members have to use two-factor authentication.

You also have access to an audit log for your organization. In many cases, you will have to ensure who did what. The audit log can also reveal if someone has gained access to your organization and tried to tamper with it.

See also

GitHub organizations are a well-documented feature of GitHub. The documentation is located at `https://help.github.com/categories/setting-up-and-managing-organizations-and-teams/`.

Creating a repository at GitHub

Using Git is all about repositories. GitHub provides a UI for creating repositories. The UI makes it easier for new Git users to get started. And for obvious reasons, GitHub does not give you access to their server directly.

In the previous recipe, we created an organization at GitHub. In this recipe, we will create a repository within the organization. As an individual user (not an organization), you can create repositories too.

Getting ready

You begin by logging in at GitHub. Before creating the repository, you have to make two decisions. First, what should the repository's name be? Second, should the repository be public or private?

Private repositories are only visible for members of the organization. But in order to create private repositories, you must be a paying customer.

How to do it...

1. Since we are going to create a repository for the organization, you will have to switch from your ordinary user to your organization. It's a dropdown with the title **Switch dashboard context**. Once you have switched context, your screen will look like this:

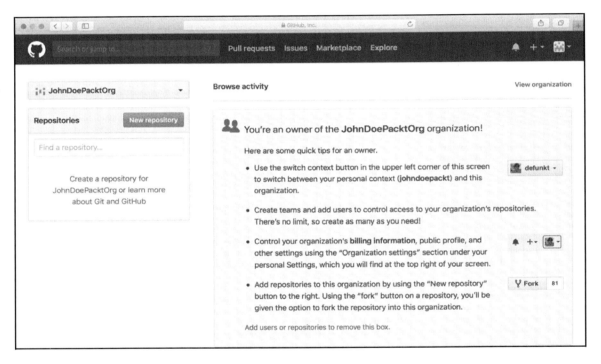

2. Now, you are ready to create the repository. You will have to set the name, a **Description (optional)**, and decide whether the repository is **Public** or **Private**. Moreover, GitHub can create .gitignore, LICENSE, and a simple README.md for you. Often you will know the main programming language, and a .gitignore based on best practices can be generated. In the following screenshot, you can see all the fields with values:

Chapter 12

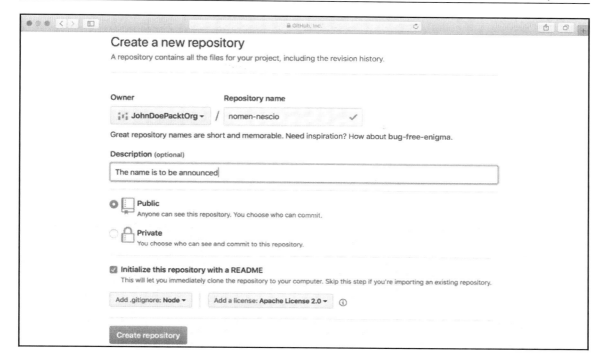

3. Once the repository is created, you can clone it on your computer as follows:

```
$ git clone https://github.com/JohnDoePacktOrg/nomen-nescio.git
$ cd nomen-nescio
$ ls -a
.            ..           .git         .gitignore LICENSE      README.md
```

How it works...

The screens you went through in the recipe are *Creating a repository at GitHub* server. In essence, it is simply creating a directory and running `git init`.

[301]

Adding the extra files (.gitignore, LICENSE, and README.md) is fairly simple too. Setting up a good .gitignore takes time, but you get a good starting point with the generated one.

GitHub also sets up access control for your repository. Only members of the organization have write permissions; that is, they have the rights to commit. In the settings of the repository, you can define more precise access control under the menu item **Collaborators & teams**. A team is a group of GitHub users who work together. In your company, you might have iOS, Android, and DevOps teams.

There's more...

With a repository at GitHub, code reviews are an integral part of pull requests. Let's update README.md and perform a code review at GitHub:

```
$ git checkout -b update-readme
Switched to a new branch 'update-readme'
$ echo "\nSoon a better name will be decided." >> README.md
$ git add README.md
$ git commit -m "Updating README.md"
[update-readme 6829c33] Updating README.md
 1 file changed, 1 insertion(+)
$ git push origin update-readme
Counting objects: 3, done.
Delta compression using up to 4 threads.
Compressing objects: 100% (3/3), done.
Writing objects: 100% (3/3), 330 bytes | 330.00 KiB/s, done.
Total 3 (delta 1), reused 0 (delta 0)
remote: Resolving deltas: 100% (1/1), completed with 1 local object.
To https://github.com/JohnDoePacktOrg/nomen-nescio.git
 * [new branch]      update-readme -> update-readme
```

You can now go to GitHub, find your repository and create a pull request. You can invite your collaborators to review your changes before they are merged, as shown in the following screenshot:

When we created the repository, we had the option to create it as a private one. Private repositories are only available for paying customers. From a Git perspective, there is no difference between public and private repositories. The major difference is who can view a repository. As you might imagine, public repositories can be viewed by everybody. You don't even have to log in to GitHub to view a public repository. These repositories are ideal for open source projects—and if you read GitHub's terms closely, you will see that a public repository is meant to be open source.

Private repositories can only be viewed by the users you have given access to. Typically, every member of your organization can view private repositories. In other words, private repositories are ideal for internal projects or proprietary software. Today, many companies are mixing public and private repositories while their software developers can fluently move between repositories.

Adding templates for issues and pull requests

In Chapter 7, *Enhancing Your Daily Work with Git Hooks, Aliases, and Scripts*, we showed how to add templates for commits. A commit template helps the developer to include the relevant information in the commit message. At GitHub, users will create issues and pull requests. It is up to the issue or pull request creator to write a meaningful description.

This recipe will explain to you how to add templates for issues and pull requests. The purpose is to help people to remember to include enough context for you to quickly understand what the issue or pull request is about.

Getting ready

We will continue to use the repository `nomen-rescio` that we created in a previous recipe. GitHub is using **Markdown** as a markup language everywhere. Markdown is developer friendly since it is plain text with some special conversions for typesetting bold, bullet lists, and so on. Going through Markdown might be a complete book on its own.

Chapter 12

How to do it...

1. To start, you will need to find **Settings** for your repository. There is a big **Set up templates** button which is what you are looking for. You can choose to use one of the precanned templates, but we will create a custom one, as shown in the next screenshot:

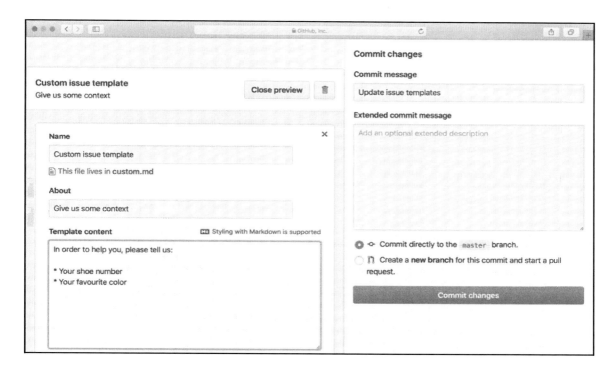

Git Providers, Integrations, and Clients

2. You save the template by clicking on **Commit changes**. When a user is creating an issue, your template will be shown. The user can choose to delete all your text but most users will read it before doing so; note the following screenshot:

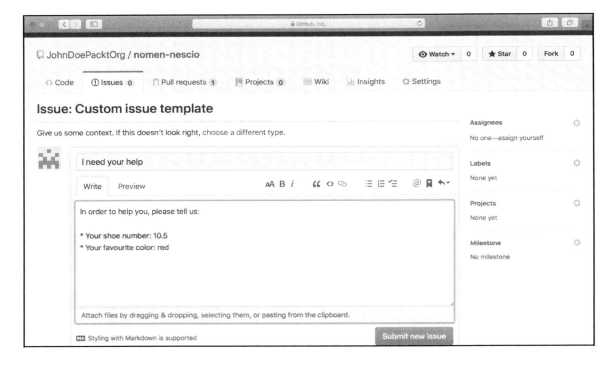

How it works...

Your templates live in the repository itself. Actually, you find them in the directory `.github`. If you prefer, you can edit a template in your favorite editor and commit changes just like any other file.

The directory `ISSUE_TEMPLATE` contains the templates for issues is the file. Similar, if you create a file under the directory `PULL_REQUEST_TEMPLATE`, you will have a template for pull requests. With multiple templates, the user will be asked to choose which template is appropriate.

Creating a GitHub API key

So far, all the work we have performed at GitHub has been manual. Programmers like to automate processes, and performing GitHub work is no exception to that rule. With the next recipe, we will show you how you can automate tasks.

Getting ready

To automate GitHub tasks you need to be able to access GitHub. Instead of logging in using a user name and password, you can use an API key or personal access token. Such a token should not be shared, and you need to keep it secret at all times.

So, this recipe begins with generating an access token and shows you a simple Python script. The Python script will find all your repositories, and find all the pull requests for each repository.

How to do it...

1. First, we need to generate the personal access token. You will have to drill down in the menu system: **Settings**, **Developer settings**, and finally, **Person access token**. We will give our token the name `basic-query` since we plan only to do that. You can specify what the token has access to. Our token will only need access to repository actions, as indicated in the following screenshot:

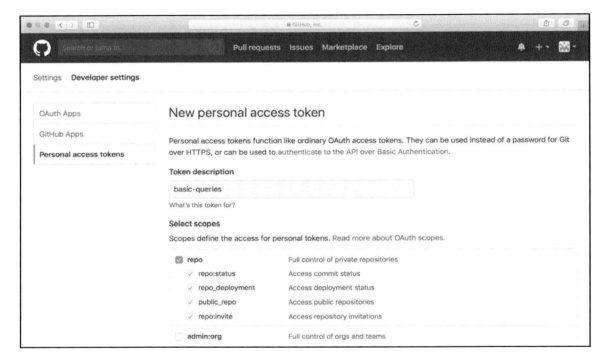

2. Once you generate the token, it will displayed. You will only see it once at GitHub, so it is important to copy it to your computer. In the following screenshot, you can see the page with the generated token (except we have added a rectangle since we need to keep it a secret):

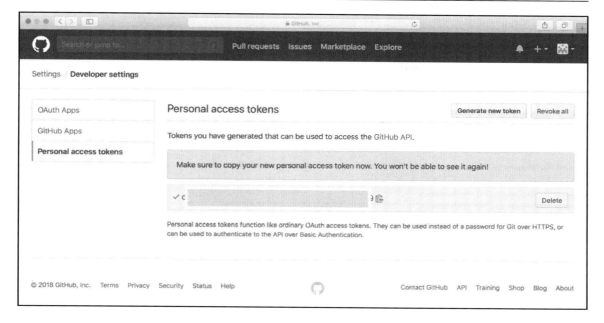

3. As already mentioned, we will use Python. You need to install the small library PyGitHub. Using Pip, the installation is easy:

    ```
    $ pip install pygithub
    ```

4. Now, we are ready to run the Python script that will fetch the repositories and the pull requests. The script is just iterating over repositories and pull requests:

    ```
    from github import Github
    import datetime

    g = Github("YOUR_PERSONAL_ACCESS_TOKEN")
    for repo in g.get_user().get_repos():
      print(repo.name)
      for pr in repo.get_pulls():
        print("  " + pr.created_at.isoformat() + " : " + pr.title)
    ```

How it works...

The token gives you access to GitHub but only the parts that were specified when you created the token. Behind the scenes, the methods of PyGitHub are implemented as HTTP calls to GitHub's API.

For example, the call `get_repos` is an HTTP GET of `/user/repos`. The HTTP request will return the result as JSON. PyGitHub is parsing the JSON result and populating Python objects so the result is more natural for a Python developer.

Python is not the only programming language. You can find libraries for almost any known language.

Of course, you can go beyond the simple scripts and develop a full-blown GitHub client. We will leave that as an exercise for you.

See also

The complete API documentation for PyGitHub can be found at `http://pygithub.readthedocs.io/en/latest/reference.html`.

Using GitHub to authenticate at Jenkins

Jenkins is the most popular continuous integration software and it allows users to continuously build, test, and release any kind of software. It is extremely flexible and configurable in every aspect, including the way users are able to log in and authorize. GitHub is able to act as an OAuth provider, which is very convenient since it makes a lot of sense to map the users working on a project with the relative area of the CI system.

Getting ready

In order to demonstrate the procedure, we will need a Jenkins instance. Every company will have a different setup so, in order to make things more predictable, we will work with a local version of Jenkins.

Jenkins is a Java app but still, the easiest way to get a running ephemeral instance of Jenkins for our example is by using Docker. With Docker installed and running on your machine, simply run:

```
$ docker run --rm -p 8080:8080 jenkinsci/blueocean
```

This instance of Jenkins won't leave behind any traces of itself once the docker container is stopped.

The logs will start appearing on your console and they will contain the password for the first login. Look for something that appears as follows:

```
*************************************************************
*************************************************************
*************************************************************

Jenkins initial setup is required. An admin user has been created and a
password generated.
Please use the following password to proceed to installation:

YOUR_PASSWORD_HERE

This may also be found at:
/Users/emanuelez/.jenkins/secrets/initialAdminPassword

*************************************************************
*************************************************************
*************************************************************
```

Git Providers, Integrations, and Clients

At this point you can point your browser to `http://localhost:8080/` and you will be prompted for your password, as shown in the next screenshot:

At this point, you will be prompted to install plugins. For this example, let's just install the suggested plugins as shown in the next screenshot:

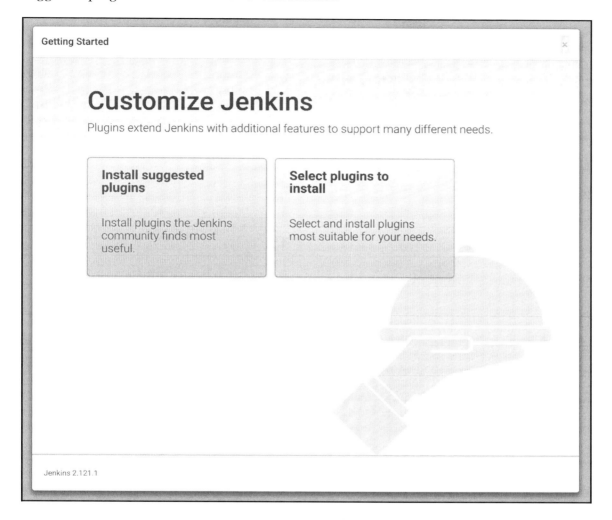

Next, you will be prompted to create an admin user, but, since this is an ephemeral image, you can just continue by clicking **Continue as admin**:

Next, you will be asked to set up the **Instance Configuration**. Just keep the default value and click **Save and Finish**.

Chapter 12

At this point, Jenkins is ready to be used. Just click on **Start using Jenkins,** as shown in the next screenshot:

Git Providers, Integrations, and Clients

You will now see the **Welcome to Jenkins!** homepage, as follows:

How to do it...

1. In order to authenticate to Jenkins using GitHub, you will have to install the **GitHub Authentication Plugin**. To do this, click on **Manage Jenkins** on the panel on the left and on the new page click on **Manage Plugins**, as shown in the following screenshot:

2. Now you can navigate to the **Available** tab and type `github auth` in the search box, as shown in the next screenshot:

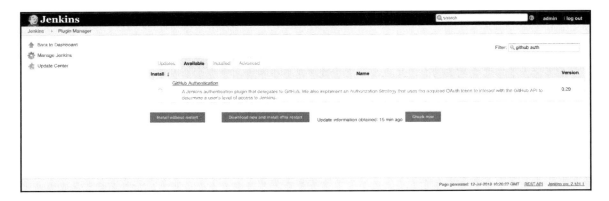

3. You can now install the plugin by checking the box on the left and clicking on **Install without restart**.
4. Once the plugin is installed you can go back to the Jenkins homepage by clicking on the Jenkins logo in the top-left corner and, once again, clicking on **Manage Jenkins**.
5. This time we will proceed by clicking on **Configure Global Security**, as shown in the next screenshot:

Chapter 12

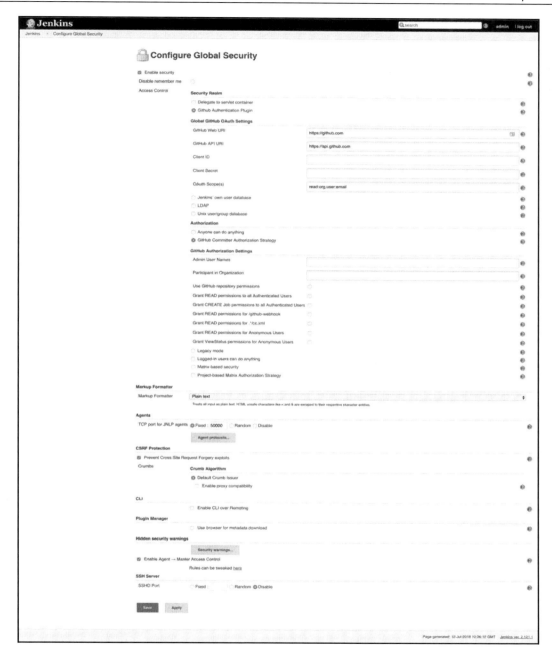

Git Providers, Integrations, and Clients

6. Now head over to GitHub and, as shown in the next screenshot, register a new application by navigating to https://github.com/settings/applications/new:

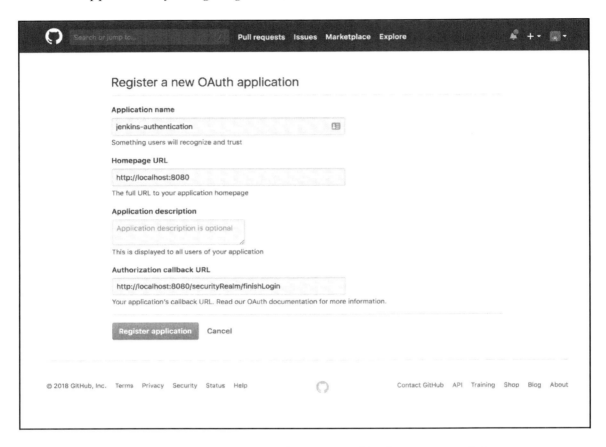

Here you will need to fill in an arbitrary **Application name** and the **Authorization callback URL** as shown. Once you register the application you will be able to see your **Client ID** and **Client Secret**. These will be needed in Jenkins in order to fill in the relative fields in the **Global Security Settings**.

7. Once you submit the form you will be able to log in to Jenkins using your GitHub credentials.

How it works...

Authentication needs to solve the question, Who is the person trying to access the service?. There are many ways to do it: login and password, tokens, and so on. OAuth is another way to answer that question. OAuth stands for Open Authentication and it is an open standard for access delegation. It allows users to have access to websites (such as our Jenkins instance) without having to provide them, and therefore trust them, with a password.

GitHub has the ability to act as an OAuth provider, which means that other websites can be configured to accept the credentials provided by GitHub to let users access their services.

This means that whenever a user tries to access a Jenkins instance configured to accept GitHub OAuth, he will be redirected to GitHub itself to authenticate and, subsequently, GitHub will redirect the user to the Jenkins instance with an attached identity token.

There's more...

Authentication is only half of the equation. Identifying a user is, of course, important, but what we do with that information is critical as well. Here is where authorization comes into play, which, keeping the question analogy, aims to answer the question: Given that the person trying to access the service is X, what is he allowed and not allowed to do?

The way we configured the Jenkins instance, anybody able to log in will be able to do anything. This might not be the desired behavior, which leads to another section of the **Global Security** page in Jenkins.

You will find a section called **Authorization**, which provides many options. One is the **GitHub Committer Authorization Strategy**, which determines if a user is allowed to see a specific Jenkins job–but only if he's allowed to access the relative GitHub repository.

See also

The documentation of the **GitHub OAuth Plugin** is available at `https://wiki.jenkins.io/display/JENKINS/GitHub+OAuth+Plugin`.

Triggering Jenkins builds

When you create a Jenkins job, how will Jenkins know when it's time to build a specific branch or pull request? Jenkins offers many ways to do this, from continuously building based on a timer, to polling the Git repository to see if anything changed. Both of these options are not very efficient, but luckily GitHub allows for a better solution.

GitHub has the concept of Webhooks, which means that it can be configured to contact a server, such as our Jenkins instance, when something important happens.

There are many ways to achieve the goal, but in this recipe we will focus on one approach, which is going to be helpful especially in an enterprise environment where a GitHub organization is used, containing several repositories. Managing a single job or more per repository can quickly become a repetitive chore and that is where the **GitHub Branch Source** plugin comes into play.

Getting ready

We are going to need a Jenkins instance so the same preparatory steps as the previous recipe are needed.

Additionally, if the Jenkins instance is not reachable from the internet, a reverse proxy will be needed in order for GitHub to send notifications to the Jenkins instance.

How to do it...

The steps are as follows:

1. The GitHub Branch Source plugin comes preinstalled with the default installation, but if your setup does not already have the plugin, you can easily install it as we did in the previous recipe. Go to the Jenkins home page and proceed to **Manage Jenkins**, **Manage Plugins**, click on the **Available** tab and look for **GitHub Branch Source**. Install the plugin.

Chapter 12

2. Now, go back to the Jenkins homepage and click on **Create New Jobs**:

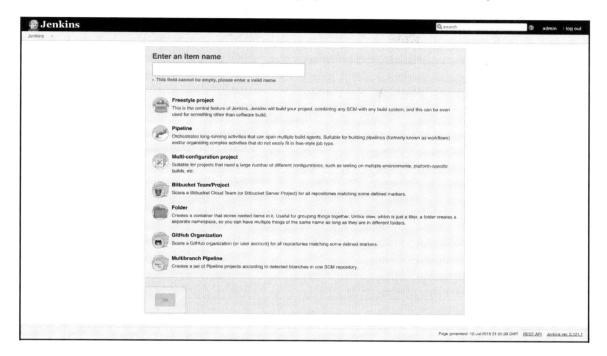

3. Choose a job name and select **GitHub Organization** before clicking **OK**. The following configuration page can look a bit daunting, so let's break it down:

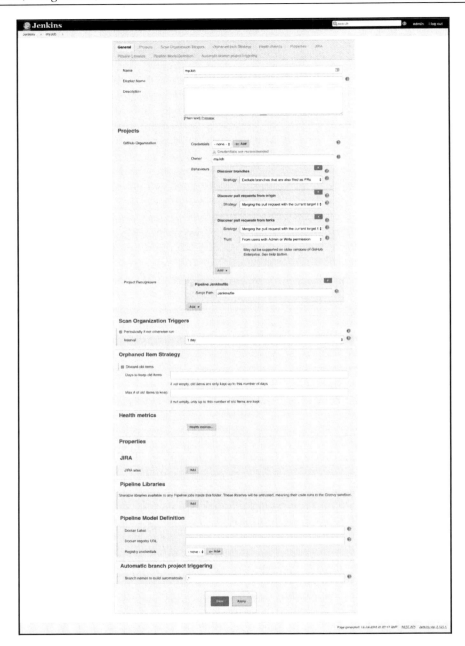

4. The only section that really needs to be taken care of is **Projects**. The first thing to set is the GitHub credentials. This will allow Jenkins to automatically set up webhooks for us. Credentials in Jenkins are treated with security in mind and are properly encrypted, so don't be afraid to save them here.
5. Next, we need to specify the **Owner**, which is simply the name of the GitHub organization we want to keep under control. The following section describes the behaviors, which are completely fine in their default form. They will allow building:
    - Branches
    - PRs coming from the repo itself
    - PRs coming from forks, but from trusted users

That is it! Now Jenkins will be able to automatically build any branch or PR as long as the code contains a Jenkinsfile. Jenkinsfiles are going to be treated in the next recipe, so stay tuned!

How it works...

The GitHub Branch Souce plugin will allow Jenkins to periodically scan the whole specified GitHub organization, and for every repository it will check all the branches and PRs, and if they contain a file called `Jenkinsfile` they will be automatically built following the directives contained in the Jenkinsfile itself.

This is quite a powerful paradigm and it allows to keep under version control not only the code of the project but also the instructions on how to build, test, and even release it in the same code base.

There's more...

The job configuration page will allow changing many different behaviors. What if, for example, we don't want to build all branches, but only the ones whose name matches a regular expression? The solution is just a few clicks away! There are so many possibilities and the Jenkins developers keep adding new ones, so it's worth taking a look periodically at what's available.

See also

The documentation for the GitHub Branch Source plugin is available at `https://go.cloudbees.com/docs/cloudbees-documentation/cje-user-guide/index.html#github-branch-source`.

Using Jenkinsfiles

Jenkinsfiles are a relatively new feature in the Jenkins world and they come in two varieties and syntaxes:

- Declarative
- Groovy DSL

The Groovy DSL is very flexible and powerful, but it also facilitates some anti-patterns, so in this recipe we're going to focus on the declarative-style Jenkinsfiles.

Getting ready

You will need a GitHub repository containing a codebase that can be built and tested. Given the sheer number of possible programming languages and build systems available, we will choose an arbitrary Java project using the popular Maven build system.

How to do it...

It will be sufficient to add a file called `Jenkinsfile` with these contents:

```
pipeline {
  agent any
  tools {
    maven 'Maven 3.3.9'
    jdk 'jdk8'
  }
  stages {
    stage ('Initialize') {
      steps {
        sh '''
          echo "PATH = ${PATH}"
          echo "M2_HOME = ${M2_HOME}"
        '''
```

```
        }
      }
      stage ('Build') {
        steps {
          sh 'mvn -Dmaven.test.failure.ignore=true install'
        }
        post {
          success {
            junit 'target/surefire-reports/**/*.xml'
          }
        }
      }
    }
  }
}
```

How it works...

The Jenkinsfile describes both how to build and test the software and the environment in which to run such an operation.

Let's take a look at the different sections:

- `agent any` specifies that this build can be run on any available executor.
- The `tools {}` section specifies the programs needed to run our build. In this case, Maven and the **Java Development Kit (JDK)** are needed and the versions are specified as well.
- `stages {}` and `stage() {}` allow splitting the run into well-defined sections which will allow better analysis of build results.
- Each stage needs to contain a `steps {}` section that will describe exactly which operations to perform. In this case, in the *Initialize* stage, we are simply running a shell script that echoes a couple of environment variables.
- The **Build** stage actually runs Maven and, if the build succeeds, it will analyze the results of the unit tests contained in an XML file.

There's more...

Jenkinsfiles are a huge topic that would be able to fill a book on its own, so the examples provided have only scratched the surface of what is possible. To give some examples, you will be able to:

- Run steps in parallel on different machines to save build time
- Save and deploy build artifacts
- Run complete releases
- Wait for some user input
- And much much more

See also

The syntax for declarative Jenkinsfiles can be found at `https://jenkins.io/doc/book/pipeline/syntax/`.

Be aware that plugins are able to contribute all kinds of steps and tools, so be sure to check the documentation of the plugin you are planning to use!

Other Books You May Enjoy

If you enjoyed this book, you may be interested in these other books by Packt:

GitHub Essentials - Second Edition

Achilleas Pipinellis

ISBN: 978-1-78913-833-7

- Create and upload repositories to your account
- Create organizations and manage teams with different access levels on repositories
- Use the issue tracker effectively and add context to issues with labels and milestones
- Create, access, and personalize your user account and profile settings
- Build a community around your project using the sophisticated tools GitHub provides
- Create GitHub pages and understand web analytics

Git Essentials - Second Edition
Ferdinando Santacroce

ISBN: 978-1-78712-072-3

- Master Git fundamentals
- Be able to "visualize," even with the help of a valid GUI tool
- Write principal commands in a shell
- Figure out the right strategy to run change your daily work with few or no annoyances
- Explore the tools used to migrate to Git from the Subversion versioning system without losing your development history
- Plan new projects and repositories with ease, using online services, or local network resources

Leave a review - let other readers know what you think

Please share your thoughts on this book with others by leaving a review on the site that you bought it from. If you purchased the book from Amazon, please leave us an honest review on this book's Amazon page. This is vital so that other potential readers can see and use your unbiased opinion to make purchasing decisions, we can understand what our customers think about our products, and our authors can see your feedback on the title that they have worked with Packt to create. It will only take a few minutes of your time, but is valuable to other potential customers, our authors, and Packt. Thank you!

Index

.
.git directory template
  creating 42, 44
  working 45

A

aliases
  creating 276, 280
archives
  creating, from tree 249, 252
autocompletion
  enabling 272
  for Linux features 272
  for Mac users 272
  for Window users 272
  of Git commands 271
automatic garbage collection
  turning off 208, 209

B

bisect
  used, for debugging 265, 267
blame command
  using 268, 269
bottleneck
  finding, in source tree 127, 130, 132
branch description
  using, in commit message 144, 145
branches
  differentiating between 75, 76
  patches, creating from 237, 238

C

commit message
  branch description, using 144
  branch message, using 146
  external information, using 153, 155, 157
  grepping 136
commit messages
  grepping 133, 135
commit template
  setting up 168
commits
  author, changing with rebase 94, 97
  auto-squashing 97, 100
  changes in staging area, retaining 177, 179
  changes to files, retaining 175, 177
  changes, reverting 187, 189
  creating, stages 14, 15, 17, 18
  finding, in history 29
  history, finding 30
  rebasing, to another branch 82, 83
  removing completely 172, 174
  squashing, with interactive rebase 89, 91, 93, 94
  tagging, in repository 118, 121
configuration examples
  about 45
  autocorrect 48
  expiry of objects 47
  rebase and merge setup 46
  working 49
configuration targets
  viewing 35
continuous integration (CI) 296

D

DAG
  viewing 18, 19, 20, 22
dirty area
  working with 180, 183
dynamic commit message template
  creating 147, 149, 150, 152

E

existing configuration
  querying 38, 40

F

files
  ignoring 289, 292
fixed issues
  extracting 22, 25

G

garbage collection
  manual execution 204, 206, 207
Git aliases
  about 49
  configuring 162, 165, 166, 167
  creating 50, 53
  using 162, 165, 167
git bisect
  used, for debugging 263
Git bundles
  creating 244, 246
  using 246, 249
Git conflicts
  merging, git reuse recorded resolution (rerere)
    used 69, 73
git fsck
  used, for tracking lost changes 198, 199
Git gui
  using, with interactive add 286, 288
Git note
  adding 104, 106, 108
git reflog
  used, for viewing past Git actions 195, 197
git reuse recorded resolution (rerere)
  used, for merging Git conflicts 69, 72, 74
Git scripts
  configuring 167
  using 167
git stash command
  using 254, 255
  working 256, 258, 260
GitHub API key
  creating 307, 309, 310

GitHub Branch Source plugin
  about 322
  documentation, reference 326
GitHub OAuth Plugin
  documentation, reference 321
GitHub organization
  reference 299
GitHub
  organization, setting up 296, 298, 299
  repository, creating 299, 300, 301, 302, 303
  used, for authentication at Jenkins 310, 313, 314, 317, 318, 320, 321
gitk
  used, for viewing history 27, 28

H

history code
  searching through 31, 32
history
  commits, finding 29
  viewing, with gtik 27, 29

I

ignored files
  cleaning 293
  displaying 293
interactive add
  using 281, 284, 286
  using, with Git Gui 286, 288

J

Java Development Kit (JDK) 327
Jenkins builds
  triggering 322, 325
Jenkins
  GitHub, used for authentication 310, 314, 317, 318, 320, 321
Jenkinsfiles
  reference 328
  using 326, 327

L

latest commit
  recreating, with new changes 183, 185, 186

layers
  configuring 35, 36, 38
list, of changed files
  obtaining 25, 26
local branches
  managing 58, 59, 61

M

Mail User Agent (MUA) 242
Markdown 304
merge commit
  forcing 65, 68
merge
  reverting 189, 191
  reverting, reference 195
Msysgit installation 272

N

non-zero status 267
notes
  pushing, to remote repository 116, 118
  retrieving, from remote repository 112, 114, 115
  separating, by category 108, 110, 112

O

objects, Git
  about 9
  blob object 12
  branch object 12
  commit object 10
  navigating 10
  tag object 13
  tree object 11
  working 13
orphan branches
  about 77
  creating 77, 80

P

past Git actions
  viewing, with git reflog 195, 197
patches
  applying 238, 240
  creating 234, 236

creating, from branches 237, 238
  reference 241
  sending 241, 243
  working 236
prompt display status information
  enabling 273, 274, 275
pull requests 296
push, specific commits
  preventing 157, 158, 161
PyGitHub documentation
  reference 310

R

rebase, with merge conflicts
  continuing 83, 85
rebase
  used, for changing author of commit 94, 97
refspec exemplified
  about 53
  repository, setting up 54, 56
  working 56
release note
  generating 136, 138
remote branches
  pruning 202, 203, 204
remote tracking branch
  about 61
  checking 61
  commands 63
  using 64
repositories
  backup, creating as mirror repositories 216, 218
repository
  achieved contents, extracting 138, 141
  commits, tagging 118, 121
  creating, at GitHub 299, 300, 302, 304
  splitting 209, 211, 213

S

selected commits
  rebasing 86, 88
single file
  modifying 214, 215
source tree
  bottleneck, finding 127, 130, 132

stashes
  applying 260, 262
  saving 260, 262
submodules
  about 219
  using 219, 223
  versus subtree merging 232
subtree merging
  about 224
  reference 231
  using 225, 228, 230
  working 231

T

templates
  adding, for issues 304, 307
  adding, for pull requests 304, 307

  creating 41
top contributor
  extracting 123, 125, 127
tree
  archives, creating 249, 252

U

UI
  coloring, in prompt 269, 271
UNIX mailbox format 236

V

version control systems (VCSs) 8

Z

zsh
  reference 276

Printed in Great Britain
by Amazon